OXFORD EARLY CHRISTIAN TEXTS

General Editor

DR. HENRY CHADWICK
Dean of Christ Church, Oxford

ATHENAGORAS

ATHENAGORAS

Legatio
AND
De Resurrectione

EDITED AND TRANSLATED
BY
WILLIAM R. SCHOEDEL

OXFORD
AT THE CLARENDON PRESS
1972

Oxford University Press, Ely House, London W. 1

GLASGOW NEW YORK TORONTO MELBOURNE WELLINGTON
CAPE TOWN IBADAN NAIROBI DAR ES SALAAM LUSAKA ADDIS ABABA
DELHI BOMBAY CALCUTTA MADRAS KARACHI LAHORE DACCA
KUALA LUMPUR SINGAPORE HONG KONG TOKYO

PRINTED IN GREAT BRITAIN
AT THE UNIVERSITY PRESS, OXFORD
BY VIVIAN RIDLER
PRINTER TO THE UNIVERSITY

PREFACE

ALTHOUGH Athenagoras is not well known and left no
deep mark on the life and thought of the ancient Church,
the two documents which come down to us under his name
may be read as fragments of larger debates and in this way
contribute significantly to our understanding of two important problems that emerged in the early period.

Athenagoras' *Plea* is especially noteworthy for the light
which it sheds on the social problem of Christianity as a
popular religious movement in the Roman Empire. The
author's careful exploration of the charge of 'atheism' sub-
ordinates traditional polemics to a controlled apologetic aim
and reveals more clearly than other early discussions something of the underlying difference between Christian and
Graeco-Roman views of 'piety'. Raffaele Pettazzoni and
others have taught us that the clash between Rome and the
Church was in part a clash between two distinct types of
religion: first, the ancient religion of city and state—that is,
the type of religion which establishes and enshrines the values
of the political and social institutions of this world; and
second, the universal religion with its message of salvation—
that is, the type of religion which (like Christianity) orients
men to values that transcend the mundane order of things.
Athenagoras knows as certainly as Varro that there is a
'political religion' which the emperors welcome for the sake of
social stability. He presents Christianity as superior to such
religion and appeals to an authority greater than that of the
state; but he also emphasizes the loyalty of Christians in
conventional terms. Unfortunately, the underlying tensions
in this marriage of themes and their practical consequences
are not adequately explored. In particular, Athenagoras
fails to realize that the mild 'atheism' of a pagan élite—the
philosophers—could not properly be compared with the
thoroughgoing 'atheism' of a popular religious movement

such as Christianity. Rome's tolerance, however broad, had limits which our apologist cannot fully grasp; consequently, he neglects the social issues for argumentation (sometimes superficial and arid) on theological and metaphysical issues. The weakness of his work, however, should not be exaggerated as it was by Johannes Geffcken in his searing attack of 1907. A more balanced view of his achievement is offered in the introduction to this edition.

The second treatise in this book, *On the Resurrection*, apparently comes from another period, despite the traditional ascription of it to Athenagoras. Reasons are presented in the introduction for viewing it as a conservative reaction to the teaching on the resurrection in the school of Origen. Alternatively, because of the close relation both historically and philosophically between Origen and the later Platonists, the treatise may be directed against the latter. In any event, we have before us a polemic which underscores the difficulties encountered by Christian theology as it attempted to come to terms more fully with Platonism.

I owe to Robert M. Grant my first interest in the text of Athenagoras and the problems of his writing on the literary, intellectual, and social side. Subsequently I have profited much from conversations with other American scholars, especially Robert L. Wilken and Lloyd G. Patterson. I wish also to recognize Brown University of Providence, R.I., for summer grants which made the writing of this book possible. The staff of the Clarendon Press has my warmest thanks, especially for its close attention to detail in the editing of this volume. Finally, I dedicate this work to my father, G. Walter Schoedel, who would have been pleased, I think, with a book of this kind.

W. R. S.

The University of Illinois
Summer 1971

CONTENTS

INTRODUCTION

ATHENAGORAS left himself almost without witness in the early Church and was recalled from obscurity only in the tenth century by Arethas, archbishop of Caesarea in Cappadocia. Before that time, one early father, Methodius (d. A.D. 311) alludes to the *Plea* (24. 2) and identifies the author as Athenagoras.[1] Epiphanius and Photius discuss the same text, but only on the authority of Methodius.[2]

One other reference to Athenagoras may be noted, but it is not encouraging. According to a fourteenth-century codex,[3] 'Philip of Side [a fifth-century Christian historian] says in his twenty-fourth book: Athenagoras was the first to head the school in Alexandria. He flourished at the time of Hadrian [A.D. 117–38] and Antoninus [A.D. 138–61], to both of whom he addressed his *Plea on behalf of the Christians*. He became a Christian while he wore the philosopher's cloak and was at the head of the Academy. Even before Celsus he was anxious to write against the Christians. He read the Sacred Scriptures in order to aim his shafts more accurately, but he was so powerfully seized by the Holy Spirit that like the great Paul he became a teacher rather than a persecutor of the faith which he was harassing. Philip says that Clement the writer of the *Stromata* was his disciple and that Pantaenus [MS. Clement] was the disciple of Clement. Pantaenus himself was also an Athenian philosopher, of the Pythagorean school. But Eusebius says the opposite: that Pantaenus was the teacher of Clement . . .' Disagreement between Philip and Eusebius on the school in Alexandria prevents us from concerning ourselves too much about the former's dating of the *Plea*. There is, as we shall see, some difficulty about the

---

[1] *De Res.* 1. 36, 37 (pp. 277–8 Bonwetsch).

[2] Epiphanius, *Pan.* 64. 20–1 (*PG* xli. 1101); Photius, *Bibl.* cod. 234 (*PG* ciii. 1109).

[3] Codex Bodl. Baroccianus 142, fol. 216 (*PG* vi. 182).

address, but the co-rulership presupposed throughout the apology is not satisfied by taking up Philip's suggestion. Antoninus, to be sure, was adopted by Hadrian before the latter's death; but it was Marcus Aurelius who first set up a co-rulership. There were, in fact, two such joint rules in his reign—one with L. Aurelius Verus (A.D. 161–9) and one with Commodus. Our text has the latter in mind, since the 'kings' addressed are regarded as father and son (18. 2).

We know practically nothing, then, about Athenagoras apart from the medieval codices which contain his work. The earliest of these, codex Paris 451, by its own account 'was written by the hand of Baanes the secretary for Arethas, archbishop of Caesarea in Cappadocia, in the year of the world 6422' (A.D. 914).[4] The codex included a number of 'apologetic' writings, among which are two works ascribed to Athenagoras—the *Plea* and *On the Resurrection*.[5]

The reason for the neglect of Athenagoras can only be conjectured. In some ways the *Plea* represents a form of pleading superior to more famous predecessors such as Justin and Tatian. But for the same reason there is much less in it that is of use to later generations who had left apologetic concerns behind and were looking to the 'Fathers' for authoritative theological statements. It is characteristic of the *Plea* that the incarnation is the subject of only one obscure remark (21. 4). In the manuscripts from the tenth to the sixteenth century the treatise *On the Resurrection* is often copied without the *Plea*, apparently because of its superior usefulness in one department of theology. The possibility that it had a separate career also before the tenth century will be discussed below.

It is likely, then, that we owe the preservation of the *Plea* to the cultural renaissance inspired especially by Photius, patriarch of Constantinople, and supported by such emperors of the Macedonian dynasty as Leo VI (A.D. 886–912), a pupil of Photius, and Constantine VII (A.D. 913–59).

---

4 Fol. 401ᵛ.   5 Fols. 322ᵛ–367ᵛ.

Arethas, as the range of his library suggests,[6] shared the scholarly ideals of this circle. His recovery of and interest in Athenagoras can best be understood against the intellectual background for which Photius' *Bibliotheca* stands.

Codex Paris 451 is the first manuscript that embodies the conception of a corpus of 'apologists'. The recognition of the existence of such a category of early Christian literature, reflecting a distinctive orientation and purpose, was an important step in the sorting out of the early materials. But there is also some artificiality inherent in the conception, and it is well to remember the wide diversity of views and temperaments of the 'apologists' of the second century.

I. THE *PLEA*

The *Plea* may be dated between A.D. 176 (the beginning of the co-rulership of M. Aurelius and Commodus) and A.D. 180 (the death of M. Aurelius) or, more narrowly, between A.D. 176 and A.D. 178 (if we assume that the 'deep peace' of 1. 2 is more than a rhetorical flourish and that no such reference was possible after the resumption of the war against the Germans in A.D. 178). The apology may have been called forth by the persecution of the Christians in Gaul in A.D. 177 (Eusebius, *H.E.* 5. 1. 1 ff.), but there is little positive evidence in favour of this (cf. 3. 1).

There is one serious difficulty with the address. M. Aurelius dropped the title 'victor of Armenia' after the death of his adoptive brother, L. Aurelius Verus, in A.D. 169; and Commodus never had it. Schwartz therefore suggested that 'victors of Germany' be read instead; Harnack suggested expunging the phrase as an interpolation; and Geffcken welcomed the confusion as evidence of the unreliability of the salutation. But Giovanni Porta has shown that in unofficial papyri and inscriptions 'victor of Armenia' *was* a title used of M. Aurelius after the death of L. Verus and that

[6] Adolph von Harnack, *Die Ueberlieferung der griechischen Apologeten des zweiten Jahrhunderts in der alten Kirche und im Mittelalter* (Texte und Untersuchungen, i. 1/2, Leipzig, J. C. Hinrichs, 1882), pp. 36–46.

it was also given to Commodus.[7] We can hardly expect our author to conform to precise official usage.

It must be admitted, however, that there is something wrong with the address. Arethas had already remarked on its incompleteness in the margin of Paris 451. In orations like those of Aelius Aristides we sometimes have addresses in the usual epistolary form 'N. to N., greeting' (*Or.* 12 and 41). The address of the *Plea* was obviously intended to conform to this formula. But the name of the sender and the greeting have fallen away. Still, in light of the internal evidence discussed above, it seems clear that the address is right as far as it goes. That the sender was Athenagoras is probably correct. The title which mentions him is old, since it is in the hand of the scribe Baanes.[8] Methodius, moreover, knew the *Plea* as a work of Athenagoras. Our apologist could also have been an Athenian as the title claims; and he had as much right to the name 'philosopher' as many others of his day.[9]

The title may be translated 'embassy' as well as 'plea'. The former translation is adopted by those who see in the *Plea* an address intended to be delivered before the emperors in person. And it must be admitted that Athenagoras writes as though he were actually addressing them (2. 6). Moreover, Philo's *Embassy* (162 ff.) and the 'Acts of the Pagan Martyrs'[10] show that emperors did receive embassies and deal with them in a loose judicial manner on matters touching whole segments of the population. But such action had some concrete situation as its focus (Athenagoras is studiously vague); and no formal apology of the length of the *Plea* was in order.[11]

---

[7] 'La dedica e la data della Πρεσβεία di Atenagora', *Didaskalion*, 5/1–2 (1916), 53–70.

[8] Oscar von Gebhardt, *Der Arethascodex Paris Gr. 451* (Texte und Untersuchungen, i. 3; Leipzig, J. C. Hinrichs, 1883), pp. 183–5.

[9] H. I. Marrou, *A History of Education in Antiquity* (New York, Sheed & Ward, 1956), pp. 287–90.

[10] H. A. Musurillo, *The Acts of the Pagan Martyrs: Acta Alexandrinorum* (Oxford, University Press, 1954).

[11] In formal trials before emperors point-for-point investigation had replaced long set speeches since the time of Nero (Max Kaser, *Das Römische Zivilprozessrecht* [München, C. H. Becker, 1966], p. 352 n. 31.

Should we wish to imagine a somewhat more likely official setting in which the *Plea* could have figured, we may follow Ehrhardt's suggestion concerning Justin's Apologies[12] (which Athenagoras knew[13]) and suppose that such a document would have been sent to the imperial department *ab epistulis*.[14] But since Athenagoras poses as a speaker, this also seems unlikely. We are driven to the conclusion that he was constructing an oration in the forensic style in obedience to the rules of rhetoric.

Despite this artificiality the peculiar mark of the *Plea* among the Apologies of the second century is its controlled apologetic aim. Exposition of Christian teaching occurs only to rebut false charges (see the outline below).[15] Athenagoras, then, seems not to be writing for himself and other Christians. As Monachino suggests,[16] the *Plea* looks like an 'open letter' to the emperors destined for the general public. It represents an elaboration of the sort of thing that Christians of an irenic bent said before tribunals (cf. Eusebius, *H.E.* 7. 11. 8). The political and legal issues involved in declining to participate in forms of pagan piety are not directly faced; instead the appeal is to a higher law felt to exonerate Christians. This

[12] 'Justin Martyr's Two Apologies', *Journal of Ecclesiastical History*, 4 (1953), 1–12.

[13] Note especially the discussion about suffering simply because of the 'name' (1. 3–2. 5). Cf. Justin, *Ap.* 1. 3. 1; 1. 4. 1.

[14] 'In the second century, the control of the Greek section [of the Secretariate] seems to have been the ambition of the Greek rhetors and sophists in a quite remarkable degree' (Ludwig Friedlaender, *Roman Life and Manners* E.T. from ed. 7 [London, George Routledge & Sons, 1914], p. 55). They were, in short, men like Athenagoras. For an example of a request of a political nature made to the emperor through the Secretariate see Josephus, *Ant.* 20. 183. Here Syrians bribe the secretary to gain a rescript from Nero to deprive the Jews of Caesarea of their political rights. Again, however, the object of the request is quite specific.

[15] Michele Pellegrino, *Studi su l'antica apologetica* (Rome, Edizioni di 'storia e letterature', 1947), pp. 46–85, also stresses the apologetic intent. He allows, however, for 'protreptic' elements as well (11. 3–4: our teachings, unlike dialectic, provide happiness and profit even the uncultured); but he regards protreptic as an extension of apologetic (the pursuit of philosophy, medicine, and music were commended, and thereby defended, in protreptic treatises). He rejects Ubaldi's category of 'propaganda' as a description of the *Plea*.

[16] 'Intento pratico e propagandistico nell'apologetica Greca del II secolo', *Gregorianum*, 32 (1951), 3–49.

flight to 'philosophy' and theology caused Geffcken to declare that the *Plea* was 'pure book literature without direct practical purposes'.[17] And Athenagoras, as we shall see, is a bookish man. But the judgement seems too strong in light of the careful elimination of materials not apologetic in character. Athenagoras was not simply providing comfort for his co-religionists. The reason for the failure to confront the practical issues more directly is that this was impossible: there was an irreconcilable clash of values. It is a mark of Athenagoras' grasp of the situation that he saw the need to redefine 'atheism'—that is, to re-orient the social and religious ideas of the cultivated—if Christians were to remain Christian and yet continue to live in the Roman empire.

This effort to re-orient conventional views on society and religion was called forth by three charges levelled against the Christians: (1) atheism, (2) Thyestean banquets, and (3) Oedipean intercourse (3. 1). It is the first that occupies Athenagoras most fully. 'Atheism' in the Roman empire was understood primarily as a refusal to recognize the gods of the 'cities' and to participate in the traditional rites. Dio Cassius (67. 14. 2) knew of capital punishment for atheism already in the reign of Domitian. But the underlying reasons for the action are unclear. Apparently Christians were suspect not because they taught a new theology but because they rejected the old ways (1. 1–2; cf. Eusebius, *H.E.* 7. 11. 6–11). As men without an ancient heritage and a national home they could not claim the immunities enjoyed by the Jews (cf. Origen, *Contra Celsum* 5. 25). It seems unlikely, then, that 'atheism' was a charge with a clearly definable legal significance. But by Athenagoras' time hostile popular sentiment may have forced governors to take the profession

---

[17] Johannes Geffcken, *Zwei Griechische Apologeten* (Leipzig, B. G. Teubner, 1907), p. 99 n. 1. Geffcken regards the beginning of chap. 37 ('let our teaching concerning the resurrection be set aside for the present') as final proof of the artificiality of the whole treatise. Again, however, the remark is motivated by a desire to avoid introducing materials that have little to do with the apologetic task. It is enough for pagans to realize that Christians are harmless even though they may be foolish.

of Christianity as proof in itself of behaviour inimical to good
social order and dangerous to the state. And the Christians'
refusal to perform honours to the emperors of a sacral
nature may often have led to the more specific charge of
treason.[18]

In his reply to this charge, Athenagoras associates himself
with the philosophical tradition against popular religion and
seeks to show that Christians are in harmony with the best
that had been thought and said. Unfortunately his train of
ideas is not always clear, and his command of materials is
not secure. A striking example is the argumentation in
chapter eight where a 'topological' proof for monotheism is
offered. So obscure is the line of thought that Eduard
Schwartz felt compelled to bracket many sentences as inter-
polations. My notes on that passage illustrate the difficulty of
understanding its logic. The background of philosophical and
theological motifs is equally clouded. Some of the language
about the One is reminiscent of the doctrine of the Eleatics[19]
which could have been known to Athenagoras in a revised
Hellenistic form.[20] The talk about the 'place' of God may
have been borrowed from the Church's anti-Gnostic debate.[21]
And inevitably Stoic and Platonic (or Philonic) themes may
be identified.[22] Yet the controlling argument is the biblical
emphasis on God's power—an argument that renders much
else in the chapter irrelevant. Such a medley of ideas would
hardly have commended itself to the pagan intellectual. Yet
the apologetic point is made, however confusedly, that, in
view of the soundness of monotheism, Christians are not
atheists.

[18] O. Sild, *Das altchristliche Martyrium in Berücksichtigung der rechtlichen Grund-
lage der Christenverfolgung* (Dorpat, 1920).
[19] Karl F. Bauer, *Die Lehre des Athenagoras von Gottes Einheit und Dreieinigkeit*
(Bamberg, Linotype-Druck der Handels-Druckerei, 1902), p. 22.
[20] Robert M. Grant, *The Early Christian Doctrine of God* (Charlottesville,
The University Press of Virginia, 1966), pp. 105–10.
[21] Grant, *Doctrine of God*, pp. 109–10.
[22] Bauer, *Gottes Einheit und Dreieinigkeit*, pp. 4–33; cf. Ludwig Richter,
Philosophisches in der Gottes- und Logoslehre des Apologeten Athenagoras aus Athen
(Meissen, C. E. Klinkicht & Sohn, 1905).

Such a theoretical view of the issue could not have interested the Roman emperors deeply. Few men desired to be counted with Diagoras the 'atheist' (4. 1);[23] but such atheism was relatively harmless. With the Christians it was otherwise. The opinion of the majority was that they were guilty of 'hatred against mankind' (Tacitus, *Annals* 15. 44), and the depth of the antipathy was symbolized by the charges of illicit sexual practices and cannibalism—charges possibly occasioned by the emphasis on universal love and by distorted views of the Eucharist. Athenagoras obsequiously proclaims the loyalty of the Christians (1. 1–2; 2. 1–3; 2. 6; 6. 2; 16. 2; 18. 2; 37) in the exaggerated language of the rhetorical schools.[24] He has nothing in common with the hostile Tatian, is even more irenic than Justin, and probably would have felt comfortable with Melito's suggestion that by divine providence the destinies of Church and Empire were intertwined (Eusebius, *H.E.* 4. 26. 7–11).

Considerable adjustment was necessary, however, before this happy state could be realized. For 'loyal' as men like Athenagoras no doubt were (1. 3), their 'philosophy' was interpenetrated by ideas that had already led to a withdrawal of Christians from full participation in the life of the 'cities'. This withdrawal seemed antisocial.

---

[23] Adolph von Harnack, *Der Vorwurf des Atheismus in den drei ersten Jahrhunderten* (Texte und Untersuchungen, xxviii. 4; Leipzig, J. C. Hinrichs, 1905), pp. 11–14.

[24] Especially important are the directions set down by Menander (C. Walz, *Rhetores Graeci*, ix [Stuttgart, J. G. Cotta, 1836], 213–31). The points that stand out are these: praise can hardly be too great for a king (213. 5–6); we are to say that kings are 'sent from god', are his 'effluences', and come 'from heaven' (217. 13–218. 1); they should be praised for their 'love of learning, their brilliance, their eagerness for studies, their easy grasp of what is taught them' (220. 1–2); if they are philosophical, that should be exploited (220. 3); one is to say that they surpassed their contemporaries (220. 6–7); on the practical side, deeds done in the pursuit of 'peace' are especially admirable (226. 3, 9); they are to be commended especially for their 'gentleness' and 'affection for men' (226. 5–7) and for their 'justice' (225. 9–13); they are to be lauded for being easy to approach (226. 7); finally 'prayer' is to be offered that god would grant them a long reign and that they be succeeded by their sons (230. 19–231. 2). Athenagoras cites biblical passages to support some of these themes; but the inspiration is clearly rhetorical.

Most important of these ideas was the emphasis on the untrammelled power of the Creator and his care for the world (13. 2). Here was a monotheism that was more radical and therefore more exclusive than any philosophical theism of the time. Only this God was to be worshipped (16. 1, 3); and Christians were willing to give up their lives for his sake (3. 2). The Christian ethic was equally uncompromising. Popular pleasures like the gladiatorial and animal fights were rejected (35. 4–5). The requirements for purity of life were severe (11. 2–4; 12. 1; 12. 3; 32. 2–34. 3). The emphasis on requital in another world (31. 4; 36. 1–3) turned Christians from things below and contributed to that stubbornness which outraged Roman officials (Pliny, *Ep.* 10. 96). The very clarity of the ethical imperative, based as it was on the prophetic voice of Scripture and the words of Jesus (11. 1; 32. 4), brought a certainty which must have looked more like *naïveté* than integrity to many. The Christians were fully conscious that it was the all-knowing God, not some shadowy mythological personages, before whom men will ultimately stand for judgement (12. 2). The uncluttered distinction between good and evil appears in another form in Athenagoras' demonology (chaps. 24–5), which echoes traditional Christian[25] and Jewish[26] themes rather than the less dualistic doctrines of the Greeks. Athenagoras is confident that God's providence guides the righteous through all difficulties.[27]

[25] Justin, *Ap.* 2. 5. 3 (cf. Enoch 6); 2. 7. 5 (cf. Tatian 7).

[26] Cf. Friedrich Andres, *Die Engellehre der griechischen Apologeten des zweiten Jahrhunderts und ihr Verhältnis zur griechische-römischen Dämonologie* (Paderborn, Ferdinand Schöningh, 1914).

[27] Similar ideas about providence may be found in Plato (*Tim.* 41 a) and, in greater detail, in Ps.-Plutarch (*De Fato* 9). But Athenagoras' view of particular providence and his explanation of disorder are Christian rather than pagan. Cf. Salvatore Pappalardo, 'La teoria degli angeli e dei demoni e la dottrina della providenza in Atenagora', *Didascalion*, N.S. 2/3 (1924), 67–130. The following scheme may be suggested: (1) There is a general providence of God connected with the 'law of reason', extending (*a*) over the whole material world and (*b*) over men as physical organisms. (2) There is a restricted providence delegated to angels who have been set over aspects of creation; some of these angels, including the prince over matter, exercised their freedom and violated their office: the angels, with their offspring the demons, move men to folly;

And his belief in the resurrection of the body (31. 4; 36. 1–3) illustrates the completeness of his reliance on God's power.

Athenagoras' doctrine of God culminates in Trinitarian theology (10. 2–5; cf. 4. 2; 6. 2; 12. 3; 18. 2). For apologetic reasons, however, he avoids its most controversial feature— the doctrine of the incarnation (cf. 21. 4). Also for apologetic reasons he matches the emphasis on the unity of God by an insistence on the reality of the three and the mutuality of their interrelation. In this connection he also presupposes (somewhat more cautiously than Justin) the veneration of angels.[28] What he is arguing is this: it is especially ridiculous to charge the Christians with atheism when their theology bears witness to a plural conception of deity (10. 5). That is why Athenagoras anticipates later 'orthodox' teaching in his emphasis on the distinctions within the godhead and the eternity of the Word; yet in harmony with his contemporaries the 'generation' of the Son is still bound up with his emission for the purpose of creation, and 'Father' is still primarily a title for God as author of all that is. In any event, Athenagoras concentrates on an aspect of Trinitarian thought which prepares the ground for a theology capable of uniting the biblical emphasis on God as Creator, the Greek fascination with a world interpenetrated by Logos, and a doctrine of prophetic authority rooted in the activity of the Spirit who touches the deepest recesses of the human intellect.

It is with some justification, then, that Athenagoras makes use of the resources of Hellenism to express Christian truth. He not only aligns himself with the best that had been thought and said by the Greeks, but he also seeks to express himself in a form that would commend his message to the cultured. His organization of materials is orderly. His style is Atticistic.[29]

---

the prince over matter creates disorder in human affairs. (3) There is a particular providence of God 'over the worthy'. This is not the Middle Platonic hierarchy with particular providence in the hands of the demons.

[28] 10. 5; cf. Justin, *Ap.* 1. 6. 2.

[29] Geffcken, *Zwei Griechische Apologeten*, pp. 163–6.

Despite weaknesses in structure,[30] the *Plea* projects an atmo-
sphere of the 'refinement' sought after by devotees of the
'second sophistic'.

Athenagoras' command of Greek philosophy and literature
reflects the learning that characterized this set of writers.
The apologist himself remarks that he has recourse to the
Hellenistic Doxographies (6. 2) in his account of Greek
philosophy—though there is a hint that he could have said
more had the occasion demanded. There are two quotations
from Empedocles,[31] seven from Plato.[32] Athenagoras probably
had read some Plato; but the quotations represent principal
texts used and reused in the Graeco-Roman period. The
close relation between Athenagoras' account of other philosophers and the summaries of their teaching in the doxographies indicates reliance on these superficial manuals.[33]

Athenagoras' acquaintance with literature and mythology
is somewhat more profound. He quotes Homer eighteen
times,[34] Hesiod twice,[35] Pindar once,[36] Aeschylus once[37] (in
a form derived from Plato), Euripides seven times,[38] Callimachus once.[39] There are four quotations from tragedies of
unknown authorship;[40] there is one spurious fragment of
Sophocles;[41] Orphic verses are cited;[42] and the Sibyl is
quoted.[43] Of prose works, his eight quotations from Herodotus stand out.[44] He also refers to a spurious letter of Alexander
the Great,[45] to Hermes Trismegistus,[46] to Ktesias,[47] and to

---

[30] Too many 'footnotes' get into the text, and Athenagoras has trouble
fully integrating some materials (such as his discussion of the 'names' of the
gods).

[31] 22. 1, 2.

[32] 6. 2; 16. 4; 19. 2; 23. 5, 7, 9 (Plato is also referred to in 12. 1; 16. 3; 30. 1;
36. 3).

[33] Thales (23. 4); Pythagoras, Heraclitus, Democritus, Socrates (31. 2);
Pythagoras (36. 3) and Pythagoreans (6. 1); Aristotle (6. 3; 25. 2) and Peripatetics (16. 3); Stoics (6. 4; 19. 3; 22. 4–5).

[34] 13. 4; 18. 1, 3; 21. 2, 3, 4, 5; 26. 4; 29. 1.

[35] 24. 6; 29. 2.   [36] 29. 2.   [37] 21. 5.

[38] 5. 1, 2; 21. 5; 25. 1, 2; 29. 3.   [39] 30. 3.

[40] 25. 2; 26. 2; 29. 4.   [41] 5. 3.   [42] 18. 3, 6; 20. 4.

[43] 30. 1.   [44] 17. 2; 28. 2, 3, 4, 6, 8, 9, 10.   [45] 28. 1.

[46] 28. 6.   [47] 30. 1.

Apollodorus' treatise 'On the Gods'.[48] Geffcken has shown in his commentary that many of these quotations were also derived from secondary works. Yet he grants the relative excellence of Athenagoras' use of literary and mythological sources and the wide range of his information. There are even a number of notices, particularly in the sphere of mythology and pagan religion (on Helen and Metaneira in 1. 1 and 14. 1; on Neryllinus in 26. 3), which are attested only by Athenagoras. Nino Scivoletto has further pressed the importance of the enrichment of traditional materials by Athenagoras himself.[49] He finds evidence for it particularly in the mythological notes in chapters one and fourteen; and he shows that Athenagoras' knowledge was probably derived from the detailed commentary that accompanied the great works of Greek culture studied at the 'secondary school' level—especially Homer's *Iliad*. He buttresses these conclusions by noting that Athenagoras is familiar for the most part with those authors recommended to the budding scholar.[50] Scivoletto does not challenge Geffcken's conclusions about Athenagoras' knowledge of philosophy, but his analysis suggests a somewhat wider breadth of literary interest and some ability in correlating materials useful to his purpose. It may be added here that Athenagoras' information on the history of art, though not profound, is also generally reliable.[51]

The appeal to such authorities arises from Athenagoras' desire to expose the weakness of polytheism and to show the agreement of the best minds on monotheism. To carry out the attack on the gods Athenagoras adopts methods already worked out by Sceptics and Epicureans. One important example of this is the rejection of the Stoic defence of polytheism by means of 'physical allegory' (5. 2; 6. 4; 22.

---

[48] 28. 7.

[49] 'Cultura e scoliastica in Atenagora', *Giornale Italiano di Filologia*, 13 (1960), 236–48.

[50] Cf. Marrou, *A History of Education*, pp. 224–8.

[51] Giuseppe Botti, 'Atenagora quale fonte per la storia dell'arte', *Didaskalion*, 4/3–4 (1915), 395–417.

1–12). Another is found in chapters one and fourteen where Athenagoras extends the sceptical complaint against diversity of opinion (cf. 7. 2) to mythological lists not originally intended for this purpose. Euhemerism is also an obvious feature of his method (28. 1–30. 6).

At the same time Athenagoras makes positive use of monotheistic expressions of poets, Stoics, and dogmatic philosophers in general. All such materials are here pulled into the orbit of the mixture of Platonic and Stoic motifs that characterizes the philosophy of the period. The emphasis on the primacy of the immaterial (15. 1; 19. 2; 36. 3) and on God's goodness (23. 7; 24. 2) points to Platonism as the prime source for Athenagoras' ontology. The clear link between God and the Good was a relatively recent development within that tradition.[52] With Athenagoras, however, God is not related to the Good in such a way that he communicates himself inevitably to the world; contrary to the explicit teaching of some Platonists,[53] the Good, though inseparable from God, is thought of as an attribute or 'accident' only; the power of God remains the decisive factor. The list of philosophical issues in 7. 2—God, matter, forms, world— reads like an outline of a Middle Platonic system. But it is a significant shift when God rather than the Ideas are connected with Being (4. 2; 7. 2); and it is an important event in religious philosophy when the created and uncreated are related as non-being to Being (4. 2; 15. 1). Athenagoras expresses these doctrines with little awareness of the difficulties involved: it is 'God' who stands over against 'matter' (4. 1; 6. 1; 15. 1); and apparently matter is still conceived as pre-existent (cf. 10. 3; 15. 2; 19. 4). Later Christian theology was to realize that the immaterial and the divine do not in all cases (e.g. angels, souls) coincide;[54] and matter was put more securely under God's control. Athenagoras' view that God can be apprehended by mind and reason alone (22. 9,

---

[52] Cf. Albinus, *Epit.* 10. 3.   [53] Albinus, *Epit.* 10. 4.
[54] Gregory of Nyssa, *Contra Eunomium* 1. 22 (Justin, *Dial.* 4–6, had already shown the way).

12; 23. 7) leaves the way open for over-exalted views of the soul; and his willingness to point to the veneration of angels to illustrate Christian theism presupposes suspiciously broad views of the divine. Yet the treatise stands as a striking example of how Christian theology came to modify Platonic metaphysics from the point of view of biblical ideas.

Aspects of Stoic 'monotheism' are also absorbed. The proof for the existence of God from the harmony of the cosmos reflects Stoic language (4. 2; 5. 3; 16. 1). More neo-Pythagorean in character is the view of the cosmos as an enclosed sphere moving in rhythm (16. 3). But all such materials are given an interpretation that brings them closely in line with the biblical emphasis on the oneness of God (9. 2).

When Christians like Athenagoras placed the Creator in the centre of their 'philosophy', it was inevitable that they would also emphasize the importance of man and his free decisions (cf. 24. 4–5; 25. 4); a characteristic point is made when human destiny is radically distinguished from that of animals (31. 4). In the philosophical tradition only Stoicism approached this conception of human nature; and only Stoicism distinguished as sharply between men and animals. There are other traces of Stoic thought in the contrast drawn between men's vices and the natural life of beasts (3. 1); in the emphasis on the production of children as the purpose of marriage (33. 1–2);[55] and in the psychological explanation given for visions (27. 1).[56] But, as Athenagoras observes, Christianity unlike philosophy demonstrates its

[55] Konrad Graf Preysing, 'Ehezweck und zweite Ehe bei Athenagoras', *Theologische Quartalschrift*, 110 (1929), 85–110. The attempt to find Stoic parallels to Athenagoras' rejection of second marriage (33. 6), however, fails. This need not be a Montanist feature (cf. Jerome, *Ep.* 41. 3; Tertullian, *Ad Uxor.* 1; *De Exh. Cast.* 9). Such rigorist ideas were probably about in many circles of the Church. Letters of Jerome (*Epp.* 54, 79, 123) illustrate how suspect second marriage remained even when it was officially condoned. Canon 7 of the Council of Neocaesarea (*c.* A.D. 314–325) forbids a presbyter to join in the celebration of a marriage of 'digamists' since 'the digamist requires repentance (penance)'. The Novatians were also rigoristic on this point (Gregory Nazianzen, *Or.* 39. 18). [56] Cf. Sextus Empiricus, *Adv. Log.* 1. 249.

power by touching the lives of men of all classes (11. 3–4). It is not the dignity of man and the nobility of rational behaviour but the answerability of man before his Maker (12. 1) that is the guarantee of clarity in theology and purity in life.

Athenagoras, then, assumes the correctness of many of the theological views of paganism. The poets and philosophers spoke as men whose souls had been touched by the 'breath' of God. But they were guilty of trusting to themselves rather than learning of God from God. This accounts for the diversity of pagan beliefs. To the poets and philosophers Athenagoras opposes the prophets who wrote under divine inspiration. The sharpness of this opposition is somewhat mitigated by the description of inspiration in a figure of speech—'as if they were musical instruments'—which has a Hellenic ring. It is clear, nevertheless, that the prophets do not give expression to merely human opinions (chap. 7). It is characteristic of Athenagoras that he follows this statement about revelation with an exposition of the rational reasons for the oneness of God (chap. 8). Revelation is the more sure guide; but 'our faith' is not devoid of rational grounds.

Athenagoras' philosophical theology, then, bears witness to the desire of a segment of Christians in the second century to exploit the most prestigious elements of Greek culture. This intellectual orientation has a social corollary; for Athenagoras finds no fundamental conflict between the Church and the Empire. The suggestion that the Church could play a role in securing the stability of the Empire is not far from his mind. Only the ignorant and prejudiced, as he sees it, can regard Christianity as atheistic and immoral.

Outline of the Plea

I. Introduction (1. 1–2. 6)

II. Defence of the Christians against charges of atheism and immorality (3. 1–36. 3)

(A) Division of topics (3. 1–2)

(B) Defence against the charge of atheism (4. 1–30. 6)

   (1) Christians not guilty of theoretical atheism (4. 1–12. 4)

      (a) The Christian doctrine of God (4. 1–10. 5)

         (i) Introductory remarks: Christians and Diagoras (4. 1–2)

         (ii) Enlightened pagan views (5. 1–6. 4)
            (a) Poets (5. 1–3)
            (b) Philosophers (6. 1–4)

         (iii) Christian views (7. 1–10. 5)
            (a) Revelation (7. 1–3)
            (b) Rational arguments (8. 1–8)
            (c) The voice of the prophets (9. 1–3)
            (d) The Christian God (10. 1–5)
               (i) Pure monotheism (10. 1)
               (ii) A rich conception of the divine: the trinity and angels (10. 2–5)

      (b) Christian morality presupposes theism (11. 1–12. 4)

   (2) The practical atheism of Christians in proper perspective (13. 1–30. 6): the refutation of paganism is undertaken to show that Christians are not atheists simply because they
      (a) do not sacrifice (13. 1–4),
      (b) do not recognize national gods (14. 1–3),
      (c) do not venerate images (15. 1–30. 6); for
         (i) idols are material and made by men (15. 1–17. 5), and
         (ii) their power is demonic (18. 1–30. 6); since
            (a) the 'gods' of myth are perishable (18. 3–19. 4),

II. *CONCERNING THE RESURRECTION OF THE DEAD*

The treatise on the resurrection must be dealt with separately from the *Plea* both because of the subject-matter and because of the doubt that has been cast on its authorship.

We owe its preservation also to Arethas. But there can be no doubt that a different textual tradition is presupposed. For the text of the treatise on the resurrection has by no means suffered the ravages which are evident in the *Plea*. Even allowing for the greater difficulty in transcribing a text like the *Plea* filled with names and quotations we can hardly avoid the conclusion that these writings had a separate history some time prior to their inclusion in codex Paris 451.

In favour of the traditional view of authorship is the fact that there is apparently no fundamental difference between the vocabulary and style of the two treatises and the fact that near the end of the *Plea* (37. 1) Athenagoras sets aside the problem of the resurrection—presumably for some other occasion. There is also the striking appearance in both treatises of the Homeric theme concerning death as the twin brother of sleep and the citation of 1 Cor. 15: 32 ('Let us eat and drink, for tomorrow we die'). What is more natural than to think that the treatise which follows is Athenagoras' fulfilment of his promise?

If, however, there are good reasons for doubting the traditional view of authorship, the announcement at the end of the *Plea* may simply have prompted the joining of the two treatises. It is significant that when Methodius looked for authorities on the resurrection he could find only the few words of Athenagoras in the *Plea*. There is, then, no trace of the treatise on the resurrection precisely where one would most expect to find it. The form of the title 'by the same . . .' reflects the critical opinion of a scholar rather than the editorial work of the author himself; Athenagoras' name occurs in the subscription, but that is in Arethas' hand.[57]

Robert M. Grant has argued vigorously for the view that the treatise on the resurrection is not by Athenagoras,[58] and we present his most important arguments here. In addition to the problems raised by the manuscript tradition and the title of the treatise the most important single argument against the traditional view of authorship is the appearance of the 'problem of chain-consumption' (4. 3–4). This argument does not yet occur in Celsus' attack on the Christian view of the resurrection; and Tertullian only alludes to the problem of bodies being eaten by fish, animals, and birds (*De Res. Carn.* 32). Origen seems to have raised the further point that such creatures may in turn be eaten by men. His

---

[57] Stählin (in Adolph von Harnack, *Die altchristliche Literatur bis Eusebius*, ii/2 [Leipzig, J. C. Hinrichs, 1897], p. 317 n. 4) says that Arethas was also responsible for the words 'by the same' in the title. One cannot be sure about that; but if Stählin is right, arguments against the traditional view are even stronger. Gebhardt, *Der Arethascodex*, pp. 183–5, regards the whole title as written by Baanes.

[58] 'Athenagoras or Pseudo-Athenagoras', *Harvard Theological Review*, 47 (1954), 121–9.

views are preserved in an epitome of his commentary on the
first psalm quoted by Methodius, a foe of Origenism (*Res.* 1.
20–4). The epitome also attacks the use of the verse 'everything is possible for God' (Luke 18: 27)—and our treatise
appeals to it for support (9. 2). Not only the *possibility* but
also the *worthiness* of the idea of the resurrection is discussed
in the epitome as well as in our treatise (2. 3; 10. 1, 6; 11.
1–2). It is probably significant that the appeal in the *Plea* to
Plato and Pythagoras in support of the resurrection (36. 3;
cf. Tertullian, *De Res. Carn.* 1) plays no role in the treatise on
the resurrection.

It is not at all clear, however, that there is any fundamental
distinction between the view of the resurrection as sketched
in the *Plea* and as developed in the treatise on the resurrection. The *Plea*'s remark that in the resurrection we shall 'not
be as flesh but as heavenly spirit' (31. 3) may mean no more
than that the resurrected body will exchange corruption for
incorruption (*De Res.* 12. 6; 12. 8–9; 13. 1; 16. 1–17. 4). And
the Aristotelian parallels to the treatise brought forward by
Pohlenz are too weak to build a case against common authorship.[59] Nevertheless, the arguments advanced by Grant are
sufficiently strong to raise serious doubts about the traditional
view.

To these may be added other considerations. In the notes
to this edition we have drawn attention not only to relevant
parallels in Methodius but also in Gregory of Nyssa and
Galen. Gregory, a 'catholic' Origenist, faced the argument

---

[59] 'Die griechische Philosophie im Dienste der christlichen Auferstehungslehre', *Zeitschrift für wissenschaftliche Theologie*, 47 (1904), 241–50. Pohlenz draws
attention to such elements as the following: man is a 'composite' (there are
parallels in Alexander of Aphrodisias, though it is granted that the term (τὸ
συναμφότερον) derived from Plato, *Symp.* 209 b, and its use by Church fathers
is noted); the affections are ascribed to man as a whole; resurrection of the
body is a logical concomitant of the Aristotelian doctrine that the soul, as form
of the body, cannot be immortal—that is, since Athenagoras assumes the immortality of the soul, the body must also be immortal. Our treatise, however,
does not work with the Aristotelian notion of the soul as the form of the body;
and the emphasis on man as a psycho-physical unity is illustrated more
adequately from other sources as we shall see shortly.

based on the problem of 'chain-consumption' and rejected it. Gregory also shows familiarity with the medical theories of Galen—theories which are brought into the discussion of the resurrection both by Methodius and by our treatise. These connections seem to provide evidence of the most natural milieu for the debate. To illustrate, attention may also be drawn to Gregory's sermon *In Sanctum Pascha*[60] which brings together many of the same points found in our treatise: the problem of the fate of parts of the body devoured by animals, birds, fish, and worms; medical theory derived from Galen; discussion of God's power in comparison with that of man; the argument from the purpose of man's creation; the truth and worthiness of the idea of the bodily resurrection; the comparison of death and sleep in Homeric terms; the quotation of 1 Cor. 15: 32; the interdependence of soul and body in performing deeds for which man is to be judged by God; the polemical tenor of the sermon. Even more important is the reference to man, the psycho-physical unity, as a 'composite'.[61] Both Gregory and our treatise use the term in connection with the theme of judgement. It is less at home in the Aristotelian framework imagined by Pohlenz. Either Athenagoras anticipated in a remarkable way the theological developments of a later period, or the treatise is not by Athenagoras. It seems more likely that the treatise is to be understood against the background of the debate over Origen's view of the resurrection. The extended life of that debate makes it unwise to attempt a more precise dating.

In addition to all this, there is little or nothing that compels the reader to think of pagan (or Gnostic) opponents. Near the beginning (1. 5) the author apparently turns from outright deniers of the resurrection (pagans) to Christians—both those who dispute the doctrine and those who are

---

[60] Edited by E. Gebhardt, in *Gregorii Nysseni Opera: Sermones, Pars I*, general editors, W. Jaeger and H. Langerbeck (Leiden, E. J. Brill, 1967), pp. 251–70. I owe this reference to Prof. Robert Wilken of Fordham University.

[61] p. 266. 20; cf. Methodius, *De Res.* 1. 54. 3; 1. 55. 4.

shaken by these disputes. In another passage (3. 3) there seems to be a reference to the disputers of the doctrine—that is, men 'admired for their wisdom' (like Origen?) yet overcome by the prejudices of 'the crowd' (pagans?). The treatise as a whole can be readily understood as directed against such doubters. Certainly the way in which the author appeals to the Law (23. 2), the Gospel (9. 2), and 'the Apostle' (18. 5) suggests an intramural debate. It is also possible, as Grant has observed, that he is improving on traditional Christian themes (cf. Tertullian, *De Res. Carn.* 14–15) when he criticizes those who stress the judgement as the primary defence of the resurrection (14. 6)—though his own long development of the argument (18. 1–23. 6) suggests that he is speaking to people who share his presuppositions.[62]

Some difference in style is also discernible. Our treatise is characterized by long periods which flow smoothly and evenly and is not ornamented by the artifices (interruptions, quotations, the heaping up of synonyms, antithesis, anaphora, etc.) which are found in the *Plea*.[63] Arguments are marshalled in an orderly fashion and find their mark with fewer diversions than is the case with the *Plea*.

The treatise on the resurrection, like the *Plea*, is in the form of an address (23. 6); but it serves a rather different purpose. Our author's rhetorical training has equipped him well for a polemical situation of the kind that we have imagined. The structure of the treatise is determined by a distinction

---

[62] It should also be noted that Porphyry (A.D. 233–c. 301) raised the problem of chain-consumption against the Christian doctrine of the resurrection and rejected the appeal to the power of God (frg. 94 Harnack). In view of the attention which Porphyry gave to Origen (Eusebius, *H.E.* 6. 19. 5–8) it is not impossible that he learnt to attack Christians with weapons provided by the Alexandrian theologian. If the defence of the resurrection in our treatise is directed against Origenists, then followers of Porphyry may be the pagans whom the author sees as exerting a baleful influence on Christian theology. Alternatively, our treatise may be directed against such Platonists themselves. In any event, the discussion seems to belong to a later period than that of the apologist Athenagoras.

[63] Schwartz, *Athenagorae Libellus*, p. 92.

between arguments 'on behalf of' the truth and arguments 'concerning' the truth (1. 3 ff.). The former serve for the refutation of error, the latter for the confirmation of truth among those 'well disposed to receive' it (cf. 11. 3–6). The text implies that refutation employs a less rigorous method, yet one that is more 'useful' for this purpose. It looks very much like a school tradition rooted in the distinction that Aristotle draws between the requirements of rhetoric and those of constructive philosophical statements (cf. *Rhet.* 1. 1, 1355ᵃ4). This impression is confirmed by a description of the tradition of the 'schools' in one of Jerome's letters (*Ep.* 48. 13). There Jerome speaks of the 'precepts of Aristotle' and distinguishes between rhetorical exercises intended to confute opponents—'those who are without'— on their own grounds and less artful approaches intended to convince disciples—'those who are within'. With Jerome there is greater emphasis on the liberty that the polemical situation provides to 'argue as one pleases, saying one thing while one means another'—doing, in short, whatever is 'needful'; but that seems to be an excuse for his own extreme style in attacking Jovinian. In any event the distinction warns us that our author regarded the arguments in the first part (with its emphasis on things like medical theory) as less final than the logical considerations of the second part. The parallel which Schwartz brings forward from Albinus (*Isag.* 6; cf. Plato, *Soph.* 230 c; Philo of Larissa, in Stobaeus, *Ecl.* 2. 7) shows that a like tradition was alive in philosophical circles: the philosopher, like the physician, must first remove diseased opinions to bring health to the understanding.

On the philosophical side, the author of our treatise shared with his opponents a belief in body and soul as separate substances. Elaborating an aspect of the view that had been worked out in the debate with Gnosticism (Irenaeus, *Adv. Haer.* 5. 6. 1) he insists that body as well as soul is required for a definition of man as he is and as he is intended to be. Yet the impact of the philosophical concept of soul has as one of its most apparent consequences the emphasis on the need for a transformation of the body in the resurrection. That which is mortal must put on immortality. Here the Pauline viewpoint is given a more precise significance in terms provided by philosophy and medical theory. If anything, the emphasis on the continuity between the earthly body and its resurrected form is even greater.

The theological point of departure is the emphasis on God's power and will in creating and recreating (2. 1–11. 2). This is taken up in the second part of the treatise in a refined form where we hear about the Creator's providence and the just judgement that such providence requires (18. 1–23. 6). Here the close relation between providence and judgement lends to the former concept a peculiarly un-Hellenic colour.

The mind of the Christian theologian is also betrayed in the treatment of the teleological argument. It is approached from two rather different points of view: (a) the reason for man's creation (12. 1–13. 2) and (b) the end to which he tends (24. 1–25. 5). The value of the two arguments is said to differ since the first deals with a consideration from 'first principles' (for whose sake does man exist?) whereas the second is based on the theological 'given' that men have the contemplation of God as their end and are subject to God's judgement (25. 4–5). Both arguments, however, as our author recognizes (24. 1), are closely related and presuppose ascribing to man an end sharply distinguished from that of other creatures. The latter were brought into being for the sake of something else whereas man was created for his own sake. Logic compels our author to add that man was not made for God's sake since God needs nothing—though this is not regarded as incompatible with saying that on a larger view God made man for his own sake as an expression of his goodness and wisdom or that man's end is the contemplation of God (12. 5; 25. 4). In any event, the other creatures which come into being for the sake of something else cease to exist when that for which they were created ceases. But reason can find nothing for the sake of which man was created. And since nothing is made in vain, man must perdure. When our author says that man was created for his own sake, he presupposes an understanding of the relation between God and man largely determined by Greek views of the divine. Yet the teleology invoked is an external one distinct from that of Plato and Aristotle who emphasize the realization of the end of all things that exist. Our author sees man as the crown of creation to whom all else is subservient; and this biblical perspective has brought him to select a teleology which is approached in the philosophical tradition only by the Stoics. There is also a tension between what is said about man philosophically (that he was made for his own sake) and what is said from a religious point of view (not only that he is destined to contemplate the divine—that would not be incompatible with his independence as a rational creature—but also that his creation was a matter of the direct concern of God and that his destiny is determined by his deeds for which he stands responsible before the Judge of all).

Even more distinctive is our author's emphasis on the community of experience between body and soul which requires their continued coexistence (15. 2–7). However much he longs for immortality, he knows that man's nature is creaturely and will continue to be determined by the basic conditions of its earthly existence. However much he desires permanence, he knows that it must be defined in a peculiar way in the case of man in accordance with the will of his Maker (16. 1–17. 4). What our author opposes is an exaggerated spiritualism in the Church—a spiritualism which seemed to conservatives to bring with it the risk of a Gnostic devaluation of creation and the Church itself. Origen's daring cosmology and his view of authority in terms of a 'charismatic and spiritual hierarchy'[64] were open to precisely such criticism. His teaching on the resurrection was simply one of the most vulnerable points in the eyes of theologians of a more traditional stamp.

[64] Jean Daniélou, *Origène* (Paris, Editions de la Table Ronde, 1948), p. 62.

Outline of the treatise

I. Introduction: the two modes of argumentation (1. 1–5)

II. Arguments 'on behalf of' the resurrection: God is both able and willing to raise the dead (2. 1–11. 2)

(A) Announcement of the theme: God's power and will (2. 1–3), with a definition of 'inability' (2. 4–6)

(B) God's power (3. 1–9. 2)

  (1) God can raise the dead (3. 1–3)

   (a) He reunites the elements of decomposed bodies (3. 1–2)

   (b) He reunites parts consumed by different animals (3. 3)

  (2) Restatement of objections (4. 1–4)

   (a) Parts of the body united with different animals (4. 1–2)

   (b) The problem of chain-consumption (4. 3–4)

  (3) Rebuttal (5. 1–9. 2)

   (a) Medical arguments (5. 1–7. 4)

    (i) A suitable food for each species (5. 1–6. 6)
    (ii) Permanent and impermanent elements in the body (7. 1–3)
    (iii) Conclusion: (*a*) men cannot assimilate human flesh (7. 4); (*b*) bodies buried in the earth can at most serve as food for other creatures (8. 1)

   (b) Moral argument: cannibalism the corollary of asserting that men can assimilate human flesh (8. 2–3)

   (c) Conclusion: (i) reduction of all parts to the elements and their reunion (8. 4); (ii) no need for further discussion on these points (8. 5); (iii) no need to take seriously those who compare God's power with that of man (9. 1–2)

(C) God's will (10. 1–11. 2)

  (1) Possible 'injustice' of the resurrection (10. 1–5)
    (a) as regards animals (10. 1–4)
    (b) as regards men (10. 5)

  (2) Possible 'unworthiness' of the resurrection as a work of God (10. 6)

  (3) Conclusion: possible, willed, worthy (11. 1–2)

III. Arguments 'concerning' the truth (11. 3–25. 5)

  (A) Excursus on the two modes of argumentation (11. 3–6)

  (B) Arguments for the resurrection (11. 7–25. 5)

    (1) Division of topics (11. 7)

    (2) Primary arguments—from first principles (12. 1–13. 2)
      (a) Man created for his own sake—that is, for his own survival (12. 1–13. 2)
      (b) The nature of man (13. 3–17. 4)
        (i) Excursus on the relation between the arguments (13. 3–15. 1)
        (ii) Man as a psycho-physical unity (15. 2–7)
        (iii) Definition of 'permanence' (16. 1–17. 4)

    (3) Secondary arguments—confirmation from God's providence (18. 1–23. 6) and man's end (24. 1–25. 5)
      (a) Reward and punishment (18. 1–23. 6)
        (i) The character of this argument (18. 1)
        (ii) Concerning just judgement (18. 2–23. 6)
          (a) Providence and just requital not maintained in this life (18. 2–19. 7), with an excursus against Epicureanism (19. 1–3)
          (b) Just requital possible only if the composite survives (20. 1–22. 5)
      (b) Man's end (24. 1–25. 5)

III. THE TEXT

The modern work on the text of Athenagoras was initiated by Adolph von Harnack in the first volume of *Texte und Untersuchungen* (1882). Though he was wholly dependent on the textual notes of Otto, he was able to make out the importance of the Arethas codex and to see that all other manuscripts had been derived directly or indirectly from it.[65] Von Gebhardt investigated the codex itself and confirmed in the main the results of Harnack's work.[66] The interdependence of the manuscripts was fully explored by Eduard Schwartz,[67] and the results are outlined here: n (codex Mutinensis III D 7), p (codex Parisinus 174), and c (codex Parisinus 450) were derived directly from A (the Arethas codex); from n were derived s (Argentoratensis 9) and four other manuscripts of lesser importance; from p were derived ten unimportant manuscripts.

The symbol A is used in this edition to refer to the manuscript as copied by Baanes, the symbol A[1] to corrections made by Arethas (we ignore the fact that breathings and accents were also added by Arethas). The present edition is based on photographs of the Arethas codex. The conjectures made by the copyists of later manuscripts and by the editors of the printed editions (Petrus Suffridius, Stephanus, Maranus, Gesner, Otto, Wilamowitz-Moellendorf, Schwartz, Geffcken, Ubaldi) have also been studied. Our main sources for this information have been the editions of Otto, Schwartz, and (in the case of the *Plea*) Geffcken. In the apparatus notations having to do with erasures and corrections in the hand of Baanes have usually been passed over when they reflect no serious uncertainty about the text. Corrections in the hand of Arethas are not indicated if they are obvious. Many are simply matters of orthography. In line with the purpose of this series of texts the emphasis is on the conjectures by

---

[65] Harnack, *Ueberlieferung*, pp. 1–89, 175–90.

[66] *Der Arethascodex.*

[67] *Athenagorae Libellus*, iii–xxx.

which successive editors have sought to elucidate the text. In general tendency the present text represents an effort to avoid the radical solutions of Schwartz. In the case of the *Plea* it is closer to the text of Geffcken, though in some particulars it is still more conservative.

The system of numbering chapters is the traditional one; the numbering of the sections within the chapters is borrowed from Ubaldi.

BIBLIOGRAPHY

(a) *Texts and studies of the* Plea *and* Concerning the Resurrection of the Dead

GEBHARDT, OSCAR VON, *Zur handschriftlichen Ueberlieferung der griechischen Apologeten: 1. Der Arethascodex Paris Gr. 451* (Texte und Untersuchungen, i. 3, pp. 154–96; Leipzig, J. C. Hinrichs, 1883).

GEFFCKEN, JOHANNES, *Zwei griechische Apologeten* (Leipzig, B. G. Teubner, 1907).

GRANT, ROBERT M., 'Athenagoras or Pseudo-Athenagoras', *Harvard Theological Review*, 47 (1954), 121–9.

—— *The Early Christian Doctrine of God* (Charlottesville, The University Press of Virginia, 1966).

HARNACK, ADOLPH VON, *Die Ueberlieferung der griechischen Apologeten des zweiten Jahrhunderts in der alten Kirche und im Mittelalter* (Texte und Untersuchungen, i. 1/2; Leipzig, J. C. Hinrichs, 1883).

KESELING, P., 'Athenagoras', *Reallexikon für Antike und Christentum*, i (1950), 881–8.

OTTO, J. K. THEODOR VON, *Corpus Apologetarum Christianorum Saeculi Secundi*, vol. vii (Jena, F. Mauke, 1858).

PELLEGRINO, MICHELE, *Gli apologeti Greci del II secolo* (Rome, Anonima Veritas Editrice, 1947).

—— *Studi su l'antica apologetica* (Rome, Edizioni di 'storia e letteratura', 1947).

POHLENZ, MAX, 'Die griechische Philosophie im Dienste der christlichen Auferstehungslehre', *Zeitschrift für wissenschaftliche Theologie*, 47 (1904), 241–50.

PUECH, AIMÉ, *Les Apologistes Grecs du IIe siècle de notre ère* (Paris, Librairie Hachette et Cie, 1912).

SCHWARTZ, EDUARD, *Athenagorae Libellus Pro Christianis, Oratio de Resurrectione Cadaverum* (Texte und Untersuchungen, iv. 2; Leipzig, J. C. Hinrichs, 1891).

UBALDI, PAULO, and PELLEGRINO, MICHELE, *Atenagora: La Supplica per i Cristiani, Della risurrezione dei morti* (Corona Patrum Salesiana, xv; Torino, Società Editrice Internazionale, 1947).

(*b*) *Sources referred to in notes and apparatus*

BONWETSCH, G. NATHANAEL (ed.), *Methodius* (Die griechischen christ-lichen Schriftsteller der ersten drei Jahrhunderten; Leipzig, J. C. Hinrichs, 1917).

DIELS, HERMANN, *Doxographi Graeci* (Berlin and Leipzig, Walter de Gruyter, 1879).

KERN, OTTO, *Orphicorum Fragmenta* (Berlin, Weidmann, 1922).

KÜHN, KARL GOTTLOB, *Medicorum Graecorum Opera Quae Exstant* (Leipzig, Carl Cnobloch, 1821–33).

NAUCK, AUGUST, *Tragicorum Graecorum Fragmenta* (2nd edn., Hildesheim, Georg Olms, 1964).

ROSE, HERBERT J., *A Handbook of Greek Mythology* (New York, E. P. Dutton, 1959).

ABBREVIATIONS

PG   J.-P. Migne, *Patrologiae Cursus Completus, Series Graeca.*

PWK   *Paulys Realenzyklopädie der klassischen Altertumswissenschaft*, ed. Georg Wissowa, Wilhelm Kroll, *et al.*

RAC   *Reallexikon für Antike und Christentum*, ed. Theodor Klauser.

TEXT AND TRANSLATION

ΑΘΗΝΑΓΟΡΟΥ ΑΘΗΝΑΙΟΥ ΦΙΛΟΣΟΦΟΥ ΧΡΙΣΤΙΑΝΟΥ ΠΡΕΣΒΕΙΑ ΠΕΡΙ ΧΡΙΣΤΙΑΝΩΝ

Αὐτοκράτορσιν Μάρκῳ Αὐρηλίῳ Ἀντωνίνῳ καὶ Λουκίῳ Αὐρηλίῳ Κομόδῳ Ἀρμενιακοῖς[1] Σαρματικοῖς, τὸ δὲ μέγιστον φιλοσόφοις.

1. Ἡ ὑμετέρα, μεγάλοι βασιλέων, οἰκουμένη ἄλλος ἄλλοις ἔθεσι χρῶνται καὶ νόμοις, καὶ οὐδεὶς αὐτῶν νόμῳ καὶ φόβῳ δίκης, κἂν γελοῖα ᾖ, μὴ στέργειν τὰ πάτρια εἴργεται, ἀλλ' ὁ μὲν Ἰλιεὺς θεὸν Ἕκτορα λέγει καὶ τὴν Ἑλένην Ἀδράστειαν ἐπιστάμενος προσκυνεῖ, ὁ δὲ Λακεδαιμόνιος Ἀγαμέμνονα Δία καὶ Φυλονόην τὴν Τυνδάρεω θυγατέρα καὶ τεννηνοδίαν†[2] σέβει, ὁ δὲ Ἀθηναῖος Ἐρεχθεῖ Ποσειδῶνι θύει καὶ Ἀγραύλῳ Ἀθηναῖοι καὶ τελετὰς καὶ μυστήρια [Ἀθηναῖοι][3] ἄγουσιν καὶ Πανδρόσῳ, αἳ ἐνομίσθησαν ἀσεβεῖν ἀνοίξασαι τὴν λάρνακα, καὶ ἑνὶ λόγῳ κατὰ ἔθνη καὶ δήμους θυσίας κατάγουσιν ἃς ἂν θέλωσιν ἄνθρωποι καὶ μυστήρια. οἱ δὲ Αἰγύπτιοι καὶ αἰλούρους καὶ κροκοδείλους καὶ ὄφεις καὶ ἀσπίδας καὶ κύνας θεοὺς νομίζουσιν. 2. καὶ τούτοις πᾶσιν ἐπιτρέπετε καὶ ὑμεῖς καὶ οἱ νόμοι, τὸ μὲν οὖν μηδ' ὅλως θεὸν ἡγεῖσθαι ἀσεβὲς καὶ ἀνόσιον νομίσαντες, τὸ δὲ οἷς ἕκαστος βούλεται χρῆσθαι ὡς θεοῖς ἀναγκαῖον, ἵνα τῷ πρὸς τὸ θεῖον δέει ἀπέχωνται τοῦ ἀδικεῖν. [ἡμῖν δέ, καὶ μὴ παρακρουσθῆτε ὡς οἱ πολλοὶ ἐξ ἀκοῆς, τῷ ὀνόματι ἀπεχθάνεται· οὐ γὰρ τὰ ὀνόματα μίσους ἄξια, ἀλλὰ τὸ ἀδίκημα δίκης καὶ τιμωρίας.][4] διόπερ τὸ πρᾶον ὑμῶν καὶ ἥμερον καὶ τὸ πρὸς ἅπαντα εἰρηνικὸν καὶ φιλάνθρωπον θαυμάζοντες οἱ μὲν καθ' ἕνα ἰσονομοῦνται, αἱ δὲ πόλεις

---

[1] Ἀρμενιακοῖς A : Γερμανικοῖς Mommsen, Schwartz   1. [2] καὶ τεννηνοδίαν A : καὶ Τέννην ὁ Τενέδιος Gesner : καθὰ τὴν Ἐνοδίαν Schwartz : καὶ Ἄρτεμιν Ὀρθρίαν Geffcken : καὶ Τέννην ὁ δὲ Τενέδιος Δία Scivoletto : fortasse Ἐνοδίαν cum glossemate Ἑκάτην   [3] Ἀθηναῖοι seclusit Gesner : Ἀθηνᾷ [καὶ τ. κ. μ. Ἀθηναῖοι ἄγουσιν] Schwartz   [4] seclusit Schwartz

A PLEA FOR CHRISTIANS
BY ATHENAGORAS THE ATHENIAN:
PHILOSOPHER AND CHRISTIAN

To the emperors Marcus Aurelius Antoninus and Lucius Aurelius Commodus, conquerors of Armenia and Sarmatia, and, above all, philosophers.

1. The inhabitants of your empire, greatest of kings, follow many different customs and laws, and none of them is prevented by law or fear of punishment from cherishing his ancestral ways, however ridiculous they may be. The Trojan calls Hector a god and worships Helen, regarding her as Adrasteia;[1] the Lacedaemonian venerates Agamemnon as Zeus and Phylonoe the daughter of Tyndareus as Enodia;[2] the Athenian sacrifices to Erechtheus as Poseidon; and the Athenians celebrate initiations and mysteries for Agraulus and Pandrosus who were considered impious for opening the chest.[3] In a word, the various races and peoples of mankind perform whatever sacrifices and mysteries they wish. The Egyptians regard even cats, crocodiles, snakes, asps, and dogs as gods. 2. All these both you and the laws permit, since you regard it as impious and irreligious to have no belief at all in a god and think it necessary for all men to venerate as gods those whom they wish, that through fear of the divine they may refrain from evil. [But in our case—and do not you be misled as are the majority by hearsay—hatred is shown because of our very name. Yet names are not deserving of hatred; only wrongdoing calls for punishment and retribution.][4] For that reason individual men, admiring your gentle and mild natures, your peaceableness and humanity toward all, enjoy equality before the law; the

1. [1] A title of Nemesis. Helen was regarded as the offspring of Zeus and Nemesis in the *Cypria* (Athenaeus, *Deipn.* 8, 334 b). Mother and Maid apparently functioned as two aspects of one reality.

[2] A title of Hecate (e.g. Euripides, *Hel.* 569–70).

[3] Athena put the infant Erichthonius into a chest, gave it into the care of the daughters of Cecrops (Agraulus, Herse, and Pandrosus), and commanded them not to open it. Two of the three could not resist the temptation and consequently were driven mad, ending their lives by leaping from the Acropolis (H. J. Rose, *A Handbook of Greek Mythology* [New York, 1959], p. 110).

[4] Although Athenagoras is not always well organized, he seems incapable of having written so dislocated a passage.

πρὸς ἀξίαν τῆς ἴσης μετέχουσι τιμῆς, καὶ ἡ σύμπασα οἰκουμένη
τῇ ὑμετέρᾳ συνέσει βαθείας εἰρήνης ἀπολαύουσιν. 3. ἡμεῖς δὲ οἱ
λεγόμενοι Χριστιανοί, ὅτι μὴ προνενόησθε καὶ ἡμῶν, συγχωρεῖτε
δὲ μηδὲν ἀδικοῦντας, ἀλλὰ καὶ πάντων, ὡς προϊόντος τοῦ λόγου
δειχθήσεται, εὐσεβέστατα διακειμένους καὶ δικαιότατα πρός τε τὸ
θεῖον καὶ τὴν ὑμετέραν βασιλείαν, ἐλαύνεσθαι καὶ φέρεσθαι καὶ
διώκεσθαι, ἐπὶ μόνῳ ὀνόματι προσπολεμούντων ἡμῖν τῶν πολλῶν,
μηνῦσαι τὰ καθ' ἑαυτοὺς ἐτολμήσαμεν (διδαχθήσεσθε δὲ ὑπὸ τοῦ
λόγου ἄτερ δίκης καὶ παρὰ πάντα νόμον καὶ λόγον πάσχοντας
ἡμᾶς) καὶ δεόμεθα ὑμῶν καὶ περὶ ἡμῶν τι σκέψασθαι, ὅπως
παυσώμεθά ποτε ὑπὸ τῶν συκοφαντῶν σφαττόμενοι. 4. οὐδὲ γὰρ
εἰς χρήματα ἡ παρὰ τῶν διωκόντων ζημία οὐδὲ εἰς ἐπιτιμίαν ἡ
αἰσχύνη ἢ εἰς ἄλλο τι τῶν μειόνων⁵ ἡ βλάβη (τούτων γὰρ καταφρονοῦμεν, κἂν τοῖς πολλοῖς δοκῇ σπουδαῖα, δέροντα οὐ μόνον
οὐκ ἀντιπαίειν⁶ οὐδὲ μὴν δικάζεσθαι τοῖς ἄγουσιν καὶ ἁρπάζουσιν
ἡμᾶς ᵃ μεμαθηκότες, ἀλλὰ τοῖς μέν, κἂν κατὰ κόρρης προπηλακί-
ζωσιν, καὶ τὸ ἕτερον παίειν παρέχειν τῆς κεφαλῆς μέρος, τοῖς δέ, εἰ
τὸν χιτῶνα ἀφαιροῖντο, ἐπιδιδόναι καὶ τὸ ἱμάτιον),ᵇ ἀλλ' εἰς τὰ
σώματα καὶ τὰς ψυχάς, ὅταν ἀπείπωμεν τοῖς χρήμασιν, ἐπιβου-
λεύουσιν ἡμῖν κατασκεδάζοντες ὄχλον ἐγκλημάτων, ἃ ἡμῖν μὲν
οὐδὲ μέχρις ὑπονοίας, τοῖς δὲ ἀδολεσχοῦσιν καὶ τῷ ἐκείνων πρόσεστι
γένει.

2. Καὶ εἰ μέν τις ἡμᾶς ἐλέγχειν ἔχει ἢ μικρὸν ἢ μεῖζον ἀδικοῦντας,
κολάζεσθαι οὐ παραιτούμεθα, ἀλλὰ καὶ ἥτις πικροτάτη καὶ ἀνηλεὴς
τιμωρία, ὑπέχειν ἀξιοῦμεν· εἰ δὲ μέχρις ὀνόματος ἡ κατηγορία
(εἰς γοῦν τὴν σήμερον ἡμέραν ἃ περὶ ἡμῶν λογοποιοῦσιν ἡ¹ κοινὴ
καὶ ἄκριτος τῶν ἀνθρώπων φήμη, καὶ οὐδεὶς ἀδικῶν Χριστιανὸς
ἐλήλεγκται), ὑμῶν ἤδη ἔργον τῶν μεγίστων καὶ φιλανθρωποτάτων²
καὶ φιλομαθεστάτων βασιλέων ἀποσκευάσαι ἡμῶν νόμῳ τὴν
ἐπήρειαν, ἵν' ὥσπερ ἡ σύμπασα ταῖς παρ' ὑμῶν εὐεργεσίαις³ καὶ
καθ' ἕνα κεκοινώνηκε καὶ κατὰ πόλεις, καὶ ἡμεῖς ἔχωμεν ὑμῖν

1. ᵃ Cf. 1 Cor. 6: 7   ᵇ Cf. Matt. 5: 39–40; Luke 6: 29

1. ⁵ μειζόνων A: corr. Schwartz   ⁶ τὸ ἀντιπαίειν A: corr. Schwartz
2. ¹ ἡ seclusit Stephanus   ² φιλανῶν A: corr. Stephanus   ³ ταῖς . . .
εὐεργεσίαις A: τῆς . . . εὐεργεσίας (cum atticissare soleat Athenagoras) Geffcken:
lacunam in vicem post κεκοινώνηκε indicavit Schwartz

cities have an equal share in honour according to their merit; and the whole empire enjoys a profound peace through your wisdom.

3. To us, however, who are called Christians, you have not given the same consideration, but allow us to be driven to and fro and persecuted, though we have done no wrong; in point of fact—as will be shown in what follows—we are the most pious and righteous of all men in matters that concern both the divine and your kingdom; for the crowd is hostile toward us only because of our name. For these reasons we have dared to set forth an account of our position—you will learn from it how unjustly and against all law and reason we suffer—and we ask you to show some concern also for us that there may be an end to our slaughter at the hands of lying informers. 4. For the penalty our persecutors exact does not affect only our goods, nor does the disgrace they bring upon us affect only our civic standing, nor does the harm they cause us have to do with some other equally trivial matter. These things we despise even though they seem matters of moment to the crowd. For we have been taught not to strike back at someone who beats us nor to go to court with those who rob and plunder us. Not only that: we have even been taught to turn our head and offer the other side when men ill use us and strike us on the jaw and to give also our cloak should they snatch our tunic. No, when our property is gone, their plots against us affect our very bodies and souls. They spread a host of charges, of which there is not the slightest suggestion that we are guilty but which are typical of those babblers and their kind.

2. Now if a man can convict us of any evil, great or small, we do not ask to be let off. On the contrary we consider it right that our punishment be severe and merciless. But if the charge stops short at our name—and to this day what is said about us amounts to only the low and untested rumour of the populace, and no Christian has yet been convicted of evil—then it is your task as mighty, humane, and learned kings to bring to an end by law the abuse we suffer, that just as all the world has enjoyed your benefactions both as individuals and as cities, we too may have reason to offer our solemn thanks to you that there has been an

χάριν σεμνυνόμενοι ὅτι πεπαύμεθα συκοφαντούμενοι. 2. καὶ γὰρ οὐ
πρὸς τῆς ὑμετέρας δικαιοσύνης τοὺς μὲν ἄλλους αἰτίαν λαβόντας
ἀδικημάτων μὴ πρότερον ἢ ἐλεγχθῆναι κολάζεσθαι, ἐφ᾽ ἡμῶν δὲ
μεῖζον ἰσχύειν τὸ ὄνομα τῶν ἐπὶ τῇ δίκῃ ἐλέγχων, οὐκ εἰ ἠδίκησέν
τι ὁ κρινόμενος τῶν δικαζόντων ἐπιζητούντων, ἀλλ᾽ εἰς τὸ ὄνομα ὡς
εἰς ἀδίκημα ἐνυβριζόντων. οὐδὲν δὲ ὄνομα ἐφ᾽ ἑαυτοῦ καὶ δι᾽ αὐτοῦ
οὐ πονηρὸν οὐδὲ χρηστὸν νομίζεται, διὰ δὲ τὰς ὑποκειμένας αὐτοῖς
ἢ πονηρὰς ἢ ἀγαθὰς ἢ φλαῦρα ἢ ἀγαθὰ δοκεῖ. 3. ὑμεῖς δὲ ταῦτα
ἴστε φανερώτερον, ὡσανεὶ ἀπὸ φιλοσοφίας καὶ παιδείας πάσης
ὁρμώμενοι. διὰ τοῦτο καὶ οἱ παρ᾽ ὑμῖν κρινόμενοι, κἂν ἐπὶ μεγίστοις
φεύγωσι, θαρροῦσιν, ⟨καὶ⟩[4] εἰδότες ὅτι ἐξετάσετε αὐτῶν τὸν βίον
καὶ οὔτε τοῖς ὀνόμασι προσθήσεσθε, ἂν ᾖ κενά, οὔτε ταῖς ἀπὸ τῶν
κατηγόρων[5] αἰτίαις, εἰ ψευδεῖς εἶεν, ἐν ἴσῃ τάξει τὴν καταδικάζουσαν
τῆς ἀπολυούσης δέχονται ψῆφον. 4. τὸ τοίνυν πρὸς ἅπαντας ἴσον καὶ
ἡμεῖς ἀξιοῦμεν, μὴ ὅτι Χριστιανοὶ λεγόμεθα μισεῖσθαι καὶ κολάζεσθαι (τί γὰρ ἡμῖν τὸ ὄνομα πρὸς κακίαν τελεῖ;), ἀλλὰ κρίνεσθαι
ἐφ᾽ ὅτῳ ἂν καὶ εὐθύνῃ τις, καὶ ἢ ἀφίεσθαι ἀπολυομένους τὰς
κατηγορίας ἢ κολάζεσθαι τοὺς ἁλισκομένους πονηρούς, μὴ ἐπὶ τῷ
ὀνόματι (οὐδεὶς γὰρ Χριστιανὸς πονηρός, εἰ μὴ ὑποκρίνεται τὸν
λόγον), ἐπὶ δὲ τῷ ἀδικήματι. 5. οὕτω καὶ τοὺς ἀπὸ φιλοσοφίας
κρινομένους ὁρῶμεν· οὐδεὶς αὐτῶν πρὸ κρίσεως διὰ τὴν ἐπιστήμην
ἢ τέχνην ἀγαθὸς ἢ πονηρὸς τῷ δικαστῇ εἶναι δοκεῖ, ἀλλὰ δόξας
μὲν εἶναι ἄδικος κολάζεται, οὐδὲν τῇ φιλοσοφίᾳ προστριψάμενος
ἔγκλημα (ἐκεῖνος γὰρ πονηρὸς ὁ μὴ ὡς νόμος φιλοσοφῶν, ἡ δὲ
ἐπιστήμη ἀναίτιος), ἀπολυσάμενος δὲ τὰς διαβολὰς ἀφίεται. ἔστω
δὴ τὸ ἴσον καὶ ἐφ᾽ ἡμῶν· ὁ τῶν κρινομένων ἐξεταζέσθω βίος, τὸ δὲ
ὄνομα παντὸς ἀφείσθω ἐγκλήματος. 6. ἀναγκαῖον δέ μοι ἀρχομένῳ
ἀπολογεῖσθαι ὑπὲρ τοῦ λόγου δεηθῆναι ὑμῶν, μέγιστοι αὐτοκράτορες, ἴσους ἡμῖν ἀκροατὰς γενέσθαι καὶ μὴ τῇ κοινῇ καὶ ἀλόγῳ
φήμῃ συναπενεχθέντας προκατασχεθῆναι, ἐπιτρέψαι δὲ ὑμῶν τὸ
φιλομαθὲς καὶ φιλάληθες καὶ τῷ καθ᾽ ἡμᾶς λόγῳ. ὑμεῖς τε γὰρ
οὐ πρὸς ἀγνοίας ἐξαμαρτήσετε καὶ ἡμεῖς τὰ ἀπὸ τῆς ἀκρίτου τῶν
πολλῶν φήμης ἀπολυσάμενοι[6] παυσόμεθα πολεμούμενοι.

2. [4] καὶ add. Stephanus: lacunam in vicem post εἶεν indicavit Schwartz
[5] κατηγοριῶν A: corr. Wilamowitz   [6] ἀποδυσάμενοι A: corr. Maranus

end to the laying of false information against us. 2. For it does not become your reputation for justice that, whereas others found guilty of crimes are not punished until convicted, in our case the mere name plays a larger role than legal tests. Our judges do not inquire whether the defendant is guilty of any crime; they simply heap abuse on our name as though that were a crime. But no name is considered good or bad in and of itself. Names appear praiseworthy or disgraceful only because of the good or bad deeds which are implied by them. 3. All this you know very well; for you make philosophy and profound learning, as it were, the ground of your actions. That is why even those who are defendants before you do not lose heart though accused of the greatest crimes; and since they know that you will examine their conduct and not pay attention to meaningless labels or to false charges from the prosecution, they are equally disposed to grant the justice of a favourable or unfavourable decision.

4. We too, then, ask to enjoy the equity you show to all that we may not be hated and punished simply because we are Christians —for how could our name make us wicked?—but to be judged on the basis of our conduct, whatever it may be that men may wish to examine, and either to be let go when we show the groundless-ness of the charges or to be punished if we are found guilty—not guilty merely because of our name (for no Christian is evil unless his profession is a pretence), but because of some crime. 5. Such is what we observe in the case of defendants who pursue philo-sophy. None of them appears good or bad to the judge before the trial because of his knowledge or skill. Only when he is shown to be guilty is he punished. He brings on himself no accusation because of his philosophy—for only the philosopher who breaks the law is evil; knowledge itself is not to blame—and when he rebuts the slanders against him, he is released. Let equity prevail also in our case. Let the conduct of the defendants be investi-gated. Let no mere name be subject to accusation.

6. As I begin the defence of our teaching, I must ask you, greatest emperors, to be fair as you listen and not to be carried away and prejudiced by low and irrational rumour, but to direct your love of learning and truth also to the following account concerning ourselves. Thus you will not go wrong through ignorance, and we shall rid ourselves of the hostility against us by showing how un-founded are the accusations arising from the uncritical gossip of the crowd.

3. Τρία ἐπιφημίζουσιν ἡμῖν ἐγκλήματα, ἀθεότητα, Θυέστεια δεῖπνα, Οἰδιποδείους μίξεις. ἀλλὰ εἰ μὲν ἀληθῆ ταῦτα, μηδενὸς γένους φείσησθε, ἐπεξέλθετε δὲ τοῖς ἀδικήμασι, σὺν γυναιξὶ καὶ παισὶ προρρίζους ἡμᾶς ἀποκτείνατε, εἴ γέ τις ἀνθρώπων[1] ζῇ δίκην θηρίων· καίτοι γε καὶ τὰ θηρία τῶν ὁμογενῶν οὐχ ἅπτεται καὶ νόμῳ φύσεως καὶ πρὸς ἕνα καιρὸν τὸν τῆς τεκνοποιίας, οὐκ ἐπ' ἀδείας, μίγνυται, γνωρίζει δὲ καὶ ὑφ' ὧν ὠφελεῖται. εἴ τις οὖν καὶ τῶν θηρίων ἀνημερώτερος, τίνα οὗτος πρὸς τὰ τηλικαῦτα ὑποσχὼν δίκην [καὶ][2] πρὸς ἀξίαν κεκολάσθαι νομισθήσεται; 2. εἰ δὲ λογο-ποιίαι ταῦτα καὶ διαβολαὶ κεναί, φυσικῷ λόγῳ πρὸς τὴν ἀρετὴν τῆς κακίας ἀντικειμένης καὶ πολεμούντων ἀλλήλοις τῶν ἐναντίων θείῳ νόμῳ, καὶ τοῦ μηδὲν τούτων ἀδικεῖν ὑμεῖς[3] μάρτυρες, κελεύοντες μὴ ὁμολογεῖν,[4] πρὸς ὑμῶν λοιπὸν ἐξέτασιν ποιήσασθαι βίου, δογμάτων, τῆς πρὸς ὑμᾶς καὶ τὸν ὑμέτερον οἶκον καὶ τὴν βασιλείαν σπουδῆς καὶ ὑπακοῆς, καὶ οὕτω ποτὲ συγχωρῆσαι ἡμῖν οὐδὲν πλέον ⟨ἢ⟩[5] τοῖς διώκουσιν ἡμᾶς. νικήσομεν γὰρ αὐτοὺς ὑπὲρ ἀληθείας ἀόκνως καὶ τὰς ψυχὰς ἐπιδιδόντες.

4. Ὅτι μὲν οὖν οὐκ ἐσμὲν ἄθεοι (πρὸς ἓν ἕκαστον ἀπαντήσω τῶν ἐγκλημάτων), μὴ καὶ γελοῖον ᾖ τοὺς λέγοντας [μὴ][1] ἐλέγχειν. Διαγόρᾳ μὲν γὰρ εἰκότως ἀθεότητα ἐπεκάλουν Ἀθηναῖοι, μὴ μόνον τὸν Ὀρφικὸν εἰς μέσον κατατιθέντι λόγον καὶ τὰ ἐν Ἐλευσῖνι καὶ τὰ τῶν Καβίρων δημεύοντι μυστήρια καὶ τὸ τοῦ Ἡρακλέους ἵνα τὰς γογγύλας ἕψοι κατακόπτοντι ξόανον, ἄντικρυς δὲ ἀποφαινομένῳ μηδὲ ὅλως εἶναι θεόν· ἡμῖν δὲ διαιροῦσιν ἀπὸ τῆς ὕλης τὸν θεὸν καὶ δεικνύουσιν ἕτερον μέν τι εἶναι τὴν ὕλην ἄλλο δὲ τὸν θεὸν καὶ τὸ διὰ μέσου πολύ (τὸ μὲν γὰρ θεῖον ἀγένητον[2] εἶναι καὶ ἀίδιον, νῷ μόνῳ καὶ λόγῳ θεωρούμενον, τὴν δὲ ὕλην γενητὴν καὶ φθαρτήν), μή τι οὐκ[3] ἀλόγως τὸ τῆς ἀθεότητος ἐπικαλοῦσιν ὄνομα; 2. εἰ μὲν γὰρ

---

3. [1] ἀνθρώπων (ἀν͞ω͞ν) A: ἄνθρωπος ὤν Schwartz   [2] καὶ seclusit Wilamowitz   [3] ὑμεῖς A: ἡμᾶς ὑμεῖς Schwartz: ἡμεῖς Geffcken   [4] ὁμονοεῖν A:
ὁμολογεῖν Lindner: μηνύειν Maranus   [5] ἢ add. Maranus
4. [1] μὴ seclusit Schwartz   [2] ἀγέννητον A (quam lectionem defendit
Ubaldi): corr. Schwartz   [3] οὐκ seclusit Wilamowitz

3. They bring three charges against us: atheism, Thyestean banquets, and Oedipean unions.[1] If these are true, spare no class among us, prosecute our crimes, destroy us root and branch, including women and children—if indeed *any* human being could be found living like wild animals in that way! Even animals, however, do not eat members of their own kind; and they mate in accordance with the law of nature and at the one season appointed for the begetting of offspring—not for any licentious purpose; and they also know by whom they are benefited.[2] If then there be a man more savage than the beasts, what punishment does he not deserve to suffer for such enormities?

2. But if these charges are fabrications and empty slanders owing their existence to the fact that by a natural principle evil opposes virtue and that by divine law opposites war against each other, and if you yourselves are our witnesses that we are not guilty of any of these crimes since you merely command us not to confess, then it is only right that you examine our conduct, our teachings, and our zeal and obedience to you, your house, and the empire. In so doing, you will at length grant us a favour equal to that enjoyed by our persecutors. We shall surely overcome them, ready as we are to give up even our lives for the truth without flinching.

4. I shall now meet each charge separately. It is so obvious that we are not atheists that it seems ridiculous even to undertake the refutation of those who make the claim. It was right for the Athenians to charge Diagoras[1] with atheism; for not only did he disclose Orphic doctrine, divulge the mysteries of Eleusis and those of the Cabiri, and chop up the wooden image of Heracles to cook his turnips, but he bluntly declared that there is no god at all. But surely it is not rational for them to apply the term atheism to us who distinguish God from matter and show that matter is one thing and God another and the difference between them immense; for the divine is uncreated and eternal and can be contemplated only by thought and reason, whereas matter is created and perishable.

3. [1] The same expressions, 'Thyestean banquets and Oedipean unions', occur in the letter from Gaul describing the persecutions of A.D. 177 (Eusebius, *H.E.* 5. 1. 14).

    [2] Each of the three clauses describing the natural powers of animals corresponds to one of the charges brought against the Christians. The last of the three is least clear; but no doubt an animal's recognition of those who tend him corresponds to man's recognition of God on whom his life depends.

4. [1] Diagoras was known to his fifth-century contemporaries primarily as a man who had disclosed the sacred mysteries of Eleusis. It was only later that he became the typical 'atheist'.

ἐφρονοῦμεν ὅμοια τῷ Διαγόρᾳ, τοσαῦτα ἔχοντες πρὸς θεοσέβειαν
ἐνέχυρα, τὸ εὔτακτον, τὸ διὰ παντὸς σύμφωνον, τὸ μέγεθος, τὴν
χροιάν, τὸ σχῆμα, τὴν διάθεσιν τοῦ κόσμου, εἰκότως ἂν ἡμῖν καὶ ἡ
τοῦ μὴ θεοσεβεῖν δόξα καὶ ἡ τοῦ ἐλαύνεσθαι αἰτία προσετρίβετο· ἐπεὶ
δὲ ὁ λόγος ἡμῶν ἕνα θεὸν ἄγει τὸν τοῦδε τοῦ παντὸς ποιητήν, αὐτὸν
μὲν οὐ γενόμενον (ὅτι τὸ ὂν οὐ γίνεται, ἀλλὰ τὸ μὴ ὄν), πάντα δὲ διὰ
τοῦ παρ᾽ αὐτοῦ λόγου πεποιηκότα, ἑκάτερα ἀλόγως πάσχομεν, καὶ
κακῶς ἀγορευόμεθα καὶ διωκόμεθα.

5. Καὶ ποιηταὶ μὲν καὶ φιλόσοφοι οὐκ ἔδοξαν ἄθεοι, ἐπιστήσαντες
περὶ θεοῦ. ὁ μὲν Εὐριπίδης ἐπὶ μὲν τῶν κατὰ κοινὴν πρόληψιν
ἀνεπιστημόνως ὀνομαζομένων θεῶν διαπορῶν

> ὤφειλε δ᾽, εἴπερ¹ ἔστ᾽ ἐν οὐρανῷ,
> Ζεὺς μὴ τὸν αὐτὸν δυστυχῆ καθιστάναι·ᵃ

ἐπὶ δὲ τοῦ κατ᾽ ἐπιστήμην νοητοῦ ὡς ἔστιν θεὸς² δογματίζων

> ὁρᾷς τὸν ὑψοῦ τόνδ᾽ ἄπειρον αἰθέρα
> καὶ γῆν πέριξ ἔχοντα ὑγραῖς ἐν ἀγκάλαις;
> τοῦτον νόμιζε Ζῆνα, τόνδ᾽ ἡγοῦ θεόν.ᵇ

2. τῶν μὲν γὰρ οὔτε τὰς οὐσίας, αἷς ἐπικατηγορεῖσθαι τὸ ὄνομα
συμβέβηκεν, ὑποκειμένας ἑώρα ("Ζῆνα γὰρ ὅστις ἐστὶ Ζεύς, οὐκ
οἶδα πλὴν λόγῳ")ᶜ οὔτε τὰ ὀνόματα καθ᾽ ὑποκειμένων κατηγορεῖ-
σθαι πραγμάτων (ὧν γὰρ αἱ οὐσίαι οὐχ ὑπόκεινται, τί πλέον αὐτοῖς
τῶν ὀνομάτων;), τὸν δὲ ἀπὸ τῶν ἔργων, ὄψιν³ τῶν ἀδήλων νοῶν τὰ
φαινόμενα, †ἀέρα αἰθέρος γῆς†.⁴ 3. οὗ οὖν τὰ ποιήματα καὶ ὑφ᾽ οὗ
τῷ πνεύματι ἡνιοχεῖται, τοῦτον κατελαμβάνετο εἶναι θεόν,ᵈ συν-
άδοντος τούτῳ καὶ Σοφοκλέους

> εἰς ταῖς ἀληθείαισιν, εἰς ἐστιν θεός,
> ὃς οὐρανόν τ᾽ ἔτευξε καὶ γαῖαν μακράν,ᵉ

5. ᵃ Frg. 900 (Nauck²) ᵇ Frg. 941 (Nauck²) ᶜ Frg. 480 (Nauck²) ᵈ Cf.
Rom. 1: 19–20 ᵉ Frg. 1025 (Nauck²)

ειλε δ᾽ ει
5. ¹ ὤφελη δὲ εἴπερ A: ὤφειλε δῆθεν Nauck: in fine supplens κρατῶν Meineke
² ἐστιν θεὸς Wilamowitz: ἐκεῖνος A ³ ὄψει A: corr. Fabricius ⁴ ἀέρα
αἰθέρος γῆς A: ἀέρος αἰθέρος γῆς Fabricius: ἑώρα αἰθέρος γῆς Maranus: ἐφώρα
[αἰθέρος γῆς] Schwartz

2. If we held opinions like those of Diagoras in spite of having such impressive signs conducive to piety in the order, the perfect harmony, the magnitude, the colours, the shapes, and the arrangement of the world, then we could not complain of having acquired a reputation for impiety and of having brought on ourselves this harassment. But since we teach that there is one God, the Maker of this universe, and that he is not created (since it is not Being that is created, but non-being) whereas all things were made by the Word that issues from him, it is irrational that either of these ills have befallen us. It is wrong that we are defamed and persecuted.

5. Poets and philosophers were not regarded as atheists for giving their attention to matters concerning God. Euripides, in expressing his perplexity concerning those whom common preconception ignorantly names gods, says:

> Zeus ought not, if he dwells in heaven,
> Reduce the same man to unhappy straits.

And in setting out his doctrine of that which may be understood of God's existence through rational insight, he says:

> Do you see aloft the boundless ether,
> Encircling the earth in its damp folds?
> This esteem Zeus! This consider God![1]

2. He could not discern the substances thought to underlie the popular gods—substances of which the word god happened to be predicated ('for as to Zeus, I know not who Zeus is, except by hearsay');[2] nor could he grant that their *names* were predicated of underlying realities[3] (for if the substances of things do not underlie them, is there anything more to them than their names?); but he discerned Another from his works, understanding the things that appear as providing a glimpse of things unseen. 3. The one whose works they are and by whose spirit they are guided he took to be God. Sophocles also agrees with him when he says:

> One in truth, yea, one is God,
> Who formed heaven and the broad earth.[4]

5. [1] Frequently quoted by pagans and Christians. Cicero (*De Nat. Deor.* 2. 25. 65) translated it into Latin.

[2] Linked with the preceding fragment in Lucian, *Iov. Trag.* 41.

[3] Apparently directed against the Stoic effort to provide a rational explanation for divine names (cf. Cicero, *De Nat. Deor.* 3. 24. 62). See also 6. 4 below, where a few standard etymologies of divine names are given.

[4] A spurious fragment derived from the work of Hellenistic-Jewish propagandists who attributed their productions to Hecataeus (cf. Clement, *Strom.* 5. 14. 114).

πρὸς τὴν τοῦ θεοῦ⁵ φύσιν τοῦ κάλλους τοῦ ἐκείνου πληρουμένην ἑκάτερα, καὶ ποῦ δεῖ εἶναι τὸν θεὸν καὶ ὅτι ἕνα δεῖ εἶναι, διδάσκων.

6. Καὶ Φιλόλαος δὲ ὥσπερ ἐν φρουρᾷ πάντα ὑπὸ τοῦ θεοῦ περιειλῆφθαι λέγων, καὶ τὸ ἕνα εἶναι καὶ τὸ ἀνωτέρω τῆς ὕλης δεικνύει. Λῦσις δὲ καὶ Ὄψιμος¹ ὁ μὲν ἀριθμὸν ἄρρητον ὁρίζεται τὸν θεόν, ὁ δὲ τοῦ μεγίστου τῶν ἀριθμῶν τὴν παρὰ τὸν ἐγγυτάτω² ὑπεροχήν. εἰ δὲ μέγιστος μὲν ἀριθμὸς ὁ δέκα κατὰ τοὺς Πυθαγορικοὺς ὁ τετρακτύς τε ὢν καὶ πάντας τοὺς ἀριθμητικοὺς καὶ τοὺς ἁρμονικοὺς³ περιέχων λόγους, τούτῳ δὲ ἐγγὺς παράκειται ὁ ἐννέα, μονάς ἐστιν ὁ θεός, τοῦτ' ἔστιν εἷς· ἑνὶ γὰρ ὑπερέχει ὁ μέγιστος τὸν ἐγγυτάτω. †ἐλάχιστον αὐτῷ.† 2. Πλάτων δὲ καὶ Ἀριστοτέλης (καὶ οὐχ ὡς ἐπιδεικνύων τὰ δόγματα τῶν φιλοσόφων ἐπ' ἀκριβές, οὕτως ἃ εἰρήκασι περὶ θεοῦ διέξειμι· οἶδα γὰρ ὅτι ὅσον συνέσει καὶ ἰσχύι τῆς βασιλείας πάντων ὑπερέχετε, τοσοῦτον καὶ τῷ πᾶσαν παιδείαν ἀκριβοῦν πάντων κρατεῖτε, οὕτω καθ' ἕκαστον παιδείας μέρος κατορθοῦντες ὡς οὐδὲ οἱ ἓν αὐτῆς μόριον ἀποτεμόμενοι· ἀλλ' ἐπειδὴ ἀδύνατον δεικνύειν ἄνευ παραθέσεως ὀνομάτων ὅτι μὴ μόνοι εἰς μονάδα τὸν θεὸν κατακλείομεν, ἐπὶ τὰς δόξας ἐτραπόμην), φησὶν οὖν ὁ Πλάτων· "τὸν μὲν οὖν ποιητὴν καὶ πατέρα τοῦδε τοῦ παντὸς εὑρεῖν τε ἔργον καὶ εὑρόντα εἰς πάντας ἀδύνατον λέγειν",ᵃ ἕνα τὸν ἀγένητον⁴ καὶ ἀίδιον νοῶν θεόν. εἰ δ' οἶδεν καὶ ἄλλους οἷον ἥλιον καὶ σελήνην καὶ ἀστέρας, ἀλλ' ὡς γενητοὺς οἶδεν αὐτούς· "θεοὶ θεῶν, ὧν ἐγὼ δημιουργὸς πατήρ τε ἔργων ἃ ἄλυτα⁵ ἐμοῦ μὴ θέλοντος, τὸ μὲν οὖν δεθὲν πᾶν λυτόν"ᵇ εἰ τοίνυν οὔκ ἐστιν ἄθεος Πλάτων, ἕνα τὸν δημιουργὸν τῶν ὅλων νοῶν ἀγένητον⁶ θεόν, οὐδὲ ἡμεῖς ἄθεοι, ὑφ' οὗ

---

6. ᵃ Tim. 28 c   ᵇ Tim. 41 a

5. ⁵ τοῦ θεοῦ: τοῦ οὐρανοῦ Schwartz: τοῦ θεοῦ seclusit Ubaldi. Post ἑκάτερα add. ex. g. ὁρῶν Geffcken
6. ¹ Ὄψιμος Meursius: ὄψει A   ² τῶν ἐγγυτάτων A: τὸν ἐγγύτατον A¹: corr. Gesner   ³ ἁρμονίους A: corr. codex Laubanensis, Otto   ⁴ ἀγένητον A   ⁵ ἃ ἄλυτα Plato: ἀδύνατα A   ⁶ ἀγέννητον A

Thus concerning God's nature which fills heaven and earth with his beauty he teaches both where God must be and that God must be one.

6. Philolaus too, by saying that God encompasses all things as in a prison,[1] shows that God is one and that he is above matter. So also Lysis and Opsimus: the one defines God as an ineffable number, the other as the excess of the greatest number over that nearest it. Now if ten is the greatest number according to the Pythagoreans, since it is the *tetractys*[2] and includes all the arithmetical and harmonic ratios, and if nine is the nearest to it, God is a unit—that is, one; for by one the greatest number exceeds that nearest it . . .

2. Plato and Aristotle—and note that it is not as one who intends to give an exact account of the doctrines of the philosophers that I run through what they say concerning God; for I know that you are as much superior to all men in an exact understanding of the whole range of learning as you exceed them in the wisdom and power of your rule, and that you can boast of having accomplished in every branch of learning what not even those who have specialized in one can lay claim to; but since it is impossible to show without mentioning names that we are not alone in insisting on the oneness of God, we have turned to the Opinions[3]—so then, Plato says: 'It is a hard task to find the Maker and Father of this universe, and having found him it is impossible to declare him to all.' Here he understands the uncreated and eternal God to be one. If he acknowledges other gods such as sun, moon, and stars, he recognizes that they are created: 'Gods, offspring of gods,[4] whose Creator am I, as well as Father of those works which are indestructible except as I will; all that is bound can be undone.' Now if Plato is no atheist when he understands the Creator of all things to be the one uncreated

6. [1] For this translation see H. Diels, *Die Fragmente der Vorsokratiker* (Berlin, 1934), i. 414.
[2] $1+2+3+4 = 10$ (Aetius, *Plac.* 1. 3. 8).
[3] That is, collections of the opinions of philosophers, more or less superficial manuals containing summaries and sometimes quotations (H. Diels, *Doxographi Graeci* [Berlin, 1879]). The passages from Plato which follow were derived from such sources, to judge from their popularity in this period (see also Diels, p. 568).
[4] This probably does not represent the original meaning of these words (see F. M. Cornford, *Plato's Cosmology* [New York, 1937], pp. 367–70). Our rendering, however, may be in line with Athenagoras' understanding of them—especially if we are justified in regarding Cicero's translation as typical (*vos qui deorum satu orti estis, Timaeus* 11. 40).

λόγῳ δεδημιούργηται καὶ τῷ παρ' αὐτοῦ πνεύματι συνέχεται τὰ
πάντα, τοῦτον εἰδότες καὶ κρατύνοντες⁷ θεόν. 3. ὁ δὲ Ἀριστοτέλης
καὶ οἱ ἀπ' αὐτοῦ ἕνα ἄγοντες οἱονεὶ ζῷον σύνθετον, ἐκ ψυχῆς καὶ
σώματος συνεστηκότα λέγουσι τὸν θεόν, σῶμα μὲν αὐτοῦ τὸ
αἰθέριον νομίζοντες τούς τε πλανωμένους ἀστέρας καὶ τὴν σφαῖραν
τῶν ἀπλανῶν κινούμενα κυκλοφορητικῶς, ψυχὴν δὲ τὸν ἐπὶ τῇ
κινήσει τοῦ σώματος λόγον, αὐτὸν μὲν οὐ κινούμενον, αἴτιον δὲ τῆς
τούτου κινήσεως γινόμενον. 4. οἱ δὲ ἀπὸ τῆς Στοᾶς, κἂν ταῖς
προσηγορίαις κατὰ τὰς παραλλάξεις τῆς ὕλης, δι' ἧς φασι τὸ
πνεῦμα χωρεῖν τοῦ θεοῦ, πληθύνωσι τὸ θεῖον τοῖς ὀνόμασι, τῷ γοῦν
ἔργῳ⁸ ἕνα νομίζουσι τὸν θεόν. εἰ γὰρ ὁ μὲν θεὸς πῦρ τεχνικὸν
ὁδῷ βαδίζον ἐπὶ γενέσει⁹ κόσμου ἐμπεριειληφὸς ἅπαντας τοὺς
σπερματικοὺς λόγους καθ' οὓς ἕκαστα καθ' εἱμαρμένην γίγνεται, τὸ
δὲ πνεῦμα αὐτοῦ διήκει δι' ὅλου τοῦ κόσμου, ὁ θεὸς εἷς κατ' αὐτούς,
Ζεὺς μὲν κατὰ τὸ ζέον τῆς ὕλης ὀνομαζόμενος, Ἥρα δὲ κατὰ τὸν
ἀέρα, καὶ τὰ λοιπὰ καθ' ἕκαστον τῆς ὕλης μέρος δι' ἧς κεχώρηκε
καλούμενος.

7. Ὅταν οὖν τὸ μὲν εἶναι ἓν τὸ θεῖον ὡς ἐπὶ τὸ πλεῖστον, κἂν μὴ
θέλωσι, τοῖς πᾶσι συμφωνῆται ἐπὶ τὰς ἀρχὰς τῶν ὅλων παραγινο-
μένοις, ἡμεῖς δὲ κρατύνωμεν τὸν διακοσμήσαντα τὸ πᾶν τοῦτο,
τοῦτον εἶναι τὸν θεόν, τίς ἡ αἰτία τοῖς μὲν¹ ἐπ' ἀδείας ἐξεῖναι καὶ
λέγειν καὶ γράφειν περὶ τοῦ θεοῦ ἃ θέλουσιν, ἐφ' ἡμῖν δὲ κεῖσθαι
νόμον, οἳ ἔχομεν ὅ τι καὶ νοοῦμεν καὶ ὀρθῶς πεπιστεύκαμεν, ἕνα
θεὸν εἶναι, ἀληθείας σημείοις καὶ λόγοις παραστῆσαι; 2. ποιηταὶ
μὲν γὰρ καὶ φιλόσοφοι, ὡς καὶ τοῖς ἄλλοις, ἐπέβαλον στοχαστικῶς,
κινηθέντες μὲν κατὰ συμπάθειαν τῆς παρὰ τοῦ θεοῦ πνοῆς ὑπὸ τῆς
αὐτὸς αὐτοῦ ψυχῆς ἕκαστος ζητῆσαι, εἰ δυνατὸς εὑρεῖν καὶ νοῆσαι
τὴν ἀλήθειαν, τοσοῦτον δὲ δυνηθέντες ὅσον περινοῆσαι, οὐχ εὑρεῖν
τὸ ὄν,² οὐ παρὰ θεοῦ περὶ θεοῦ ἀξιώσαντες μαθεῖν, ἀλλὰ παρ'
αὐτοῦ ἕκαστος· διὸ καὶ ἄλλος ἄλλως ἐδογμάτισεν αὐτῶν καὶ περὶ
θεοῦ καὶ περὶ ὕλης καὶ περὶ εἰδῶν καὶ περὶ κόσμου. 3. ἡμεῖς δὲ
ὧν νοοῦμεν καὶ πεπιστεύκαμεν ἔχομεν προφήτας μάρτυρας, οἳ

6. ⁷ κρατοῦντες A: corr. Schwartz (cf. 7. 1)   ⁸ τὸ γοῦν ἔργον A: corr. A¹
⁹ γενέσεις A: corr. s
7. ¹ inter τοῖς μὲν et ἐπ' ἀδείας inseruit A verba ἀδοκιμάζουσιν ἐπειδὴ οἱ πολλοὶ
κτλ. usque ad κνίσῃ τε παρατροπῶσιν ex 12. 4–13. 4   ² εὕρηντο ὂν A: corr.
Schwartz

God, neither are we atheists when we acknowledge him by whose Word all things were created and upheld by his Spirit and assert that he is God.

3. Aristotle[5] and his school bring before us one God whom they liken to a composite living being and say that he consists of soul and body. They consider his body to be the ether, the planets, and the sphere of the fixed stars, all of which have a circular motion, and his soul to be the reason that controls the motion of the body—itself unmoved, yet cause of the body's motion.

4. The Stoics, although they multiply names for the divine being by means of titles corresponding to the permutations of matter through which they say the Spirit of God moves, in reality think of God as one. For if God is an artisan fire systematically proceeding to the production of the world, containing in itself all the generative principles by which everything takes place in accord with Destiny, and if his Spirit penetrates the whole world, then it follows from their teaching that God is one, receiving the name 'Zeus' to correspond to the 'seething' element of matter or 'Hera' to correspond to the 'air', and being given all his other names to correspond to every part of matter, which he pervades.

7. Seeing, then, that by and large all admit, though reluctantly, when they get down to the first principles of everything, that the divine being is one, and since we insist that he who ordered our universe is God, why is it that *they* enjoy the licence to speak and write what they want concerning the divine being, whereas a law has been imposed upon *us* who can establish with compelling proofs and arguments the correctness of what we think and believe—that God is one?

2. For poets and philosophers have gone at this and other matters by guesswork, each of them moved by his own soul through some affinity with the breath of God to seek, if possible, to find and understand the truth. But they were able to gain no more than a peripheral understanding; they could not find Being since they would not stoop to learn about God from God, but each relied upon himself. That is why they all came up with different doctrines concerning God, matter, the forms, and the world. 3. We, however, have prophets as witnesses of what we think and believe. They have spoken out by a divinely inspired

---

6. [5] Possibly derived from Aetius, *Plac.* 1. 7. 32; but it is more likely that Athenagoras reflects the early (Platonizing) Aristotle here (G. Lazzati, *L'Aristotele perduto e gli antichi scrittori cristiani* [Milan, 1938], pp. 69–72; cf. Aetius, *Plac.* 5. 20. 1).

πνεύματι ἐνθέῳ ἐκπεφωνήκασι καὶ περὶ τοῦ θεοῦ καὶ περὶ τῶν τοῦ
θεοῦ. εἴποιτε δ' ἂν καὶ ὑμεῖς συνέσει καὶ τῇ περὶ τὸ ὄντως θεῖον
εὐσεβείᾳ τοὺς ἄλλους προὔχοντες ὡς ἔστιν ἄλογον παραλιπόντας
πιστεύειν τῷ παρὰ τοῦ θεοῦ πνεύματι ὡς ὄργανα κεκινηκότι[3] τὰ[4] τῶν
προφητῶν στόματα, προσέχειν δόξαις ἀνθρωπίναις.

8. Ὅτι τοίνυν εἷς ἐξ ἀρχῆς ὁ τοῦδε τοῦ παντὸς ποιητὴς θεός,
οὑτωσὶ σκέψασθε, ἵν' ἔχητε[1] καὶ τὸν λογισμὸν ἡμῶν τῆς πίστεως.
εἰ δύο ἐξ ἀρχῆς ἢ πλείους ἦσαν θεοί, ἤτοι ἐν ἑνὶ καὶ ταὐτῷ[2] ἦσαν ἢ
ἰδίᾳ ἕκαστος αὐτῶν. 2. ἐν μὲν οὖν ἑνὶ καὶ ταὐτῷ εἶναι οὐκ ἠδύναντο.[3]
οὐ γάρ, εἰ θεοί, ὅμοιοι, ἀλλ' ὅτι ἀγένητοι,[4] οὐχ ὅμοιοι· τὰ μὲν γὰρ
γενητὰ ὅμοια τοῖς παραδείγμασιν, τὰ δὲ ἀγένητα ἀνόμοια, οὔτε ἀπό
τινος οὔτε πρός τινα γενόμενα. 3. εἰ δέ, ὡς χεὶρ καὶ ὀφθαλμὸς καὶ
ποὺς περὶ ἓν σῶμά εἰσιν συμπληρωτικὰ[5] μέρη, ἕνα ἐξ αὐτῶν
συμπληροῦντες, ὁ θεὸς εἷς· καίτοι ὁ μὲν Σωκράτης, παρὸ γενητὸς
καὶ φθαρτός, συγκείμενος καὶ διαιρούμενος εἰς μέρη, ὁ δὲ θεὸς
ἀγένητος[6] καὶ ἀπαθὴς καὶ ἀδιαίρετος· οὐκ ἄρα συνεστὼς ἐκ μερῶν.
4. εἰ δὲ ἰδίᾳ ἕκαστος[7] αὐτῶν, ὄντος τοῦ τὸν κόσμον πεποιηκότος
ἀνωτέρω τῶν γεγονότων καὶ περὶ[8] ἃ ἐποίησέ τε καὶ ἐκόσμησεν, ποῦ
ὁ ἕτερος ἢ οἱ λοιποί; εἰ γὰρ ὁ μὲν κόσμος σφαιρικὸς ἀποτελεσθεὶς

---

7. [3] κεκινηκότα A: corr. m. rec. A   [4] τὰ om. A: add. A[1]
8. [1] ἔχητε: ἔχοιτε A   [2] καὶ ταὐτῷ: καὶ ταῦ add. A[1]   [3] ἠδύνατο A:
corr. A[1]   [4] ἀλλοτ///ια///ενητοι A: ἀλλ' ὅτ///ι ἀγενητοι τε και γενητοὶ
A[1]   [5] συμπληρωτικὰ Schwartz: συμπληροῦντες τὰ A   [6] ἀγέννητος
A   [7] ἑκάστου A: corr. s   [8] περὶ A: ὑπὲρ Wilamowitz,
Schwartz, Geffcken

Spirit about God and the things of God. You too would admit, since you surpass others in wisdom and reverence for the truly divine, that it would be irrational to abandon belief in the Spirit from God which had moved the mouths of the prophets like musical instruments and to pay attention to human opinions.

8. Consider, in light of the following arguments, the teaching that God, the Creator of this universe, is one from the beginning so that you may also understand the reasoning which supports our faith: if there were two or more gods from the beginning, either (a) they would be in one and the same category or (b) each of them would be independent. 2. (a) They could not be in one and the same category.[1] [i] For if they were gods, they would not be similar; but, because they were uncreated, they would be dissimilar. For created things are similar to their exemplars,[2] whereas uncreated things are dissimilar, deriving their existence from no one and without reference to models. 3. [ii] If it is suggested that God is one, as in the case of one body a hand and eye and foot are complementary parts forming one being, we reply: Socrates, since he is created and perishable, is indeed composite and divisible into parts; but God is uncreated, impassible, and indivisible; he does not consist of parts.

4. (b) If on the other hand each of the two or more gods were independent, and we assume that the Maker of the world is above the things created and around what he has made and adorned, where would the other god or the other gods be?[3] For

---

8. [1] Athenagoras deals with two possibilities in this connection: (i) that the gods form a community in one and the same genus (a suggestion built up in Platonic terms); (ii) that the gods form a community in one and the same organism (a suggestion built up in Stoic terms; cf. Sextus Empiricus, *Hyp.* 3. 100; M. Aurelius 7. 13; 8. 34). For Athenagoras' critique of the latter compare Philo (*Leg. Alleg.* 1. 66).

[2] A reference to the Platonic Ideas.

[3] For 'above' and 'around' compare 6. 1 (above); Hermas, *Man.* 1. 1; Philo, *Leg. Alleg.* 1. 44; *De Somn.* 1. 63, 185; *De Sobr.* 63; *De Conf. Ling.* 136; Cicero, *De Nat. Deor.* 1. 37. 103. Even Aristotle's unmoved mover, for whom Aristotle himself as well as the later Platonists used all the predicates of the Platonic Idea (especially that of the Good), could be described as 'encompassing' all the spheres (Diels, *Doxographi Graeci*, p. 450; cf. Aristotle, *Phys.* 267b6-9). 'To encompass' and 'to fill' (for the latter see 8. 6 below) probably mean to be 'infinite' as in Hippolytus (*Pasch.* 3). Athenagoras' God is in fact 'infinite' or 'encompassed by none' (10. 1). The spatial terminology may have received special impetus in Christian circles from the debate with Gnostics (Irenaeus, *Adv. Haer.* 2. 1. 1; Tertullian, *Adv. Marc.* 1. 3-11; Adamantius, *Dial.* 2. 1-2; cf. R. M. Grant, *The Early Christian Doctrine of God* [Charlottesville, Va., 1966], pp. 109-10).

οὐρανοῦ κύκλοις ἀποκέκλεισται, ὁ δὲ τοῦ κόσμου ποιητὴς ἀνωτέρω
τῶν γεγονότων ἐπέχων αὐτόν⁹ τῇ τούτων προνοίᾳ, τίς ὁ τοῦ
ἑτέρου θεοῦ ἢ τῶν λοιπῶν τόπος; οὔτε γὰρ ἐν τῷ κόσμῳ ἐστίν, ὅτι
ἑτέρου ἐστίν· οὔτε περὶ τὸν κόσμον, ὑπὲρ γὰρ τοῦτον ὁ τοῦ κόσμου
ποιητὴς θεός. 5. εἰ δὲ μήτε ἐν τῷ κόσμῳ ἐστὶν μήτε περὶ τὸν
κόσμον (τὸ γὰρ περὶ αὐτὸν πᾶν ὑπὸ τούτου κατέχεται), ποῦ ἐστιν;
ἀνωτέρω τοῦ κόσμου καὶ¹⁰ τοῦ θεοῦ, ἐν ἑτέρῳ κόσμῳ καὶ περὶ
ἕτερον; ἀλλ᾽ εἰ μέν ἐστιν ἐν ἑτέρῳ καὶ περὶ ἕτερον, οὔτε περὶ ἡμᾶς
ἐστιν ἔτι (οὐδὲ¹¹ γὰρ κόσμου κρατεῖ), οὔτε αὐτὸς δυνάμει μέγας
ἐστίν (ἐν γὰρ περιωρισμένῳ τόπῳ ἐστίν). 6. εἰ δὲ οὔτε ἐν ἑτέρῳ
κόσμῳ ἐστὶν (πάντα γὰρ ὑπὸ τούτου πεπλήρωται) οὔτε περὶ
ἕτερον (πάντα γὰρ ὑπὸ τούτου κατέχεται), καὶ οὐκ ἔστιν, οὐκ
ὄντος ἐν ᾧ ἐστιν. ἢ τί ποιεῖ, ἑτέρου μὲν ὄντος οὗ ἐστιν ὁ κόσμος,
αὐτὸς δὲ ἀνωτέρω ὢν τοῦ ποιητοῦ τοῦ κόσμου, οὐκ ὢν δὲ οὔτε ἐν
κόσμῳ οὔτε περὶ κόσμον; 7. ἀλλ᾽ ἔστι τι ἕτερον ἵνα που στῇ ὁ
γενόμενος κατὰ τοῦ ὄντος; ἀλλ᾽ ὑπὲρ αὐτὸν ὁ θεὸς καὶ τὰ τοῦ θεοῦ.
καὶ τίς ἔσται τόπος τὰ ὑπὲρ τὸν κόσμον τούτου πεπληρωκότος;
8. ἀλλὰ προνοεῖ;¹² καὶ μὴν οὐδὲ προνοεῖ,¹³ εἰ μὴ πεποίηκεν. εἰ δὲ
μὴ ποιεῖ¹⁴ μήτε προνοεῖ μήτε ἐστὶ τόπος ἕτερος, ἐν ᾧ ἐστίν, εἷς
οὗτος ἐξ ἀρχῆς καὶ μόνος ὁ ποιητὴς τοῦ κόσμου θεός.

9. Εἰ μὲν οὖν ταῖς τοιαύταις ἐννοίαις ἀπηρκούμεθα, ἀνθρωπικὸν ἄν
τις εἶναι τὸν καθ᾽ ἡμᾶς ἐνόμιζεν¹ λόγον· ἐπεὶ δὲ αἱ φωναὶ τῶν

8. ⁹ ἐπέχων αὐτὸν A: παρέχων αὐτὸν Schwartz   ¹⁰ καὶ Schwartz: ἢ A ex
corr.   ¹¹ οὐδὲ Schwartz: οὔτε A   ¹² ἀλλὰ προνοεῖ: in mg. οὐ A¹
¹³ καὶ μὴν οὐδὲ εἰ μὴ προνοῇ πεποίηκεν A: corr. Gesner   ¹⁴ μὴ ποιεῖ seclusit Wilamowitz: μήτε ποιεῖ Bauer
9. ¹ ἐνόμισεν A: corr. Wilamowitz

if the world is spherical in shape and is enclosed by the orbits of
the heavenly bodies, and if the Maker of the world is above
created things and governs the world by exercising his providence
over them, what place is there for the other god or the other gods?
[i] He cannot be (*a*) in the world since that belongs to another;
nor can he be (*b*) around the world since it is God the Maker of
the world who is above it. 5. [ii] Now if he is neither in the world
nor around the world (for everything around the world is controlled by God its Maker), where is he? Above the world and God;
in another world and around it? But (*a*) if he is in another world
and around it, he is in no way around us (for he does not rule our
world), nor is he great in power (for he is in a circumscribed
place).⁴ 6. And if (*b*) he is not in another world (for all things are
filled by God the Maker)⁵ nor around another (for all things are
controlled by God the Maker), he does not exist, since there is no
place for him in which to be; otherwise what would there be for
him to do, since there is another to whom the world belongs,
whereas he himself would be above the Maker of the world yet
would be neither in a world nor around a world?⁶

7. Is there anything else that will make it possible for one
pitted against Being to find a place to stand? No, for God and the
things of God are above him. And what place can there be since
God fills that which is above the world? 8. Can he then exercise
providence? He cannot even exercise providence, if he has not
made anything. If he cannot make anything, if he cannot exercise
providence over anything, and if there is no other place in which
he can be, God the Maker of the world is from the beginning one
and alone.

9. Now if we were satisfied with considerations of this kind, one
could regard our doctrine as man-made. But since the voices of

---

8. ⁴ i.e. even if he exists, he has nothing to do with us and does not concern us.

⁵ Cf. Philo, *De Conf. Ling.* 136 (see n. 3 above).

⁶ Athenagoras works out the consequences of the supposition that this god
controls no world (but is somewhere above the Creator). First the supposition
that this god controls no world is shown—parenthetically—to be fact: there is
no place for such a world; the Creator controls everything. (This is already
implicit in the preceding remarks: a god who is 'great in power' is not 'in a
circumscribed place'.) So sweeping is the argument, however, that it all but
suffices to rule out the possibility of any place in which this god might exist.
Nevertheless Athenagoras returns to the bare supposition that this god is
somewhere above the Creator but controls no world. In this connection he
argues that if a god controls nothing, he does not exist (see also 8. 8). For the
presupposition involved see Tertullian (*Adv. Hermog.* 3) and Origen (*De Princ.*
1. 2. 10; 3. 5. 3).

προφητῶν πιστοῦσιν ἡμῶν τοὺς λογισμούς (νομίζω ⟨δὲ⟩² καὶ
ὑμᾶς φιλομαθεστάτους καὶ ἐπιστημονεστάτους ὄντας οὐκ ἀνοήτους³
γεγονέναι οὔτε τῶν Μωσέως οὔτε τῶν Ἠσαΐου καὶ Ἰερεμίου καὶ
τῶν λοιπῶν προφητῶν, οἳ κατ' ἔκστασιν τῶν ἐν αὐτοῖς λογισμῶν,
κινήσαντος αὐτοὺς τοῦ θείου πνεύματος, ἃ ἐνηργοῦντο ἐξεφώνησαν,
συγχρησαμένου τοῦ πνεύματος, ὡς εἰ καὶ αὐλητὴς αὐλὸν ἐμπνεύσαι)
—τί οὖν οὗτοι; 2. "κύριος ὁ θεὸς ἡμῶν· οὐ λογισθήσεται ἕτερος
πρὸς αὐτόν." ᵃ καὶ πάλιν· "ἐγὼ θεὸς πρῶτος καὶ μετὰ ταῦτα, καὶ
πλὴν ἐμοῦ οὐκ ἔστι θεός." ᵇ ὁμοίως·⁴ "ἔμπροσθεν ἐμοῦ οὐκ ἐγένετο
ἄλλος θεὸς καὶ μετ' ἐμὲ οὐκ ἔσται· ἐγὼ ὁ θεὸς⁵ καὶ οὐκ ἔστι παρὲξ
ἐμοῦ".ᶜ καὶ περὶ τοῦ μεγέθους· "ὁ οὐρανός μοι θρονός, ἡ δὲ γῆ ὑπο-
πόδιον τῶν ποδῶν μου. ποῖον οἶκον οἰκοδομήσετέ μοι, ἢ τίς τόπος
τῆς καταπαύσεώς μου;" ᵈ 3. καταλείπω δὲ ὑμῖν ἐπ' αὐτῶν τῶν
βιβλίων γενομένοις ἀκριβέστερον τὰς ἐκείνων ἐξετάσαι προφητείας,
ὅπως μετὰ τοῦ προσήκοντος λογισμοῦ τὴν καθ' ἡμᾶς ἐπήρειαν
ἀποσκευάσησθε.

10. Τὸ μὲν οὖν ἄθεοι μὴ εἶναι, ἕνα τὸν¹ ἀγένητον² καὶ ἀίδιον καὶ
ἀόρατον καὶ ἀπαθῆ καὶ ἀκατάληπτον καὶ ἀχώρητον, νῷ μόνῳ
καὶ λόγῳ καταλαμβανόμενον, φωτὶ καὶ κάλλει καὶ πνεύματι
δυνάμει ἀνεκδιηγήτῳ περιεχόμενον, ὑφ' οὗ γεγένηται τὸ πᾶν διὰ
⟨τοῦ παρ'⟩ αὐτοῦ³ λόγου καὶ διακεκόσμηται καὶ συγκρατεῖται,
θεὸν ἄγοντες, ἱκανῶς μοι δέδεικται.⁴ 2. νοοῦμεν γὰρ καὶ υἱὸν τοῦ
θεοῦ. καὶ μή μοι γελοῖόν τις νομίσῃ τὸ υἱὸν εἶναι τῷ θεῷ. οὐ γὰρ
ὡς ποιηταὶ μυθοποιοῦσιν οὐδὲν βελτίους τῶν ἀνθρώπων δεικνύντες
τοὺς θεούς, ἢ περὶ τοῦ θεοῦ καὶ πατρὸς ἢ περὶ τοῦ υἱοῦ πεφρονή-
καμεν, ἀλλ' ἐστὶν ὁ υἱὸς τοῦ θεοῦ λόγος τοῦ πατρὸς ἐν ἰδέᾳ καὶ
ἐνεργείᾳ· πρὸς αὐτοῦ γὰρ καὶ δι' αὐτοῦ πάντα ἐγένετο,ᵃ ἑνὸς ὄντος
τοῦ πατρὸς καὶ τοῦ υἱοῦ. ὄντος δὲ τοῦ υἱοῦ ἐν πατρὶ καὶ πατρὸς ἐν
υἱῷᵇ ἑνότητι καὶ δυνάμει πνεύματος, νοῦς καὶ λόγος τοῦ πατρὸς ὁ

---

9. ᵃ Baruch 3: 36   ᵇ Isa. 44: 6   ᶜ Isa. 43: 10–11   ᵈ Isa. 66: 1
10. ᵃ Cf. John 1: 3   ᵇ Cf. John 10: 38

9. ² δὲ add. Gesner   ³ ἀνοήτους A: ἀνηκόους Schwartz: ἀμήτους
Geffcken   ⁴ ὅμοιος A: corr. Otto   ⁵ σώζ(ων) in mg. add. A¹
10. ¹ τὸν p: τὸ A   ² ἀγέννητον A   ³ διανοῦ A: διὰ τοῦ αὐτοῦ A¹: corr.
Schwartz (cf. 4. 2)   ⁴ post δέδεικται lacunam indicavit Schwartz: νοοῦμεν
δὲ Gesner

the prophets affirm our arguments—and I expect that you who are so eager for knowledge and so learned are not without understanding of the teachings either of Moses or of Isaiah and Jeremiah and the rest of the prophets who in the ecstasy of their thoughts, as the divine Spirit moved them, uttered what they had been inspired to say, the Spirit making use of them as a flautist might blow into a flute[1]—what, then, do they say? 2. 'The Lord is our God; no other shall be reckoned in addition to him.' And again: 'I am God, first and last; and except for me there is no God.' Similarly: 'There was no other God before me and there will be none after me; I am God and there is none beside me.' And concerning his greatness: 'Heaven is my throne and the earth my footstool. What house will you build for me, or what place for me to rest?' 3. I leave it to you to apply yourselves to these very books and to examine more carefully these men's prophecies, that you may with fitting discernment bring to an end the abuse with which we are treated.

10. We have brought before you a God who is uncreated, eternal, invisible, impassible, incomprehensible, and infinite, who can be apprehended by mind and reason alone, who is encompassed by light, beauty, spirit, and indescribable power, and who created, adorned, and now rules the universe through the Word that issues from him. I have given sufficient evidence that we are not atheists on the basis of arguments presenting this God as one.[1]

2. For we think there is also a Son of God. Now let no one think that this talk of God having a Son is ridiculous. For we have not come to our views on either God the Father or his Son as do the poets, who create myths in which they present the gods as no better than men. On the contrary, the Son of God is the Word of the Father in Ideal Form and Energizing Power;[2] for in his likeness and through him all things came into existence, which presupposes that the Father and the Son are one. Now since the Son is in the Father and the Father in the Son by a powerful

---

9. [1] For the imagery see Plutarch (*De Def. Orac.* 436 f) and Philo (*Quis Rer. Div. Heres* 259).

10. [1] The implication is that arguments on other grounds are also possible. These Athenagoras proceeds to elaborate. This interpretation of the text fits in well with what is said below in 10. 5.

[2] It appears that a Platonic term (Form, Idea) is linked with one that is Aristotelian (Energizing Power, Act). The phrase as a whole, however, is probably modelled on the Stoic–Philonic distinction between the (cosmic) *logos endiathetos* (containing all the Forms) and the *logos prophorikos* (as agent in creation). Cf. Theophilus, *Ad Autol.* 2. 10, 22.

υἱὸς τοῦ θεοῦ. 3. εἰ δὲ δι' ὑπερβολὴν συνέσεως σκοπεῖν ὑμῖν
ἔπεισιν, ὁ παῖς τί βούλεται, ἐρῶ διὰ βραχέων· πρῶτον γέννημα
εἶναι τῷ πατρί, οὐχ ὡς γενόμενον (ἐξ ἀρχῆς γὰρ ὁ θεός, νοῦς
ἀίδιος ὤν, εἶχεν αὐτὸς ἐν ἑαυτῷ τὸν λόγον, ἀιδίως λογικὸς ὤν), ἀλλ'
ὡς τῶν ὑλικῶν ξυμπάντων ἀποίου φύσεως^c καὶ †γῆς οχιας†⁵ ὑποκειμένων δίκην, μεμιγμένων τῶν παχυμερεστέρων πρὸς τὰ κου-
φότερα,^d ἐπ' αὐτοῖς ἰδέα καὶ ἐνέργεια εἶναι, προελθών. 4. συνᾴδει
δὲ τῷ λόγῳ καὶ τὸ προφητικὸν πνεῦμα·⁶ "κύριος γάρ", φησίν,
"ἔκτισέν με ἀρχὴν ὁδῶν αὐτοῦ εἰς ἔργα αὐτοῦ."^e καίτοι καὶ αὐτὸ
τὸ ἐνεργοῦν τοῖς ἐκφωνοῦσι προφητικῶς ἅγιον πνεῦμα ἀπόρροιαν^f
εἶναί φαμεν τοῦ θεοῦ, ἀπορρέον καὶ ἐπαναφερόμενον ὡς ἀκτῖνα
ἡλίου. 5. τίς οὖν οὐκ ἂν ἀπορήσαι ⟨τοὺς⟩⁷ ἄγοντας⁸ θεὸν πατέρα
καὶ υἱὸν θεὸν καὶ πνεῦμα ἅγιον, δεικνύντας αὐτῶν⁹ καὶ τὴν ἐν τῇ
ἑνώσει δύναμιν καὶ τὴν ἐν τῇ τάξει διαίρεσιν, ἀκούσας¹⁰ ἀθέους
καλουμένους; καὶ οὐδ'¹¹ ἐπὶ τούτοις τὸ θεολογικὸν ἡμῶν ἵσταται
μέρος, ἀλλὰ καὶ πλῆθος ἀγγέλων καὶ λειτουργῶν φαμεν, οὓς ὁ
ποιητὴς καὶ δημιουργὸς κόσμου θεὸς διὰ τοῦ παρ' αὐτοῦ λόγου
διένειμε καὶ διέταξεν περί τε τὰ στοιχεῖα εἶναι καὶ τοὺς οὐρανοὺς
καὶ τὸν κόσμον καὶ τὰ ἐν αὐτῷ καὶ τὴν τούτων εὐταξίαν.

11. Εἰ δὲ ἀκριβῶς διέξειμι τὸν καθ' ἡμᾶς λόγον, μὴ θαυμάσητε· ἵνα
γὰρ μὴ τῇ κοινῇ καὶ ἀλόγῳ συναποφέρησθε γνώμῃ, ἔχητε δὲ
τἀληθὲς εἰδέναι, ἀκριβολογοῦμαι· ἐπεὶ καὶ δι' αὐτῶν τῶν δογμάτων
οἷς προσέχομεν, οὐκ ἀνθρωπικοῖς οὖσιν ἀλλὰ θεοφάτοις καὶ θεο-
διδάκτοις, πεῖσαι ὑμᾶς μὴ ὡς περὶ ἀθέων ἔχειν δυνάμεθα. 2. τίνες
οὖν ἡμῶν οἱ λόγοι, οἷς ἐντρεφόμεθα; "λέγω ὑμῖν· ἀγαπᾶτε τοὺς
ἐχθροὺς ὑμῶν, εὐλογεῖτε τοὺς καταρωμένους, προσεύχεσθε ὑπὲρ τῶν
διωκόντων ὑμᾶς, ὅπως γένησθε υἱοὶ τοῦ πατρὸς τοῦ ἐν τοῖς οὐρανοῖς,
ὃς τὸν ἥλιον αὐτοῦ ἀνατέλλει ἐπὶ πονηροὺς καὶ ἀγαθοὺς καὶ βρέχει

---

10. ^c Cf. Plato, Tim. 50 c–51 b   ^d Cf. Plato, Tim. 53 a–b   ^e Prov. 8: 22
^f Cf. Wisd. 7: 25

---

10. ⁵ γῆς οχιας A: γῆς ἀχρείας Maranus: ἀργῆς συστοιχίας Schwartz: μεγάλης
aut πολλῆς ἀψυχίας Geffcken: fortasse ὑποδόχης   ⁶ πνι A: corr. n p
⁷ τοὺς add. Wilamowitz   ⁸ ἄγοντας Schwartz: ///γοντας A: λέγοντας
A¹   ⁹ αὐτὸν A: corr. m. rec.   ¹⁰ ἀκούσασα A: corr. A¹   ¹¹ οὐδ'
Wilamowitz: οὐκ A

unity of spirit, the Son of God is the mind and reason of the Father.

3. If in your great wisdom you would like to know what 'Son' means, I will tell you in a few brief words: it means that he is the first begotten of the Father. The term is used not because he came into existence (for God, who is eternal mind, had in himself his Word or Reason from the beginning, since he was eternally rational) but because he came forth to serve as Ideal Form and Energizing Power for everything material which like an entity without qualities and ... underlies things in a state characterized by the mixture of heavier and lighter elements.

4. The prophetic Spirit also agrees with this account. 'For the Lord', it says, 'made me the beginning of his ways for his works.' Further, this same holy Spirit, which is active in those who speak prophetically, we regard as an effluence of God which flows forth from him and returns like a ray of the sun.

5. Who then would not be amazed if he heard of men called atheists who bring forward God the Father, God the Son, and the Holy Spirit and who proclaim both their power in their unity and their diversity in rank. Nor does our teaching concerning the Godhead stop there, but we also say that there is a host of angels and ministers whom God, the Maker and Artificer of the world, set in their places through the Word that issues from him and whom he commanded to be concerned with the elements, the heavens, and the world with all that is in it and the good order of all that is in it.

11. Do not be surprised that I go through our teaching in detail. I am making my points carefully to prevent you from being carried away by low and irrational opinion and to put you in a position to know the truth. For we can persuade you that you are not dealing with atheists precisely through the doctrines which we hold—doctrines not man-made but ordained and taught by God.

2. What then are the teachings on which we are brought up? 'I say to you, love your enemies, bless them who curse you, pray for them who persecute you, that you may be sons of your Father

ἐπὶ δικαίους καὶ ἀδίκους."ᵃ 3. ἐπιτρέψατε¹ ἐνταῦθα τοῦ λόγου
ἐξακούστου μετὰ πολλῆς κραυγῆς γεγονότος ἐπὶ παρρησίαν
ἀναγαγεῖν, ὡς ἐπὶ βασιλέων φιλοσόφων ἀπολογούμενον. τίνες γὰρ ἢ
τῶν τοὺς συλλογισμοὺς ἀναλυόντων καὶ τὰς ἀμφιβολίας διαλυόντων
καὶ τὰς ἐτυμολογίας σαφηνιζόντων ἢ τῶν τὰ ὁμώνυμα καὶ συνώ-
νυμα καὶ κατηγορήματα καὶ ἀξιώματα καὶ τί τὸ ὑποκείμενον καὶ
τί τὸ κατηγορούμενον†² εὐδαίμονας ἀποτελεῖν διὰ τούτων καὶ τῶν
τοιούτων λόγων ὑπισχνοῦνται τοὺς συνόντας, οὕτως ἐκκεκαθαρ-
μένοι εἰσὶ τὰς ψυχὰς ὡς ἀντὶ τοῦ μισεῖν τοὺς ἐχθροὺς ἀγαπᾶν καὶ
ἀντὶ τοῦ, τὸ μετριώτατον, κακῶς ἀγορεύειν τοὺς προκατάρξαντας
λοιδορίας εὐλογεῖν, καὶ ὑπὲρ τῶν ἐπιβουλευόντων εἰς τὸ ζῆν
προσεύχεσθαι; οἳ τοὐναντίον ἀεὶ διατελοῦσι κακῶς τὰ ἀπόρρητα
ἑαυτοὺς ταῦτα μεταλλεύοντες καὶ ἀεί τι ἐργάσασθαι ἐπιθυμοῦντες
κακόν, τέχνην λόγων καὶ οὐκ ἐπίδειξιν ἔργων τὸ πρᾶγμα πεποιημένοι. 4. παρὰ δ' ἡμῖν εὕροιτε ἂν ἰδιώτας καὶ χειροτέχνας καὶ
γραΐδια, εἰ λόγῳ τὴν ὠφέλειαν παριστᾶν εἰσιν ἀδύνατοι τὴν παρὰ τοῦ
λόγου, ἔργῳ τὴν ἀπὸ τῆς προαιρέσεως ὠφέλειαν ἐπιδεικνυμένους·
οὐ γὰρ λόγους διαμνημονεύουσιν, ἀλλὰ πράξεις ἀγαθὰς ἐπιδεικνύ-
ουσιν, παιόμενοι μὴ ἀντιτύπτειν καὶ ἁρπαζόμενοι μὴ δικάζεσθαι,
τοῖς αἰτοῦσιν διδόναι καὶ τοὺς πλησίον ἀγαπᾶν ὡς ἑαυτούς.ᵇ

12. Ἆρα τοίνυν, εἰ μὴ ἐφεστηκέναι θεὸν τῷ τῶν ἀνθρώπων γένει
ἐνομίζομεν, οὕτως ἂν ἑαυτοὺς ἐξεκαθαίρομεν; οὐκ ἔστιν εἰπεῖν,
ἀλλ' ἐπεὶ πεπείσμεθα ὑφέξειν παντὸς τοῦ ἐνταῦθα βίου λόγον τῷ
πεποιηκότι καὶ ἡμᾶς καὶ τὸν κόσμον θεῷ, τὸν μέτριον καὶ φιλάνθρωπον καὶ εὐκαταφρόνητον βίον αἱρούμεθα, οὐδὲν τηλικοῦτον
πείσεσθαι κακὸν ἐνταῦθα νομίζοντες κἂν τῆς ψυχῆς¹ ἡμᾶς ἀφαι-
ρῶνταί τινες, ὧν ἐκεῖ κομιούμεθα² τοῦ πράου καὶ φιλανθρώπου καὶ
ἐπιεικοῦς βίου παρὰ τοῦ μεγάλου δικαστοῦ. 2. Πλάτωνᵃ μὲν οὖν
Μίνω καὶ Ῥαδάμανθυν δικάσειν καὶ κολάσειν τοὺς πονηροὺς ἔφη,

11. ᵃ Matt. 5: 44–5 (cf. Luke 6: 27–8)   ᵇ Cf. Matt. 5: 39–40; Luke 6: 29–
30; Matt. 22: 39   12. ᵃ Gorg. 523 c–524 a

11. ¹ ἐπιστρέψατε A: corr. n   ² post κατηγορούμενον lacuna esse videtur:
διδασκόντων add. Gesner
12. ¹ τῆς ψυχῆς A: τὴν ψυχὴν Schwartz: τὰς ψυχὰς Geffcken   ² ὧν ἐκεῖ
κομιούμεθα fortasse non sanum: οἷον ἐκεῖ κομιούμεθα μισθὸν Wilamowitz

in heaven who makes his sun rise upon the evil and the good, and sends rain on the just and the unjust.'

3. Since this teaching has made itself heard with a loud cry, allow me here to proceed with full liberty of speech as one who is making his defence before philosopher kings. For which of those who solve syllogisms and eliminate ambiguities and trace etymologies or who . . . homonyms and synonyms, predicates and propositions, what the subject is and what the predicate . . . promise to make their followers happy with these and similar teachings—which of those, I say, are so pure in soul that they love rather than hate their enemies, bless (as most befits a man of moderation) rather than speak evil of those who are prompt with reproach for them, and pray for those who plot against their life? On the contrary, with ill will they constantly dig up just such abuse against one another and constantly seek to bring off some wickedness, for they have made the concoction of words their business rather than the doing of deeds.

4. In our ranks, however, you could find common men, artisans, and old women who, if they cannot establish by reasoned discourse the usefulness of their teaching, show by deed the usefulness of the exercise of their will. For they do not rehearse words but show forth good deeds: when struck they do not strike back; when robbed they do not prosecute; they give to those who ask; and they love their neighbours as themselves.

12. So then, if we did not think that God presided over the human race, would we remain so pure? Certainly not! But since we are convinced that we shall render an account of all our life here below to the God who made both us and the world, we choose the way of life that is moderate, that shows affection for men, and that is thoughtlessly despised. We do not think that we shall suffer so great an evil here below, even if they rob us of our lives, that it may be compared to what we shall gain beyond from the great Judge in return for a way of life that is gentle, affectionate, and kind. 2. Plato said that Minos and Rhadamanthys would judge and punish evil men; we say that no one, not a Minos

26 ATHENAGORAS 12. 2

ἡμεῖς δὲ κἂν Μίνως τις κἂν Ῥαδάμανθυς ἦ κἂν ὁ τούτων πατήρ,
οὐδὲ τοῦτόν³ φαμεν διαφεύξεσθαι τὴν κρίσιν τοῦ θεοῦ. 3. εἶθ᾽ οἱ
μὲν τὸν βίον τοῦτον νομίζοντες "φάγωμεν καὶ πίωμεν, αὔριον γὰρ
ἀποθνήσκομεν"ᵇ καὶ τὸν θάνατον βαθὺν ὕπνον καὶ λήθην τιθέμενοι—
"ὕπνος καὶ θάνατος διδυμάονε"⁴, ᶜ—πιστεύονται θεοσεβεῖν· ἄνθρωποι
δὲ τὸν μὲν ἐνταῦθα ὀλίγου καὶ μικροῦ τινος ἄξιον βίον λελογισμένοι,
ὑπὸ μόνου δὲ παραπεμπόμενοι τοῦ τὸν⁵ ὄντως⁶ θεὸν καὶ τὸν παρ᾽
αὐτοῦ λόγον εἰδέναι, τίς ἡ τοῦ παιδὸς πρὸς τὸν πατέρα ἑνότης, τίς
ἡ τοῦ πατρὸς πρὸς τὸν υἱὸν κοινωνία, τί τὸ πνεῦμα, τίς ἡ τῶν
τοσούτων ἕνωσις καὶ διαίρεσις ἑνουμένων, τοῦ πνεύματος, τοῦ
παιδός, τοῦ πατρός, πολὺ δὲ καὶ κρεῖττον᾽ ἢ εἰπεῖν λόγῳ τὸν ἐκ-
δεχόμενον⁷ βίον εἰδότες, ἐὰν καθαροὶ ὄντες ἀπὸ παντὸς παρα-
πεμφθῶμεν ἀδικήματος, μέχρι τοσούτου δὲ φιλανθρωπότατοι ὥστε
μὴ μόνον στέργειν τοὺς φίλους ("ἐὰν γὰρ ἀγαπᾶτε", φησί, "τοὺς
ἀγαπῶντας καὶ δανείζητε⁸ τοῖς δανείζουσιν ὑμῖν, τίνα μισθὸν
ἕξετε;"),ᵈ τοιοῦτοι δὲ ἡμεῖς ὄντες καὶ τὸν τοιοῦτον βιοῦντες βίον
ἵνα κριθῆναι διαφύγωμεν, ἀπιστούμεθα θεοσεβεῖν;

4. Ταῦτα μὲν οὖν μικρὰ ἀπὸ μεγάλων καὶ ὀλίγα ἀπὸ πολλῶν, ἵνα
μὴ ἐπὶ πλεῖον ὑμῖν ἐνοχλοίημεν· καὶ γὰρ τὸ μέλι καὶ τὸν ὀρὸν δοκι-
μάζοντες μικρῷ μέρει τοῦ παντὸς τὸ πᾶν εἰ καλὸν δοκιμάζουσιν.⁹, ¹⁰

13. Ἐπεὶ δὲ¹ οἱ πολλοὶ τῶν ἐπικαλούντων ἡμῖν τὴν ἀθεότητα οὐδ᾽
ὄναρ τί ἐστι θεὸν² ἐγνωκότες, ἀμαθεῖς καὶ ἀθεώρητοι ὄντες τοῦ
φυσικοῦ καὶ τοῦ θεολογικοῦ λόγου, μετροῦντες τὴν εὐσέβειαν θυσιῶν
νόμῳ, ἐπικαλοῦσιν τὸ μὴ καὶ τοὺς αὐτοὺς ταῖς πόλεσι θεοὺς ἄγειν,
σκέψασθέ μοι, αὐτοκράτορες, ὧδε περὶ ἑκατέρων, καὶ πρῶτόν γε
περὶ τοῦ μὴ θύειν. 2. ὁ τοῦδε τοῦ παντὸς δημιουργὸς καὶ πατὴρ οὐ
δεῖται αἵματος οὐδὲ κνίσης οὐδὲ τῆς ἀπὸ τῶν ἀνθῶν καὶ θυμια-
μάτων εὐωδίας, αὐτὸς ὢν ἡ τελεία εὐωδία, ἀνενδεὴς καὶ ἀπροσδεής·

12. ᵇ Isa. 22: 13; 1 Cor. 15: 32   ᶜ Homer, *Iliad* 16. 672   ᵈ Matt. 5: 46;
Luke 6: 32, 34

12. ³ τούτων A: corr. A¹   ⁴ ὕπνῳ καὶ θανάτῳ διδυμάονε A: corr.
Wilamowitz   ⁵ τοῦ τὸν Maranus: τοῦτον A: τούτου A¹   ⁶ ὄντως
Schwartz: ὃν ἴσως A   ⁷ ἐκδεχομένων A: corr. A¹   ⁸ δανείζετε A:
corr. Wilamowitz   ⁹ ἀδοκιμάζουσιν ἐπειδὴ οἱ πολλοὶ . . . κνίσῃ τε
παρατροπῶσιν (13. 4): ea quae supra (vide 7. 1) addidit A siglo a indicavi
¹⁰ ἀδοκιμάζουσιν a
13. ¹ ἐπειδὴ a   ² τί ἐστιν ὁ θεὸς a

or a Rhadamanthys or the father of them both,[1] will escape the judgement of God.

3. And yet are those to be credited with piety who think that the way to live is this, 'Let us eat and drink, for tomorrow we die', and claim that death is a deep sleep and a forgetting ('sleep and death are twin brothers')? And are we at the same time to be considered irreligious despite the fact that to escape condemnation our behaviour and our way of life are of so different a character? For we are men who consider life here below of very little worth. We are attended only by the knowledge of him who is truly God and of the Word that issues from him—a knowledge as to what is the unity of the Son with the Father, what is the communion of the Father with the Son, what is the Spirit, what is the unity of these powers—the Spirit, the Son, and the Father—and their diversity when thus united. We know that the life we await is far better than words can tell if we are brought there pure from all blame. We show such affection for men that we love not only our friends; 'for', it says, 'if you love them who love you and lend to them who lend to you, what reward will you have?'

4. These points, then, represent a few small matters from among many important ones—few and small that we may not further burden you; for those who test the quality of honey and whey can tell if the whole is good by tasting one small sample.

13. Since the majority of those accusing us of atheism—though they have not even the foggiest notion of the nature of God, are ignorant of scientific or theological doctrine and have no acquaintance with them, and measure piety in terms of sacrifices—since they accuse us of not recognizing the same gods as do the cities, I ask you to take the following into account, my sovereigns, in dealing with both issues. First, concerning our refusal to sacrifice.

2. The Artificer and Father of this universe needs no blood, fat, or the fragrance of flowers and incense. He himself is the perfect fragrance and is in need of nothing from within or without. The best sacrifice to him is for us to know who stretched out

12. [1] Zeus.

ἀλλὰ θυσία αὐτῷ μεγίστη, ἂν γινώσκωμεν τίς ἐξέτεινε καὶ συνεσφαίρωσεν τοὺς οὐρανοὺς καὶ τὴν γῆν κέντρου δίκην ἤδρασε, τίς συνήγαγεν τὸ ὕδωρ εἰς θαλάσσας καὶ διέκρινεν τὸ φῶς ἀπὸ τοῦ σκότους, τίς ἐκόσμησεν ἄστροις τὸν αἰθέρα καὶ ἐποίησεν πᾶν σπέρμα τὴν γῆν ἀναβάλλειν, τίς ἐποίησεν ζῷα καὶ ἄνθρωπον ἔπλασεν.ᵃ 3. ὅταν ⟨οὖν⟩³ ἔχοντες τὸν δημιουργὸν θεὸν συνέχοντα καὶ ἐποπτεύοντα⁴ ἐπιστήμῃ καὶ τέχνῃ καθ' ἣν ἄγει τὰ πάντα, ἐπαίρωμεν ὁσίους χεῖραςᵇ αὐτῷ, ποίας ἔτι χρείαν ἑκατόμβης ἔχει;

4. καὶ τοὺς μὲν θυσίῃσι καὶ εὐχωλῇς ἀγανῇσι
λοιβῇ τε κνίσῃ τε παρατρωπῶσ' ἄνθρωποι,
λισσόμενοι, ὅτε κέν τις ὑπερβαίῃ καὶ ἁμάρτῃ.ᶜ

τί δὲ⁵ μοι ὁλοκαυτώσεων, ὧν μὴ δεῖται ὁ θεός; καὶ⁶ προσφέρειν, δέον ἀναίμακτον θυσίαν⁷ τὴν λογικὴν προσάγειν λατρείαν;ᵈ

14. Ὁ δὲ περὶ τοῦ μὴ¹ προσιέναι καὶ τοὺς αὐτοὺς ταῖς πόλεσιν θεοὺς ἄγειν πάνυ αὐτοῖς εὐήθης λόγος· ἀλλ' οὐδὲ οἱ ἡμῖν ἐπικαλοῦντες ἀθεότητα, ἐπεὶ μὴ τοὺς αὐτοὺς οἷς ἴσασι νομίζομεν, σφίσιν αὐτοῖς συμφωνοῦσιν περὶ θεῶν [μάτην],² ἀλλ' Ἀθηναῖοι³ μὲν Κελεὸν καὶ Μετάνειραν ἵδρυνται θεούς, Λακεδαιμόνιοι δὲ Μενέλεων καὶ θύουσιν αὐτῷ καὶ ἑορτάζουσιν, Ἰλιεῖς δὲ οὐδὲ τὸ ὄνομα ἀκούοντες Ἕκτορα φέρουσιν, Κεῖοι⁴ Ἀρισταῖον,⁵ τὸν αὐτὸν καὶ Δία καὶ Ἀπόλλω⁶ νομίζοντες, Θάσιοι Θεαγένην, ὑφ' οὗ καὶ φόνος Ὀλυμπίασιν ἐγένετο, Σάμιοι Λύσανδρον ἐπὶ τοσαύταις σφαγαῖς καὶ τοσούτοις κακοῖς, †Ἀλκμὰν καὶ Ἡσίοδος Μήδειαν ἢ Νιόβην† Κίλικες, Σικελοὶ Φίλιππον τὸν Βουτακίδου, Ὀνησίλαον Ἀμαθούσιοι, Ἀμίλκαν Καρχηδόνιοι· ἐπιλείψει με ἡ ἡμέρα τὸ πλῆθος καταλέγοντα.

---

13. ᵃ Cf. Gen. 1   ᵇ Cf. 1 Tim. 2: 8   ᶜ Homer, Iliad 9. 499–501 (cf. Plato, Rep. 364 d)   ᵈ Cf. Rom. 12: 1

---

13. ³ οὖν add. Maranus   ⁴ lacunam post ἐποπτεύοντα indicavit Schwartz
⁵ τί δὲ A: τί δεῖ Schwartz   ⁶ καὶ A: καίτοι A¹: lacunam indicavit
Schwartz   ⁷ post θυσίαν add. καὶ A¹
14. ¹ μὴ περὶ τοῦ A: corr. Gesner   ² μάτην seclusit Maranus
³ Ἀθήναισι A   ⁴ Κεῖοι Otto: καὶ χιοι A   ⁵ ἀριστέων A: corr. p
⁶ Ἀπόλλω: πολλῷ A

the heavens and gave them their spherical form and established the earth as a centre, who brought together water into seas and divided the light from the darkness, who adorned the sky with stars and caused the earth to make every seed spring up, who made animals and formed man. 3. So then, when we regard the Artificer as a God who conserves and governs all things with the knowledge and skill by which he guides them and we raise up holy hands to him, what further need does he have of any hecatomb?

4. And men in their petitions, when one sins and errs,
Turn some of them[1] aside with sacrifices
And pleasing votive gifts, with libation and with fat.

But what have I to do with whole burnt offerings which God does not need? And what have I to do with sacrificing, since what is required is to offer up our rational worship as an unbloody sacrifice?

14. What they have to say about our not coming forward and recognizing the same gods as the cities is very silly. Even those who accuse us of atheism for not acknowledging the same gods they know do not agree with each other about the gods: the Athenians set up Celeus and Metaneira[1] as gods; the Lacedaemonians, Menelaus (to whom they sacrifice and celebrate festivals); the Trojans (who do not even want to hear the name of Menelaus) bring forward Hector; the Chians, Aristaeus[2] (acknowledging him as both Zeus and Apollo); the Thasians, Theagenes (who even committed murder at the Olympian games);[3] the Samians, Lysander[4] for so much slaughter and destruction; the Cilicians, . . .; the Sicilians, Philip the son of Butacides; the Amathusians, Onesilaus; the Carthaginians, Hamilcar.[5] A day would not suffice for me to complete the catalogue.

13. [1] i.e. some of the gods.
14. [1] King and queen at Eleusis at the time of Demeter's visit. Evidence for divine honours paid to the pair is at best obscure (cf. Pausanias 1. 39. 2).
    [2] Son of Apollo and Cyrene of Thessaly. A rustic deity known as the inventor of bee-keeping, olive-growing, and some kinds of hunting (Rose, *Handbook*, p. 144).
    [3] There is some confusion here since the athlete's statue alone seems to have been charged with murder (Pausanias 6. 11). Ubaldi suggests that accounts concerning Theagenes and a certain Cleomedes became mixed (cf. Pausanias 6. 9).
    [4] For this famous case see Plutarch (*Lys.* 18).
    [5] The last three names appear to be derived from Herodotus (5. 47; 5. 104–14; 7. 167).

2. ὅταν οὖν αὐτοὶ αὑτοῖς διαφωνῶσιν περὶ τῶν κατ' αὐτοὺς θεῶν, τί ἡμῖν μὴ συμφερομένοις ἐπικαλοῦσιν; τὸ δὲ κατ' Αἰγυπτίους μὴ καὶ γελοῖον ᾖ· τύπτονται γὰρ ἐν τοῖς ἱεροῖς τὰ στήθη κατὰ τὰς πανηγύρεις ὡς ἐπὶ τετελευτηκόσιν καὶ θύουσιν ὡς θεοῖς. καὶ οὐδὲν θαυμαστόν· οἵ γε καὶ τὰ θηρία θεοὺς ἄγουσιν καὶ ξυρῶνται ἐπεὶ ἀποθνήσκουσιν, καὶ θάπτουσιν ἐν ἱεροῖς καὶ δημοτελεῖς κοπετοὺς ἐγείρουσιν. 3. ἂν τοίνυν ἡμεῖς, ὅτι μὴ κοινῶς ἐκείνοις θεοσεβοῦμεν, ἀσεβῶμεν, πᾶσαι μὲν πόλεις, πάντα δὲ ἔθνη ἀσεβοῦσιν· οὐ γὰρ τοὺς αὐτοὺς πάντες ἄγουσι θεούς.

15. Ἀλλ' ἔστωσαν τοὺς αὐτοὺς ἄγοντες. τί οὖν; ἐπεὶ οἱ πολλοὶ διακρῖναι οὐ δυνάμενοι, τί μὲν ὕλη, τί δὲ θεός, πόσον δὲ τὸ διὰ μέσου αὐτῶν, προσίασι τοῖς ἀπὸ τῆς ὕλης εἰδώλοις, δι' ἐκείνους καὶ ἡμεῖς οἱ διακρίνοντες καὶ χωρίζοντες τὸ ἀγένητον[1] καὶ τὸ γενητόν, τὸ ὂν καὶ τὸ οὐκ ὄν, τὸ νοητὸν καὶ τὸ αἰσθητόν, καὶ ἑκάστῳ αὐτῶν τὸ προσῆκον ὄνομα ἀποδιδόντες, προσελευσόμεθα καὶ προσκυνήσομεν τὰ ἀγάλματα; 2. εἰ μὲν γὰρ ταὐτὸν ὕλη καὶ θεός, δύο ὀνόματα καθ' ἑνὸς πράγματος, τοὺς λίθους καὶ τὰ ξύλα, τὸν χρυσὸν καὶ τὸν ἄργυρον οὐ νομίζοντες θεοὺς ἀσεβοῦμεν· εἰ δὲ διεστᾶσι πάμπολυ ἀπ' ἀλλήλων καὶ τοσοῦτον ὅσον τεχνίτης καὶ ἡ πρὸς τὴν τέχνην αὐτοῦ παρασκευή, τί ἐγκαλούμεθα; ὡς γὰρ ὁ κεραμεὺς καὶ ὁ πηλός, ὕλη μὲν ὁ πηλός, τεχνίτης δὲ ὁ κεραμεύς, καὶ ὁ θεὸς[2] δημιουργός, ὑπακούουσα δὲ αὐτῷ ἡ ὕλη πρὸς τὴν τέχνην. ἀλλ' ὡς ὁ πηλὸς καθ' ἑαυτὸν σκεύη γενέσθαι χωρὶς τέχνης ἀδύνατος, καὶ ἡ πανδεχὴς ὕλη ἄνευ τοῦ θεοῦ τοῦ δημιουργοῦ διάκρισιν καὶ σχῆμα καὶ κόσμον οὐκ ἐλάμβανεν. 3. ὡς δὲ οὐ τὸν κέραμον προτιμότερον τοῦ ἐργασαμένου αὐτὸν ἔχομεν οὐδὲ τὰς φιάλας καὶ χρυσίδας τοῦ χαλκεύσαντος, ἀλλ' εἴ τι περὶ ἐκείνας δεξιὸν κατὰ τὴν τέχνην, τὸν τεχνίτην ἐπαινοῦμεν καὶ οὗτός ἐστιν ὁ τὴν ἐπὶ τοῖς σκεύεσι δόξαν καρπούμενος, καὶ ἐπὶ τῆς ὕλης καὶ τοῦ θεοῦ τῆς διαθέσεως τῶν κεκοσμημένων οὐχ[3] ἡ[4] ὕλη τὴν δόξαν καὶ τὴν τιμὴν δικαίαν ἔχει, ἀλλ' ὁ δημιουργὸς αὐτῆς θεός. 4. ὥστε,[5] εἰ τὰ εἴδη τῆς ὕλης ἄγοιμεν θεούς, ἀναισθητεῖν τοῦ ὄντως θεοῦ δόξομεν, τὰ λυτὰ καὶ φθαρτὰ τῷ ἀιδίῳ ἐξισοῦντες.

2. Since they themselves are in disagreement about their own gods, why do they accuse us of not conforming? I cannot help thinking that what goes on among the Egyptians is ridiculous. For on their festivals they go to the temples and beat their breasts as though lamenting the dead, and yet they sacrifice to them as though to gods! And no wonder, considering the fact that they regard animals as gods, shave themselves when the creatures die, bury them in temples, and initiate public laments. 3. If we are irreligious because our religiosity has nothing in common with theirs, all cities and all nations are irreligious; for all men do not recognize the same gods.

15. But suppose that they all did recognize the same ones. What then? Since the crowd, in its inability to distinguish what is matter, what is god, and what a gulf there is between them, reverently approaches material images, are we on their account also to draw near and worship statues—we who do distinguish and divide the uncreated from the created, being from non-being, the intelligible from the perceptible, and who give each of them its proper name?

2. To be sure, if matter and God are the same—two names for one thing—then we are irreligious if we do not regard stones and wood, gold and silver, as gods. But if there is a vast difference between them, as much as there is between the artisan and the materials provided for his craft, why are we accused? As with the potter and the clay, the clay is the matter and the potter the artisan, so God is the artificer and matter is subservient to him for the exercise of his craft. As the clay by itself cannot turn into vessels without a man's craft, so also matter, which is receptive to all modifications, did not receive articulation, form, and order without God the artificer. 3. Now we do not regard the pottery as worth more honour than its maker nor the cups and gold vessels as worth more honour than the smith; but we praise the craftsman if there is something fine about his craftsmanship, and he is the one who gains a reputation for his vessels. Similarly, in the case of matter and God, not matter but God its artificer justly receives the praise and honour for the arrangement and good order of things.

4. Consequently, if we should recognize material forms as gods, it will be seen that we are blind to him who is truly God by equating perishable and corruptible things with that which is eternal.

16. Καλὸς μὲν γὰρ ὁ κόσμος καὶ τῷ μεγέθει περιέχων καὶ τῇ διαθέσει τῶν τε ἐν τῷ λοξῷ κύκλῳ καὶ τῶν περὶ τὴν ἄρκτον καὶ τῷ σχήματι σφαιρικῷ ὄντι· ἀλλ' οὐ τοῦτον, ἀλλὰ τὸν τεχνίτην αὐτοῦ προσκυνητέον. 2. οὐδὲ γὰρ οἱ πρὸς ὑμᾶς ἀφικνούμενοι ὑπήκοοι παραλιπόντες ὑμᾶς τοὺς ἄρχοντας καὶ δεσπότας θεραπεύειν παρ' ὧν ἄν, ⟨ὧν⟩¹ δέοιντο, καὶ τύχοιεν, ἐπὶ τὸ σεμνὸν τῆς καταγωγῆς ὑμῶν καταφεύγουσιν,² ἀλλὰ τὴν μὲν βασιλικὴν ἑστίαν, τὴν ἄλλως ἐντυχόντες αὐτῇ, θαυμάζουσι καλῶς ἠσκημένην, ὑμᾶς δὲ πάντα ἐν πᾶσιν ἄγουσι τῇ δόξῃ. 3. καὶ ὑμεῖς μὲν οἱ βασιλεῖς ἑαυτοῖς ἀσκεῖτε τὰς καταγωγὰς βασιλικάς, ὁ δὲ κόσμος οὐχ ὡς δεομένου τοῦ θεοῦ γέγονεν· πάντα γὰρ ὁ θεός ἐστιν αὐτὸς αὑτῷ, φῶς ἀπρόσιτον,ᵃ κόσμος τέλειος, πνεῦμα, δύναμις, λόγος. εἰ τοίνυν ἐμμελὲς ὁ κόσμος ὄργανον κινούμενον ἐν ῥυθμῷ, τὸν ἁρμοσάμενον καὶ πλήσσοντα τοὺς φθόγγους καὶ τὸ σύμφωνον ἐπᾴδοντα μέλος, οὐ τὸ ὄργανον προσκυνῶ· οὐδὲ γὰρ ἐπὶ τῶν ἀγωνιστῶν παραλιπόντες οἱ ἀθλοθέται τοὺς κιθαριστάς, τὰς κιθάρας στεφανοῦσιν αὐτῶν· εἴτε,³ ὡς ὁ Πλάτωνᵇ φησί, τέχνη τοῦ θεοῦ, θαυμάζων αὐτοῦ τὸ κάλλος τῷ τεχνίτῃᶜ πρόσειμι· εἴτε οὐσία καὶ σῶμα, ὡς οἱ ἀπὸ τοῦ Περιπάτου, οὐ παραλιπόντες προσκυνεῖν τὸν αἴτιον τῆς κινήσεως τοῦ σώματος θεὸν ἐπὶ τὰ πτωχὰ καὶ ἀσθενῆ στοιχεῖαᵈ καταπίπτομεν, τῷ ἀπαθεῖ ἀέρι κατ' αὐτοὺς τὴν παθητὴν ὕλην προσκυνοῦντες· εἴτε δυνάμεις τοῦ θεοῦ τὰ μέρη τοῦ κόσμου νοεῖ τις, οὐ τὰς δυνάμεις προσιόντες θεραπεύομεν, ἀλλὰ τὸν ποιητὴν αὐτῶν καὶ δεσπότην. 4. οὐκ αἰτῶ τὴν ὕλην ἃ μὴ ἔχει, οὐδὲ παραλιπὼν τὸν θεὸν τὰ στοιχεῖα θεραπεύω, οἷς μηδὲν πλέον ἤ⁴ ὅσον ἐκελεύσθησαν ἔξεστιν· εἰ γὰρ καὶ καλὰ ἰδεῖν τῇ τοῦ δημιουργοῦ τέχνῃ, ἀλλὰ λυτὰ⁵ τῇ τῆς ὕλης φύσει. μαρτυρεῖ δὲ τῷ λόγῳ τούτῳ καὶ Πλάτων· "ὃν" γὰρ "οὐρανόν", φησί, "καὶ κόσμον ἐπωνομάκαμεν, πολλῶν μὲν μετέσχηκε ⟨καὶ⟩⁶ μακαρίων παρὰ τοῦ πατρός, ἀτὰρ οὖν δὴ κεκοινώνηκε ⟨καὶ⟩⁶ σώματος· ὅθεν αὐτῷ μεταβολῆς ἀμοίρῳ τυγχάνειν ἀδύνατον."ᵉ 5. εἰ τοίνυν θαυμάζων τὸν οὐρανὸν καὶ τὰ στοιχεῖα τῆς τέχνης οὐ

---

16. ᵃ Cf. 1 Tim. 6: 16   ᵇ Cf. *Tim.* 33 c   ᶜ Cf. Wisd. 13: 1; Rom. 1: 25
ᵈ Cf. Gal. 4: 9   ᵉ *Politic.* 269 d

---

16. ¹ ὧν add. Wilamowitz   ² φεύγουσιν A: κατα superscr. A¹   ³ εἴτε
p in mg.: ἐστε A   ⁴ ἢ add. in mg. m. rec. A   ⁵ ἀλλὰ λυτὰ Schwartz:
ἀλλ' αὐτὰ A   ⁶ καὶ bis add. Schwartz

16. The world, to be sure, is beautiful and excels in its size, in its arrangement of the things in the ecliptic and about the pole, and in its spherical shape. Not the world, however, but its Maker ought to be worshipped. 2. Your subjects who come to you do not neglect waiting upon you, their rulers and masters, and run for help to the splendour of your lodging (for it is from you that they would receive their requests); they casually admire the imperial residence for its beautiful appointments when they reach it, but it is you whom they honour as all in all. 3. Now you as emperors adorn imperial lodgings for yourselves; but the world did not come into being because God needed it. For God is himself all things to himself: inaccessible light, a complete world, spirit, power, reason. Thus if the world is a harmonious instrument rhythmically moved, I worship not the instrument but the one who tuned and strikes the strings and sings to its accompaniment the melodious strain. Judges do not neglect the players in a contest and crown their lyres instead! If, as Plato says, the world is God's craftsmanship, though I admire its beauty, I reverently draw near to the craftsman. If it is substance and body as the Peripatetics say,[1] we do not neglect worshipping God, the cause of bodily motion, and fall back upon the beggarly and weak elements, worshipping passible matter because of the air which they regard as impassible.[2] If a man regards the parts of the world as powers of God, we will not draw near and serve these powers, but their Maker and Ruler.

4. I do not ask of matter what it does not have; nor do I neglect God to serve the elements which can do no more than what they have been commanded. For though they are beautiful to see because of the Artificer's craftsmanship, they are perishable because of the very nature of matter. Plato too supports this teaching: 'For', he says, 'that which we call heaven and the world has received many blessed qualities from the Father; but then too it has a share in bodily nature; consequently it cannot be free from change.' 5. If then I admire the sky and the elements as

---

16. [1] Possibly an echo of the early Aristotle (Lazzati, *L'Aristotele perduto*, pp. 70–2; cf. Aetius, *Plac.* 5. 20. 1).

[2] Aristotle is said to have taught that the 'aether' was 'impassible' (Aetius, *Plac.* 2. 7. 5); but some manuscripts read 'air' instead of 'aether'.

προσκυνῶ αὐτὰ ὡς θεοὺς εἰδὼς τὸν ἐπ' αὐτοῖς τῆς λύσεως λόγον, ὧν οἶδα ἀνθρώπους δημιουργούς, πῶς ταῦτα προσείπω θεούς;

17. Σκέψασθε δέ μοι διὰ βραχέων (ἀνάγκη δὲ ἀπολογούμενον ἀκριβεστέρους παρέχειν τοὺς λογισμοὺς καὶ περὶ τῶν ὀνομάτων, ὅτι νεώτερα, καὶ περὶ τῶν εἰκόνων, ὅτι χθὲς καὶ πρῴην γεγόνασιν ὡς λόγῳ¹ εἰπεῖν· ἴστε δὲ καὶ ὑμεῖς ταῦτα ἀξιολογώτερον ὡς ἂν ἐν πᾶσιν καὶ ὑπὲρ πάντας τοῖς παλαιοῖς συγγιγνόμενοι)· φημὶ οὖν Ὀρφέα καὶ Ὅμηρον καὶ Ἡσίοδον εἶναι τοὺς καὶ γένη καὶ ὀνόματα δόντας² τοῖς ὑπ' αὐτῶν λεγομένοις θεοῖς. 2. μαρτυρεῖ δὲ καὶ Ἡρόδοτος· "Ἡσίοδον γὰρ καὶ Ὅμηρον ἡλικίην τετρακοσίοισι ἔτεσι³ δοκέω πρεσβυτέρους ἐμοῦ γενέσθαι, καὶ οὐ πλείοσι· οὗτοι δέ εἰσιν οἱ ποιήσαντες θεογονίην Ἕλλησι καὶ τοῖσι θεοῖσι τὰς ἐπωνυμίας δόντες καὶ τιμάς τε καὶ τέχνας διελόντες καὶ εἴδεα αὐτῶν σημήναντες."ᵃ 3. αἱ δ' εἰκόνες μέχρι μήπω πλαστικὴ καὶ γραφικὴ καὶ ἀνδριαντοποιητικὴ ἦσαν, οὐδὲ ἐνομίζοντο· Σαυρίου δὲ τοῦ Σαμίου καὶ Κράτωνος τοῦ Σικυωνίου καὶ Κλεάνθους τοῦ Κορινθίου καὶ κόρης Κορινθίας ἐπιγενομένων καὶ σκιαγραφίας μὲν εὑρεθείσης ὑπὸ Σαυρίου ἵππον ἐν ἡλίῳ περιγράψαντος, γραφικῆς δὲ ὑπὸ Κράτωνος ἐν πίνακι λελευκωμένῳ σκιὰς ἀνδρὸς καὶ γυναικὸς ἐναλείψαντος,—ἀπὸ δὲ τῆς κόρης ἡ κοροπλαθικὴ⁴ εὑρέθη (ἐρωτικῶς γάρ τινος ἔχουσα περιέγραψεν αὐτοῦ κοιμωμένου ἐν τοίχῳ τὴν σκιάν, εἶθ' ὁ πατὴρ ἡσθεὶς ἀπαραλλάκτῳ οὔσῃ τῇ ὁμοιότητι— κέραμον δὲ εἰργάζετο—ἀναγλύψας τὴν περιγραφὴν πηλῷ προσανεπλήρωσεν· ὁ τύπος ἔτι καὶ νῦν ἐν Κορίνθῳ σῴζεται),—τούτοις δὲ ἐπιγενόμενοι Δαίδαλος, Θεόδωρος, Σμῖλις⁵ ἀνδριαντοποιητικὴν καὶ πλαστικὴν προσεξεῦρον. 4. ὁ μὲν δὴ χρόνος ὀλίγος τοσοῦτος ταῖς εἰκόσι καὶ τῇ περὶ τὰ εἴδωλα πραγματείᾳ, ὡς ἔχειν εἰπεῖν τὸν ἑκάστου τεχνίτην θεοῦ. τὸ μὲν γὰρ ἐν Ἐφέσῳ τῆς Ἀρτέμιδος καὶ τὸ τῆς Ἀθηνᾶς (μᾶλλον δὲ Ἀθηλᾶς· †ἀθήλη⁶ γὰρ ὡς οἱ μυστικώτερον οὕτω γὰρ†) τὸ ἀπὸ τῆς ἐλαίας τὸ παλαιὸν καὶ τὴν Καθημένην

17. ᵃ Herod. 2. 53

17. ¹ λόγος A: corr. Ducaeus, Stephanus δόντας infra post πλείοσι coll. A: corr. Otto κοσίοις ἔτεσι A¹: τετρακοσίοισι ἔτεσι Herodotus corr. p ⁵ Σμῖλις Schwartz: ὁ μιλίσιος A ἀθηλᾶ A

² τοὺς καὶ γένη καὶ ὀνόματα ³ τετρακοσιετεσι A: τετρα- ⁴ κοροπαλθική A: ⁶ ἀθήλη Wilamowitz:

products of his craftsmanship and yet do not worship them as gods, since I know the law of dissolution which governs them, how can I call things gods which I know were made by men?

17. I ask you to examine them briefly. For it is necessary in defending my cause to make precise observations both about their names, showing that they are very recent, and about their images, showing that they were made, so to speak, only yesterday or the day before. You yourselves know these things better than I, since you are deeply versed beyond all others in the ancients. I say, then, that it was Orpheus, Homer, and Hesiod who gave genealogies and names to those they called gods. 2. Herodotus also provides proof of this: 'For I think that Hesiod and Homer preceded me by four hundred years, and not more. They are the ones who provided the Greeks with a genealogy of the gods, gave names to the gods, distributed to them their honours and crafts, and described their appearances.'

3. Images were not in use before the discovery of moulding, painting, and sculpture. Then came Saurius of Samos, Crato of Sicyon, Cleanthes of Corinth, and the Corinthian maid. Tracing out shadows was discovered by Saurius, who drew the outline of a horse standing in the sun. Painting was discovered by Crato, who coloured in the outlines of the shadows of a man and woman on a whitened tablet. Relief modelling was discovered by the Corinthian maid: she fell in love with someone and traced the outline of his shadow on the wall as he slept; then her father, a potter, delighted with so precise a likeness, made a relief of the outline and filled it with clay; the relief is preserved to this very day in Corinth. After these there came Daedalus, Theodore, and Smilis, who went further and discovered sculpture and moulding.

4. So short, then, is the time since the introduction of images and the making of statues that it is possible to name the craftsman of each God. Endoios, a disciple of Daedalus, made the statue of Artemis in Ephesus and the ancient olive statue of Athene (or rather of Athela; for she is Athela, the unsuckled, as those . . . the more mystical sense . . .) and the Seated Athena.

Ἔνδοιος[7] εἰργάσατο μαθητὴς Δαιδάλου, ὁ δὲ Πύθιος ἔργον Θεο-
δώρου καὶ Τηλεκλέους καὶ ὁ Δήλιος καὶ ἡ Ἄρτεμις Τεκταίου[8] καὶ
Ἀγγελίωνος τέχνη, ἡ δὲ ἐν Σάμῳ Ἥρα καὶ ἐν Ἄργει Σμίλιδος
χεῖρες καὶ †Φειδίου τὰ λοιπὰ εἴδωλα†[9] ἡ Ἀφροδίτη ἐν Κνίδῳ
ἑτέρα Πραξιτέλους τέχνη, ὁ ἐν Ἐπιδαύρῳ Ἀσκληπιὸς ἔργον
Φειδίου. 5. συνελόντα φάναι, οὐδὲν αὐτῶν διαπέφευγεν τὸ μὴ ὑπ'
ἀνθρώπου γεγονέναι. εἰ τοίνυν θεοί, τί οὐκ ἦσαν ἐξ ἀρχῆς; τί
δέ εἰσιν νεώτεροι τῶν πεποιηκότων; τί δὲ ἔδει αὐτοῖς[10] πρὸς τὸ
γενέσθαι ἀνθρώπων καὶ τέχνης; γῆ ταῦτα καὶ λίθοι καὶ ὕλη καὶ
περίεργος τέχνη.

18. Ἐπεὶ τοίνυν φασί τινες εἰκόνας μὲν εἶναι ταύτας, θεοὺς δὲ ἐφ'
οἷς αἱ εἰκόνες, καὶ τὰς προσόδους ἃς ταύταις[1] προσίασιν καὶ τὰς
θυσίας ἐπ' ἐκείνους ἀναφέρεσθαι καὶ εἰς ἐκείνους γίνεσθαι μὴ εἶναί
τε ἕτερον τρόπον τοῖς θεοῖς ἢ τοῦτον προσελθεῖν ("χαλεποὶ δὲ θεοὶ
φαίνεσθαι ἐναργεῖς")[a] καὶ τοῦ ταῦθ' οὕτως ἔχειν τεκμήρια παρέχουσιν τὰς ἐνίων εἰδώλων ἐνεργείας, φέρε ἐξετάσωμεν τὴν ἐπὶ
τοῖς ὀνόμασι δύναμιν αὐτῶν. 2. δεήσομαι δὲ ὑμῶν, μέγιστοι αὐτο-
κρατόρων, πρὸ τοῦ λόγου ἀληθεῖς παρεχομένῳ τοὺς λογισμοὺς
συγγνῶναι· οὐ γὰρ προκείμενόν μοι ἐλέγχειν τὰ εἴδωλα, ἀλλὰ
ἀπολυόμενος τὰς διαβολὰς λογισμὸν τῆς προαιρέσεως ἡμῶν
παρέχω.[2] ἔχοιτε[3] ἀφ' ἑαυτῶν καὶ τὴν ἐπουράνιον βασιλείαν[4]
ἐξετάζειν· ὡς γὰρ ὑμῖν πατρὶ καὶ υἱῷ πάντα κεχείρωται ἄνωθεν τὴν
βασιλείαν εἰληφόσιν ("βασιλέως γὰρ ψυχὴ ἐν χειρὶ θεοῦ",[b] φησὶ τὸ
προφητικὸν πνεῦμα), οὕτως ἑνὶ τῷ θεῷ καὶ τῷ παρ' αὐτοῦ λόγῳ
υἱῷ νοουμένῳ ἀμερίστῳ πάντα ὑποτέτακται. 3. ἐκεῖνο τοίνυν
σκέψασθέ μοι πρὸ τῶν ἄλλων. οὐκ ἐξ ἀρχῆς, ὥς φασιν, ἦσαν οἱ
θεοί, ἀλλ' οὕτως γέγονεν αὐτῶν ἕκαστος ὡς γιγνόμεθα ἡμεῖς· καὶ
τοῦτο πᾶσιν αὐτοῖς ξυμφωνεῖται,[5] Ὁμήρου μὲν [γὰρ][6] λέγοντος

Ὠκεανόν τε, θεῶν γένεσιν, καὶ μητέρα Τηθύν,[c]

18. [a] Homer, Iliad 20. 131   [b] Prov. 21: 1   [c] Iliad 14. 201, 302

17. [7] Ἔνδυος A: corr. Otto   [8] Τεκταίου Otto: ἰδεκταίου A   [9] καὶ
Φειδίου τὰ λοιπὰ εἴδωλα: haec verba infra post ἔργον Φειδίου coll. Botti
[10] αὐτοὺς A
18. [1] ταύταις Otto: τούτοις A   [2] παρέχων A   [3] ἔχοιτε δ' ἂν
Schwartz: αὐτοὶ δ' ἂν ἔχοιτε Wilamowitz   [4] post βασιλείαν ins. εἰληφόσιν
(v. infra) A   [5] ξυμφωνεῖ A: corr. Schwartz   [6] γὰρ seclusit Schwartz

The Pythian Apollo is the work of Theodore and Telecles. The Delian Apollo and the Artemis are the craftsmanship of Tectaeus and Angelio. The Hera in Samos and in Argos are the works of Smilis . . . The Aphrodite in Cnidus is another work of Praxiteles. The Asclepius in Epidaurus is the work of Phidias.

5. To put it in a word, not one of their images eludes identification as the work of a man. If, then, they are gods, why were they not so from the beginning? Why are they more recent than those who have made them? Why did they need human craftsmanship for their existence? They are earth, stones, matter, and futile craftsmanship.

18. Now some say that these are only images but that there are gods for whose sake the images exist. They say that their processions to the images and their sacrifices are offered up to the gods and celebrated for them because there is no way other than this to approach them ('dangerous are the gods when they appear visibly'). As evidence that this is so they refer to the activities associated with certain statues. With this in mind let us investigate the power of the divine names.

2. I shall request you, greatest of sovereigns, before beginning my examination, to excuse me if I bring forward my arguments polemically to establish their truth. Certainly I do not consider it my task to condemn images; but in dismissing the slanders against us I must provide the reason for the decision that we have made. May you find it possible to examine by your own efforts also the heavenly kingdom; for as all things have been subjected to you, a father and a son, who have received your kingdom from above ('for the king's life is in God's hand', as the prophetic spirit says), so all things are subordinated to the one God and the Word that issues from him whom we consider his inseparable Son.

3. I ask you then to examine the following point before all else. The gods, so they say, were not in existence from the beginning, but each of them came into being as we do. And this is agreed to by them all: Homer speaks of 'Ocean, the origin of the gods, and Tethys their mother'. Orpheus (who was the first to

'Ορφέως δέ, ὃς καὶ τὰ ὀνόματα αὐτῶν πρῶτος ἐξηῦρεν καὶ τὰς γενέσεις διεξῆλθεν καὶ ὅσα ἑκάστοις πέπρακται εἶπεν καὶ πεπίστευται⁷ παρ' αὐτοῖς ἀληθέστερον θεολογεῖν, ᾧ καὶ Ὅμηρος τὰ πολλὰ καὶ περὶ θεῶν μάλιστα ἕπεται, καὶ αὐτοῦ τὴν πρώτην γένεσιν αὐτῶν ἐξ ὕδατος συνιστάντος

Ὠκεανός, ὅσπερ γένεσις πάντεσσι τέτυκται.ᵈ

4. ἦν γὰρ ὕδωρ ἀρχὴ κατ' αὐτὸν τοῖς ὅλοις, ἀπὸ δὲ τοῦ ὕδατος ἰλὺς κατέστη, ἐκ δὲ ἑκατέρων ἐγεννήθη ζῷον δράκων προσπεφυκυῖαν ἔχων κεφαλὴν λέοντος,⁸ διὰ μέσου δὲ αὐτῶν θεοῦ πρόσωπον, ὄνομα Ἡρακλῆς καὶ Χρόνος. 5. οὗτος ὁ Ἡρακλῆς ἐγέννησεν ὑπερμέγεθες ᾠόν, ὃ συμπληρούμενον ὑπὸ βίας τοῦ γεγεννηκότος ἐκ παρατριβῆς εἰς δύο ἐρράγη. τὸ μὲν οὖν κατὰ κορυφὴν αὐτοῦ Οὐρανὸς εἶναι ἐτελέσθη, τὸ δὲ κάτω ἐνεχθὲν⁹ Γῆ· προῆλθε δὲ καὶ θεὸς †γη δισώματος.¹⁰ 6. Οὐρανὸς δὲ Γῆ μιχθεὶς γεννᾷ θηλείας μὲν Κλωθώ, Λάχεσιν, Ἄτροπον,¹¹ ἄνδρας δὲ¹² Ἑκατόγχειρας Κόττον,¹³ Γύγην,¹⁴ Βριάρεων καὶ Κύκλωπας,¹⁵ Βρόντην¹⁶ καὶ Στερόπην καὶ Ἄργην·¹⁷ οὓς καὶ δήσας κατεταρτάρωσεν, ἐκπεσεῖσθαι αὐτὸν ὑπὸ τῶν παίδων τῆς ἀρχῆς μαθών. διὸ καὶ ὀργισθεῖσα ἡ Γῆ τοὺς Τιτᾶνας ἐγέννησεν·

Κούρους δ' Οὐρανίωνας ἐγείνατο πότνια Γαῖα,
οὓς δὴ καὶ Τιτῆνας ἐπίκλησιν καλέουσιν,
οὕνεκα τισάσθην¹⁸ μέγαν Οὐρανὸν ἀστερόεντα.ᵉ

19. Αὕτη ἀρχὴ γενέσεως περὶ τοὺς κατ' αὐτοὺς θεούς τε καὶ τῷ παντί. †ἐκεῖνο τοίνυν ἕκαστον γὰρ τῶν τεθεολογημένων ὡς τὴν ἀρχήν ονειναι†.¹ εἰ γὰρ γεγόνασιν οὐκ ὄντες, ὡς οἱ περὶ αὐτῶν

---

18. ᵈ Iliad 14. 246   ᵉ Frg. 57 (Kern)

18. ⁷ post πεπίστευται ins. βασιλείαν ἐξετάζειν ὡς παρ' ὑμῖν πῦρ καὶ υἱῷ πάντα κεχείρωται ἄνωθεν (v. supra) A   ⁸ post λέοντος add. e Damascio (frg. 54 Kern) καὶ ἄλλην ταύρου Zoega : sed textus sanus videtur secundum Norden collato scholio in Gregor. Nazianz. *Or.* 31. 16   ⁹ κάτω κατενεχθὲν A : corr. Schwartz   ¹⁰ γη (γῇ A¹) διὰ σώματος A : τις δισώματος Lobeck   ¹¹ ἄτραπον A   ¹² δὲ: τε A   ¹³ κόττυν A   ¹⁴ γυνη A : γύνην A¹   ¹⁵ κύκλοπας A   ¹⁶ κρότην A : corr. A¹   ¹⁷ ἄργον A   ¹⁸ οὕνεκα τιτιμωρήσωσιν ἢ τιμήσωσινσασθην A
19. ¹ τὸ πᾶν. τί ἐκεῖνο τοίνυν; ἕκαστον γὰρ τῶν τεθεολογημένων ὡς τὴν ἀρχὴν ὃν νοεῖται (ὃν δεῖ εἶναι Otto) Maranus : τῷ παντί. ἐκεῖνο τοίνυν σκέψασθε ἕκαστον πάντων τῶν τεθεολογημένων, ὡς τὴν ἀρχήν, γεγονέναι Schwartz : τῷ παντί. ἐκεῖνο τοίνυν σκέψασθε· ἕκαστον γὰρ τῶν τεθεολογημένων, ὡς τὴν ἀρχὴν ἔχει, οὕτως δεῖ καὶ φθαρτὸν εἶναι (ὡς τὴν ἀρχὴν ἔχον, φθαρτὸν εἶναι δεῖ Ubaldi) Geffcken

invent their names, to describe their births, and to recount the deeds of each, who is generally believed by them to treat of the gods with great accuracy, and who for the most part is followed even by Homer, especially in his treatment of the gods) affirms their ultimate origin from water—'Ocean, in whom is to be found the origin of all'. 4. For according to him water was the beginning of everything. From water came slime. From both an animal was born—a serpent with the head of a lion attached, and between them the face of a god. Its name was Heracles and Chronos. 5. This Heracles generated a huge egg which, when filled by the power of him who generated it, broke into two through friction. The upper part of it was fashioned into Heaven; the part which descended became Earth; a sort of two-bodied god came forth. 6. Heaven in union with Earth begot female offspring—Clotho, Lachesis, and Atropus—and the male Hundred-hands[1]—Cottus, Gyges, Briareus—and the Round-eyes[2]—Brontes, Steropes, and Arges. Heaven bound and cast them into Tartarus when he learned that he would be deprived of his rule by his offspring. Consequently Earth in her anger brought forth the Titans:

> Our mistress the Earth brought forth children of Heaven
> To whom men also give the name of 'Titans'
> Because they 'took vengeance'[3] on the starry expanse of
>   Heaven.

19. This is their version of the beginning of the generation of the gods and the universe. Take this then into consideration: each of the beings divinized by them, since it has a beginning, must also be perishable. For if they came into being from nothing, as those

18. [1] Hecatoncheires.
   [2] Cyclopes.
   [3] A play on words (*Titan–tinō*). Cf. Hesiod, *Theog.* 207–11.

θεολογοῦντες λέγουσιν, οὐκ εἰσίν· ἢ γὰρ ἀγένητόν² τι, καὶ ἔστιν
ἀίδιον, ἢ γενητόν,³ καὶ φθαρτόν ἐστιν. 2. καὶ οὐκ ἐγὼ μὲν οὕτως,
ἑτέρως δὲ οἱ φιλόσοφοι. "τί τὸ ὂν ἀεὶ γένεσίν τε οὐκ ἔχον, ἢ τί τὸ
γενόμενον μέν, ὂν δὲ οὐδέποτε;" ᵃ περὶ νοητοῦ καὶ αἰσθητοῦ δια-
λεγόμενος ὁ Πλάτων τὸ μὲν ἀεὶ ὄν, τὸ νοητόν, ἀγένητον⁴ εἶναι
διδάσκει, τὸ δὲ οὐκ ὄν, τὸ αἰσθητόν, γενητόν,⁵ ἀρχόμενον εἶναι καὶ
παυόμενον. 3. τούτῳ τῷ λόγῳ καὶ οἱ ἀπὸ τῆς Στοᾶς⁶ ἐκπυρω-
θήσεσθαι τὰ πάντα καὶ πάλιν ἔσεσθαί φασιν, ἑτέραν ἀρχὴν τοῦ
κόσμου λαβόντος. εἰ δέ, καίτοι δισσοῦ αἰτίου κατ᾽ αὐτοὺς ὄντος,
τοῦ μὲν δραστηρίου καὶ καταρχομένου, καθὸ ἡ πρόνοια, τοῦ δὲ
πάσχοντος καὶ τρεπομένου, καθὸ ἡ ὕλη, ἀδύνατον [δέ]⁷ ἐστιν καὶ
προνοούμενον ἐπὶ ταὐτοῦ μεῖναι τὸν κόσμον γενόμενον, πῶς ἡ
τούτων μένει σύστασις, οὐ φύσει ὄντων ἀλλὰ γενομένων; τί δὲ τῆς
ὕλης κρείττους οἱ θεοὶ τὴν σύστασιν ἐξ ὕδατος ἔχοντες; 4. ἀλλ᾽ οὔτε⁸
κατ᾽ αὐτοὺς ὕδωρ τοῖς πᾶσιν ἀρχή (ἐκ γὰρ⁹ ἁπλῶν καὶ μονοειδῶν
στοιχείων τί ἂν συστῆναι¹⁰ δύναιτο; δεῖ δὲ καὶ τῇ ὕλῃ τεχνίτου
καὶ ὕλης τῷ τεχνίτῃ· ἢ πῶς ἂν γένοιτο τὰ ἐκτυπώματα χωρὶς τῆς
ὕλης ἢ τοῦ τεχνίτου;)· οὔτε πρεσβυτέραν λόγον ἔχει εἶναι τὴν ὕλην
τοῦ θεοῦ· τὸ γὰρ ποιητικὸν αἴτιον προκατάρχειν τῶν γιγνομένων
ἀνάγκη.

20. Εἰ μὲν οὖν μέχρι τοῦ φῆσαι γεγονέναι τοὺς θεοὺς καὶ ἐξ
ὕδατος τὴν σύστασιν ἔχειν τὸ ἀπίθανον ἦν αὐτοῖς τῆς θεολογίας,
ἐπιδεδειχὼς ὅτι οὐδὲν γενητὸν¹ ὃ οὐ καὶ διαλυτόν, ἐπὶ τὰ λοιπὰ ἂν
παρεγενόμην τῶν ἐγκλημάτων. 2. ἐπεὶ δὲ τοῦτο μὲν διατεθείκασιν
αὐτῶν τὰ σώματα, τὸν μὲν Ἡρακλέα, ὅτι θεὸς δράκων ἑλικτός,
τοὺς δὲ Ἑκατόγχειρας εἰπόντες, καὶ τὴν θυγατέρα τοῦ Διός, ἣν
ἐκ τῆς μητρὸς Ῥέας †καὶ Δήμητρος ἢ δημήτορος τὸν αὐτῆς†²
ἐπαιδοποιήσατο, δύο μὲν κατὰ φύσιν [εἶπον]³ ἔχειν ὀφθαλμοὺς καὶ

---

19. ᵃ Tim. 27 d

19. ² ἀγέννητόν A   ³ γεννητὸν A   ⁴ ἀγέννητον A   ⁵ γεννητὸν A:
del. Wilamowitz, Schwartz, Geffcken   ⁶ τουτῳ καὶ οἱ ἀπὸ τῆς Στοᾶς τῷ
λόγῳ A: corr. Schwartz   ⁷ δὲ del. Dechair, Lindner   ⁸ ἀλλ᾽ οὐδὲ A:
corr. Schwartz   ⁹ ἐκ γὰρ Schwartz: ἐκ τε A   ¹⁰ μονοειδῶν τί ἂν
συστῆναι στοιχείων A: στοιχείων del. Wilamowitz, Schwartz: στοιχείων post
μονοειδῶν coll. Geffcken
20. ¹ γεννητὸν A   ² ἢ Δήμητρος αὐτῆς Otto: καὶ Δήμητρος ἤδη προσ-
αγορευθείσης Schwartz   ³ εἶπον seclusit Schwartz

who theologize about them say, then they do not exist; for either they are something uncreated and so eternal; or they are created and so perishable.

2. On this point there is no disagreement between myself and the philosophers. 'What is that which always is and does not come to be, or what is that which comes to be but never is?' Plato in his dialogues on the intelligible and perceptible teaches that that which always is, the intelligible, is uncreated, whereas that which is not, the perceptible, is created, having a beginning to its existence and an end.

3. For this same reason the Stoics say that there will be a cosmic conflagration and that all will be restored as the world begins again. According to them there are two causes, one active and efficacious in so far as it is Providence, the other passive and mutable in so far as it is matter; if it is impossible for the world which is subject to becoming to remain unaltered even though guided by Providence, how can these gods avoid dissolution, since they do not exist by nature but come into being? How can the gods be superior to matter when they derive their substance from water? 4. But neither on their view can it be said that water is the beginning of all things. For what could arise from simple and uniform elements? Matter needs a craftsman and the craftsman needs matter. Or how could there be shapes without matter or a craftsman? Nor does it make sense to say that matter is more ancient than God, for the active cause necessarily precedes those things that come into being.

20. Now if the absurdity of their theology extended only to their saying that the gods came into being and have their substance from water, I would simply show that there is nothing created which is not also subject to dissolution and would pass on to the other charges. 2. They go on, however, to give a description of the bodies of their gods. They say that Heracles is a coiled serpent-god and the others Hundred-handed. They say that the daughter of Zeus, whom he fathered by his mother Rhea, also called Demeter[1] . . . had two eyes in the natural place and two more on

20. [1] Rhea, according to the Orphics, became known as Demeter after she had given birth to Zeus (Kern, *Orphicorum Fragmenta*, pp. 188–9, no. 145).

ἐπὶ τῷ μετώπῳ δύο καὶ προτομὴν κατὰ τὸ ὄπισθεν τοῦ τραχήλου
μέρος, ἔχειν δὲ καὶ κέρατα, διὸ καὶ τὴν 'Ρέαν φοβηθεῖσαν τὸ τῆς
παιδὸς τέρας φυγεῖν οὐκ ἐφεῖσαν αὐτῇ τὴν θηλήν, ἔνθεν μυστικῶς
μὲν Ἀθηλᾶ κοινῶς δὲ Φερσεφόνη καὶ Κόρη κέκληται, οὐχ ἡ αὐτὴ
οὖσα τῇ Ἀθηνᾷ τῇ ἀπὸ τῆς κόρης λεγομένῃ· 3. τοῦτο δὲ τὰ
πραχθέντα αὐτοῖς ἐπ᾽ ἀκριβὲς⁴ ὡς οἴονται διεξεληλύθασιν, Κρόνος
μὲν ὡς ἐξέτεμεν τὰ αἰδοῖα τοῦ πατρὸς καὶ κατέρριψεν αὐτὸν ἀπὸ τοῦ
ἅρματος καὶ ὡς ἐτεκνοκτόνει καταπίνων τῶν παίδων τοὺς ἄρσενας,
Ζεὺς δὲ ὅτι τὸν μὲν πατέρα δήσας κατεταρτάρωσεν, καθὰ καὶ τοὺς
υἱεῖς ὁ Οὐρανός, καὶ πρὸς Τιτᾶνας περὶ τῆς ἀρχῆς ἐπολέμησεν καὶ
ὅτι τὴν μητέρα 'Ρέαν ἀπαγορεύουσαν αὐτοῦ τὸν γάμον ἐδίωκε,
δρακαίνης δ᾽ αὐτῆς γενομένης καὶ αὐτὸς εἰς δράκοντα μεταβαλὼν
συνδήσας αὐτὴν τῷ καλουμένῳ 'Ηρακλειωτικῷ ἅμματι ἐμίγη (τοῦ
σχήματος τῆς μίξεως σύμβολον ἡ τοῦ 'Ερμοῦ ῥάβδος), εἶθ᾽ ὅτι
Φερσεφόνῃ τῇ θυγατρὶ ἐμίγη βιασάμενος καὶ ταύτην ἐν δράκοντος
σχήματι, ἐξ ἧς παῖς Διόνυσος αὐτῷ· 4. ἀνάγκη κἂν τοσοῦτον
εἰπεῖν· τί τὸ σεμνὸν ἢ χρηστὸν τῆς τοιαύτης ἱστορίας, ἵνα πιστεύ-
σωμεν θεοὺς εἶναι τὸν Κρόνον, τὸν Δία, τὴν Κόρην, τοὺς λοιπούς;
αἱ διαθέσεις τῶν σωμάτων; καὶ τίς ἂν ἄνθρωπος κεκριμένος⁵
καὶ ἐν θεωρίᾳ γεγονὼς ὑπὸ θεοῦ γεννηθῆναι πιστεύσαι ἔχιδναν—
'Ορφεύς·

ἂν δὲ Φάνης ἄλλην γενεὴν τεκνώσατο δεινήν
νηδύος ἐξ ἱερῆς, προσιδεῖν φοβερωπὸν Ἔχιδναν,
ἧς χαῖται μὲν ἀπὸ κρατὸς καλόν τε πρόσωπον
ἦν ἐσιδεῖν, τὰ δὲ λοιπὰ μέρη φοβεροῖο δράκοντος
αὐχένος ἐξ ἄκρου—ᵃ

ἢ αὐτὸν τὸν Φάνητα δέξαιτο, θεὸν ὄντα πρωτόγονον (οὗτος γάρ
ἐστιν ὁ ἐκ τοῦ ᾠοῦ προχυθείς), ἢ σῶμα⁶ ἢ σχῆμα ἔχειν δράκοντος ἢ
καταποθῆναι ὑπὸ τοῦ Διός, ὅπως ὁ Ζεὺς ἀχώρητος γένοιτο; 5. εἰ
γὰρ μηδὲν διενενηνόχασιν τῶν φαυλοτάτων θηρίων (δῆλον γὰρ
ὅτι ὑποδιαλλάσσειν δεῖ τῶν γηΐνων καὶ τῶν ἀπὸ τῆς ὕλης
ἀποκρινομένων τὸ θεῖον), οὐκ εἰσὶν θεοί. τί δὲ καὶ πρόσιμεν

---

20. ᵃ Frg. 58 (Kern)

20. ⁴ ἐπ᾽ ἀκριβὲς αὐτοῖς A: corr. Schwartz   ⁵ κεκριμένος dubitanter
retineo: νοῦν κεκτημένος Schwartz   ⁶ ἢ σῶμα del. Wilamowitz, Schwartz,
Geffcken

her forehead and the face of an animal on the back of her neck and that she had horns. Consequently Rhea in a fright abandoned the monstrous child and did not offer her the breast. That is why she is called by the initiates Athela, but commonly Persephone and Core [Maid]; though she is not the same as Athena, who is also named from the fact that she is a 'maid'.[2]

3. They also go on to recount, accurately as they suppose, the deeds performed by the gods: that Cronus cut off the genitals of his father and threw him down from his chariot and that he slew his children by devouring his male offspring; that Zeus bound his father and cast him into Tartarus (just as Heaven had done with his sons) and fought with the Titans for sovereignty; and that he pursued his mother Rhea when she resisted marriage with him; that when she became a serpent, he likewise turned himself into a serpent, entangled her in the so-called knot of Heracles, and had intercourse with her (the rod of Hermes is a symbol of that kind of union); then that he had intercourse with his daughter Persephone, violating her also in the form of a serpent, and so having his son Dionysus by her.

4. Since this is their teaching, this much at least must be said: what nobility or value is there in such an account for us to believe that Cronus, Zeus, Core, and the rest are gods? The forms of their bodies?! And what man of discernment habituated to reflection would believe that a viper was the offspring of a god? Thus Orpheus:

> Phanes brought forth yet another fearful child
> From his sacred belly: the Viper, terrible to look upon.
> Hair indeed streamed from its head, and beautiful to see
> Was its face; but what remained below its neck
> Were the parts of a fearful serpent.

Or could he allow that this very Phanes, the first-born of the gods (for he was the one who emerged from the egg), had the body or form of a serpent or was devoured by Zeus so that Zeus could become infinite? 5. For if their gods differ in no way from the vilest beasts (for it is clear that the divine must differ somewhat from earthly things and things derived from matter!), they are not gods. Why indeed do we reverently draw near to them who

---

20. [2] Core—'daughter', 'maid'—was a name regularly used for Persephone, daughter of Demeter. But the name Pallas, regularly given to Athena, is also plausibly associated with terms for 'virgin' and 'maid'. Apparently Athenagoras had this in mind; and especially since Athena was also known as Athela (cf. 17. 4; *Schol. Hes. Op.* 76), he was probably anxious to avoid confusion.

αὐτοῖς, ὧν κτηνῶν μὲν δίκην ἔχει ἡ γένεσις, αὐτοὶ δὲ θηριόμορφοι καὶ δυσειδεῖς;

21. Καίτοι εἰ σαρκοειδεῖς μόνον ἔλεγον αὐτοὺς καὶ αἷμα ἔχειν καὶ σπέρμα¹ καὶ πάθη ὀργῆς καὶ ἐπιθυμίας, καὶ τότε ἔδει λῆρον καὶ γέλωτα² λόγους τούτους νομίζειν· οὔτε γὰρ ὀργὴ οὔτε ἐπιθυμία καὶ ὄρεξις οὐδὲ παιδοποιὸν σπέρμα ἐν τῷ θεῷ. 2. ἔστωσαν τοίνυν σαρκοειδεῖς, ἀλλὰ κρείττους μὲν θυμοῦ καὶ ὀργῆς, ἵνα μὴ Ἀθηνᾶ μὲν βλέπηται "σκυζομένη Διὶ πατρί, χόλος δέ μιν ἄγριος ᾕρει",³˒ ᵃ Ἥρα δὲ θεωρῆται "'Ήρῃ δ᾽ οὐκ ἔχαδε στῆθος χόλον, ἀλλὰ προσηύδα",ᵇ κρείττους δὲ λύπης,

ὢ πόποι, ἦ φίλον ἄνδρα διωκόμενον περὶ τεῖχος
ὀφθαλμοῖσιν ὁρῶμαι· ἐμὸν δ᾽ ὀλοφύρεται ἦτορ.ᶜ

ἐγὼ μὲν γὰρ καὶ ἀνθρώπους ἀμαθεῖς καὶ σκαιοὺς λέγω τοὺς ὀργῇ καὶ λύπῃ εἴκοντας· ὅταν δὲ ὁ "πατὴρ ἀνδρῶν τε θεῶν τε" ὀδύρηται μὲν τὸν υἱὸν

αἲ αἲ ἐγών,⁴ ὅτε μοι Σαρπηδόνα φίλτατον ἀνδρῶν
μοῖρ᾽⁵ ὑπὸ Πατρόκλοιο Μενοιτιάδαο δαμῆναι,ᵈ

ἀδυνατῇ δὲ ὀδυρόμενος τοῦ κινδύνου ἐξαρπάσαι

Σαρπηδὼν Διὸς υἱός, ὁ δ᾽ οὐδ᾽ ᾧ παιδὶ ἀμύνει,ᵉ

τίς οὐκ ἂν τοὺς ἐπὶ τοῖς τοιούτοις μύθοις φιλοθέους, μᾶλλον δὲ ἀθέους, τῆς ἀμαθίας καταμέμψαιτο;⁶ 3. ἔστωσαν σαρκοειδεῖς, ἀλλὰ μὴ τιτρωσκέσθω μηδὲ Ἀφροδίτη ὑπὸ Διομήδους τὸ σῶμα, "οὐτά με Τυδέος υἱὸς ὑπέρθυμος Διομήδης",ᶠ ἢ ὑπὸ Ἄρεως τὴν ψυχήν,

ὡς ἐμὲ χωλὸν ἐόντα Διὸς θυγάτηρ Ἀφροδίτη
αἰὲν ἀτιμάζει, φιλέει δ᾽ ἀΐδηλον Ἄρηα.ᵍ

21. ᵃ Homer, Iliad 4. 23   ᵇ Iliad 4. 24   ᶜ Iliad 22. 168–9   ᵈ Iliad 16. 433–4
ᵉ Iliad 16. 522   ᶠ Iliad 5. 376   ᵍ Odyssey 8. 308–9

21. ¹ καὶ σπέρμα : σπέρμα A : καὶ add. A¹ vel m. rec. : σπέρμα seclusit Wilamowitz
² γέλωτος A : corr. Schwartz   ³ αἱρεῖ A : ᾕρει Homerus   ⁴ αἲ αἲ λέγων
A : ὤμοι ἐγών Homerus : αἲ αἲ ἐγών Platon (Resp. 388 c)   ⁵ μοῖραι A
⁶ καταμέμψοιτο A : καταμέμφοιτο Schwartz : καταμέμψαιτο Geffcken

are born like dumb beasts and who themselves look like animals and are ugly in form?

21. Yet if all they said was that their gods were corporeal and had blood, semen, and the passions of anger and lust, even then one would be bound to consider these doctrines laughable nonsense; for in God there is neither anger nor lust and desire nor yet semen for producing offspring.

2. Well then, let us suppose that they are corporeal yet superior to wrath and anger, so that Athena will not be seen 'incensed with Zeus her father, as fierce anger seized her', and Hera will not be described as follows: 'Hera's heart could not contain her anger, but she cried out.' And let them be superior to grief like this:

> Alas, I see pursued about the wall
> A man I cherish; and my heart grieves.

For my part I regard even men who yield to anger and grief as ignorant and foolish; but when the 'Father of men and gods' bewails his son—

> Woe is me, when Fate decrees that by Patroclus, Menoetius' son,
> Sarpedon, dearest of men to me, is now to be subdued—

and when for all his grief he cannot rescue him from danger—

> Sarpedon is son of Zeus, yet Zeus saves not his own child—

who would not condemn the foolishness of those who are ardent theists, or rather atheists, on the basis of such myths?

3. Let us suppose that they are corporeal, but let us not have Aphrodite's body wounded by Diomedes—'Diomedes, proud son of Tydeus, has wounded me'—or her soul by Ares:

> Aphrodite, daughter of Zeus, always dishonours me
> Because I am lame; and she loves destructive Ares.

. . .⁷ "διὰ δὲ χρόα καλὸν ἔδαψεν",ʰ ὁ δεινὸς ἐν πολέμοις, ὁ σύμ-
μαχος κατὰ Τιτάνων τοῦ Διός, ἀσθενέστερος Διομήδους φαίνεται.
"μαίνετο δ' ὡς ὅτ' Ἄρης ἐγχέσπαλος"ⁱ—σιώπησον, Ὅμηρε, θεὸς
οὐ μαίνεται· σὺ δέ μοι καὶ μιαιφόνον καὶ βροτολοιγόν, "Ἄρες,
Ἄρες βροτολοιγέ, μιαιφόνε",ʲ διηγῇ τὸν θεὸν καὶ τὴν μοιχείαν
αὐτοῦ διέξει καὶ τὰ δεσμά·

τὼ δ' ἐς δέμνια βάντε κατέδραθον, ἀμφὶ δὲ δεσμοί
τεχνήεντες ἔχυντο πολύφρονος Ἡφαίστοιο,
οὐδέ τι κινῆσαι μελέων ἦν.ᵏ

4. οὐ καταβάλλουσι τὸν πολὺν τοῦτον ἀσεβῆ λῆρον περὶ τῶν θεῶν;
Οὐρανὸς ἐκτέμνεται, δεῖται καὶ καταταρταροῦται Κρόνος, ἐπαν-
ίστανται Τιτᾶνες, Στὺξ ἀποθνήσκει κατὰ τὴν μάχην—ἤδη καὶ
θνητοὺς αὐτοὺς δεικνύουσιν—ἐρῶσιν ἀλλήλων, ἐρῶσιν ἀνθρώπων·

Αἰνείας, τὸν ὑπ' Ἀγχίσῃ τέκε δι' Ἀφροδίτη,
Ἴδης ἐν κνημοῖσι θεὰ βροτῷ εὐνηθεῖσα.ˡ

οὐκ ἐρῶσιν, οὐ πάσχουσιν· ἢ⁸ γὰρ θεοὶ καὶ οὐχ ἅψεται αὐτῶν
ἐπιθυμία . . .⁹ κἂν σάρκα θεὸς κατὰ θείαν οἰκονομίαν λάβῃ, ἤδη
δοῦλός ἐστιν ἐπιθυμίας;

5. οὐ γὰρ πώποτέ μ' ὧδε θεᾶς ἔρος¹⁰ οὐδὲ γυναικός
θυμὸν ἐνὶ στήθεσσι περιπροχυθεὶς ἐδάμασσεν,
οὐδ' ὁπότ' ἠρασάμην Ἰξιονίης¹¹ ἀλόχοιο,
οὐδ' ὅτε περ Δανάης καλλισφύρου Ἀκρισιώνης,
οὐδ' ὅτε Φοίνικος κούρης τηλεκλειτοῖο,
οὐδ' ὅτε περ Σεμέλης, οὐδ' Ἀλκμήνης ἐνὶ Θήβῃ,
οὐδ' ὅτε Δήμητρος καλλιπλοκάμοιο ἀνάσσης,
οὐδ' ὅτε περ Λητοῦς ἐρικυδέος, οὐδὲ σεῦ αὐτῆς.ᵐ

21. ʰ Iliad 5. 858 ⁱ Iliad 15. 605 ʲ Iliad 5. 31 ᵏ Odyssey 8. 296-8 ˡ Iliad
2. 820-1 ᵐ Iliad 14. 315-27 (omitting lines 318, 320, 322, 324, 325)

21. ⁷ post Ἄρηα lacuna dimidiae lineae in A ⁸ ἢ A: εἰ Ubaldi ⁹ post
ἐπιθυμία lacunam indicavit Schwartz ¹⁰ ante οὐδὲ ins. ἀμφεκάλυψεν A:
punctis superpositis seclusit A vel A¹: fortasse ex Il. 14. 343 (vel 3. 442) Grant
¹¹ ἐξηιονίης A

'Fair flesh he tore asunder'[1]—the mighty one in battle, ally of Zeus against the Titans, shows himself weaker than Diomedes! 'He raged as when Ares with his spear'—be silent, Homer, a god does not rage! Yet you tell me of a god who is bloodthirsty and a bane of men—'Ares, Ares bane of men, bloodthirsty one'—and you tell a story of his adultery and bonds:

> They went to bed and slept together; but there fell about them
> Bonds cunningly contrived by the skilled Hephaestus,
> Not a limb could they move.

4. Do they not reject this mass of impious nonsense concerning the gods? Heaven is castrated; Cronus is bound and cast down into Tartarus; the Titans revolt; the Styx dies in battle (already this shows that they regard them as mortal); they fall in love with each other; they fall in love with human beings—

> Aeneas, whom fair Aphrodite bore to Anchises,
> A goddess who slept with a mortal on the slopes of mount Ida.

They do not fall in love. They experience no passion. For either they are gods and lust does not touch them ... Yet if a god assumes flesh by divine dispensation, is he forthwith a slave of lust?[2]

> 5. For never did love for goddess or woman
> Poured out in my breast so overcome my heart,
> Not when I loved the wife of Ixion,
> Nor when I loved Danaë, fair daughter of Acrisius,
> Nor the daughter of far-famed Phoenix,
> Nor Semele, or Alcmene in Thebes,
> Nor the fair queen Demeter,
> Nor famed Leto, nor thyself.

---

21. [1] This line comes from a part of Homer widely separated from the preceding lines. In Homer it is Diomedes who wounds Ares and tears his flesh. In Athenagoras the quotation was possibly preceded by a few simple words such as 'And the same Ares' (Geffcken, Ubaldi) grammatically related to what follows the quotation ('the mighty one in battle').

[2] Athenagoras anticipates objections which could be directed on the same grounds against the Christian 'dispensation'—a term by now virtually technical for 'incarnation'. (Compare the similar treatment of a related issue in 10. 2–3.) Probably this concern explains Athenagoras' willingness to grant the corporeal nature of the gods and to go on from there in his criticism of them.

γενητός ἐστιν, φθαρτός ἐστιν, οὐδὲν ἔχων θεοῦ. ἀλλὰ καὶ θητεύουσιν
ἀνθρώποις·

> ὦ δώματ' Ἀδμήτεια, ἐν οἷς ἔτλην ἐγώ
> θῆσσαν τράπεζαν αἰνέσαι θεός περ ὤν,[n]

καὶ βουκολοῦσιν·

> ἐλθὼν δ' ἐς αἶαν τήνδ' ἐβουφόρβουν ξένῳ,[12]
> καὶ τόνδ' ἔσῳζον οἶκον.[o]

οὐκοῦν κρείττων Ἄδμητος τοῦ θεοῦ. 6. ὦ μάντι καὶ σοφὲ καὶ
προειδὼς τοῖς ἄλλοις τὰ ἐσόμενα, οὐκ ἐμαντεύσω τοῦ ἐρωμένου τὸν
φόνον, ἀλλὰ καὶ ἔκτεινας αὐτοχειρὶ τὸν φίλον·

> κἀγὼ τὸ[13] Φοίβου θεῖον ἀψευδὲς στόμα
> ἤλπιζον εἶναι, μαντικῇ βρύον τέχνῃ,

ὡς ψευδόμαντιν κακίζει τὸν Ἀπόλλω ὁ Αἰσχύλος,

> ὁ δ' αὐτὸς ὑμνῶν, αὐτὸς ἐν θοίνῃ παρών,
> αὐτὸς τάδ' εἰπών, αὐτός ἐστιν ὁ κτανών
> τὸν παῖδα τὸν ἐμόν.[p]

22. Ἀλλὰ ταῦτα μὲν ἴσως πλάνη ποιητική, φυσικὸς[1] δέ τις ἐπ'
αὐτοῖς καὶ τοιοῦτος λόγος· "Ζεύς ἀργής", ὥς φησιν Ἐμπεδοκλῆς,
'"Ἥρη τε[2] φερέσβιος ἠδ' Ἀϊδωνεύς

> Νῆστίς θ',[3] ἣ δακρύοις τέγγει κρούνωμα[4] βρότειον".[a]

2. εἰ τοίνυν Ζεὺς μὲν τὸ πῦρ, Ἥρα δὲ ἡ γῆ καὶ ὁ ἀὴρ Ἀϊδωνεὺς καὶ
τὸ ὕδωρ Νῆστις, στοιχεῖα δὲ ταῦτα, τὸ πῦρ, τὸ ὕδωρ, ὁ ἀήρ,[5] οὐδεὶς
αὐτῶν θεός, οὔτε Ζεύς, οὔτε Ἥρα, οὔτε Ἀϊδωνεύς· ἀπὸ γὰρ τῆς
ὕλης διακριθείσης ὑπὸ τοῦ θεοῦ ἡ τούτων σύστασίς τε καὶ γένεσις,

> πῦρ καὶ ὕδωρ καὶ γαῖα καὶ ἠέρος ἤπιον ὕψος,
> καὶ φιλίη μετὰ τοῖσιν.[b]

---

21. [n] Euripides, Alcest. 1–2   [o] Alcest. 8–9   [p] Aeschylus, frg. 350 (Nauck²)
22. [a] Frg. 6 (Diels)   [b] Frg. 17. 18, 20 (Diels)

---

21. [12] ξένων A   [13] τό: τοι A
22. [1] φυσικῶς A   [2] Ἥρη τε: εἴρηται A   [3] θ': τε A   [4] τέγγει
κρούνωμα: τ' ἐπικούρου νωμᾶι A   [5] τὸ πῦρ τὸ ὕδωρ ὁ ἀήρ expunxit Diels

He is created, he is perishable, with nothing of a god about him. They even serve men—

> O halls of Admetus, in which I, though a god,
> Brought myself to praise menial fare—

and they tend cattle—

> I came to this land and herded cattle for a stranger
> And preserved this house.

Admetus then is superior to the god! 6. Wise seer, you who foreknow what will befall others, you did not foresee the murder of your darling, but killed your friend with your own hand![3]

> I deemed Apollo's divine mouth to be unerring,
> Welling up with prophetic lore—

thus Aeschylus reproaches Apollo as a false seer—

> But he himself who sung the hymn, was present at the feast,
> And spoke these words, he it is who slew
> My son.

22. But perhaps all this is the deceit of poets, and there is a scientific explanation concerning the gods along lines such as this:

> Shining Zeus [as Empedocles says] and life-giving Hera with
>   Aidoneus
> And Nestis who with her tears fills the springs of mortals.

2. If then Zeus represents fire, Hera earth, Aidoneus air, and Nestis water, they are elements—fire, water, air—and none of them a god, neither Zeus, nor Hera, nor Aidoneus. For they have their substance and origin from matter which has been given its diversity by God:

> Fire, water, earth, and the calm height of air,
> And with them all, Love.

---

21. [3] Hyacinth, beloved of Apollo, was killed accidentally (or through the jealousy of Zephyrus) by a discus thrown by the god (Rose, *Handbook*, p. 142).

3. ἃ χωρὶς τῆς φιλίας οὐ δύναται μένειν ὑπὸ τοῦ νείκους συγχεόμενα,
πῶς ἂν οὖν εἴποι τις ταῦτα εἶναι θεούς; ἀρχικὸν ἡ φιλία κατὰ
τὸν Ἐμπεδοκλέα, ἀρχόμενα τὰ συγκρίματα, τὸ δὲ ἀρχικὸν κύριον·
ὥστε,⁶ ἐὰν μίαν καὶ τὴν ⟨αὐτὴν⟩⁷ τοῦ τε ἀρχομένου καὶ τοῦ
ἄρχοντος δύναμιν θῶμεν, λήσομεν ἑαυτοὺς ἰσότιμον τὴν ὕλην τὴν
φθαρτὴν καὶ ῥευστὴν καὶ μεταβλητὴν τῷ ἀγενήτῳ⁸ καὶ ἀϊδίῳ καὶ
διὰ παντὸς συμφώνῳ ποιοῦντες θεῷ. 4. Ζεὺς ἡ ζέουσα οὐσία κατὰ
τοὺς Στωϊκούς, Ἥρα ὁ ἀήρ, καὶ τοῦ ὀνόματος εἰ αὐτὸ αὐτῷ
ἐπισυνάπτοιτο συνεκφωνουμένου, Ποσειδῶν ἡ πόσις. ἄλλοι δὲ
ἄλλως φυσιολογοῦσιν· οἱ μὲν γὰρ ἀέρα διφυῆ ἀρσενόθηλυν τὸν Δία
λέγουσιν, οἱ δὲ καιρὸν εἰς εὐκρασίαν τρέποντα τὸν χρόνον, διὸ καὶ
μόνος Κρόνον διέφυγεν. 5. ἀλλ' ἐπὶ μὲν τῶν ἀπὸ τῆς Στοᾶς ἔστιν
εἰπεῖν· εἰ ἕνα τὸν ἀνωτάτω θεὸν ἀγένητόν⁹ τε καὶ ἀΐδιον νομίζετε,
συγκρίματα δὲ εἰς ἃ¹⁰ ἡ τῆς ὕλης ἀλλαγή, καὶ τὸ πνεῦμα τοῦ
θεοῦ διὰ τῆς ὕλης κεχωρηκὸς κατὰ τὰς παραλλάξεις αὐτῆς ἄλλο καὶ
ἄλλο ὄνομα μεταλαγχάνειν φατέ, σῶμα μὲν τὰ εἴδη τῆς ὕλης τοῦ
θεοῦ γενήσεται, φθειρομένων δὲ τῶν στοιχείων κατὰ τὴν ἐκπύρωσιν
ἀνάγκη συμφθαρῆναι ὁμοῦ τοῖς εἴδεσι τὰ ὀνόματα, μόνου μένοντος
τοῦ πνεύματος τοῦ θεοῦ. ὧν οὖν σωμάτων φθαρτὴ ἡ κατὰ τὴν
ὕλην παραλλαγή, τίς ἂν ταῦτα πιστεύσαι θεούς; 6. πρὸς δὲ τοὺς
λέγοντας τὸν μὲν Κρόνον χρόνον, τὴν δὲ Ῥέαν γῆν, τὴν μὲν συλ-
λαμβάνουσαν ἐκ τοῦ Κρόνου καὶ ἀποτίκτουσαν, ἔνθεν καὶ μήτηρ
πάντων νομίζεται, τὸν δὲ γεννῶντα καὶ καταναλίσκοντα, καὶ εἶναι
τὴν μὲν τομὴν τῶν ἀναγκαίων ὁμιλίαν τοῦ ἄρρενος πρὸς τὸ θῆλυ,
τέμνουσαν καὶ καταβάλλουσαν σπέρμα εἰς μήτραν καὶ γεννῶσαν
ἄνθρωπον ἐν ἑαυτῷ τὴν ἐπιθυμίαν, ὅ ἐστιν Ἀφροδίτη, ἔχοντα, τὴν δὲ
μανίαν τοῦ Κρόνου τροπὴν καιροῦ φθείρουσαν ἔμψυχα καὶ ἄψυχα,
τὰ δὲ δεσμὰ καὶ τὸν Τάρταρον χρόνον ὑπὸ καιρῶν τρεπόμενον καὶ
ἀφανῆ γινόμενον, πρὸς τοίνυν τούτους φαμέν· εἴτε χρόνος ἐστὶν ὁ
Κρόνος, μεταβάλλει, εἴτε καιρός, τρέπεται, εἴτε σκότος ἢ πάγος ἢ
οὐσία ὑγρά, οὐδὲν αὐτῶν μένει· τὸ δὲ θεῖον καὶ ἀθάνατον καὶ
ἀκίνητον καὶ ἀναλλοίωτον· οὔτε ἄρα ὁ Κρόνος οὔτε τὸ ἐπ' αὐτῷ
εἴδωλον θεός. 7. περὶ δὲ τοῦ Διός, εἰ μὲν ἀήρ ἐστι γεγονὼς ἐκ
Κρόνου, οὗ τὸ μὲν ἄρσεν ὁ Ζεύς, τὸ δὲ θῆλυ Ἥρα (διὸ καὶ ἀδελφὴ

22. ⁶ ὥστε Gesner: ὡς A   ⁷ αὐτὴν add. Gesner   ⁸ ἀγεννήτῳ A
⁹ ἀγένητόν A   ¹⁰ εἰς ἃ Schwartz: ἴσα A: ὅσα Gesner: εἴδη τῆς ὕλης κατ'
ἀλλαγήν Geffcken

3. Without Love the elements cannot be kept from being thrown into confusion by Strife. How then could anyone say that they are gods? Love is the ruling principle according to Empedocles, the composite entities are the ruled, and the ruling principle is their master. If then we attribute one and the same power to the ruled and the ruling, we shall inadvertently make perishable, unstable, and changeable matter equal in rank to the uncreated, eternal, and ever self-same God.

4. 'Zeus' according to the Stoics is the element which 'seethes', 'Hera' the 'air' (if the name is repeated in quick succession, both terms are actually sounded together),[1] 'Poseidon' what is 'potable'. Some give physical explanations of one kind, some of another. For some say that Zeus is air—dipolar, male–female. Others say that he is the season that turns time [*chronos*] and brings fine weather; consequently he alone escaped Cronus.

5. But in the case of the Stoics this can be said: 'If you think that the supreme God is one, both uncreated and eternal, and you say that there are composite entities resulting from the mutation of matter and that the spirit of God pervading matter in its permutations receives now one name, now another, then material things will be God's body, and when the elements perish at the cosmic conflagration, such names must perish together with these things and the spirit of God alone remain.' Who then could believe those to be gods whose bodies the permutation of matter destroys?

6. We have a reply to those who say that Cronus is time [*chronos*]; that Rhea is earth; that she conceived by Cronus and brought forth and is regarded, therefore, as mother of all; that he begat and consumed his offspring, and that the severing of his vital organs signifies the intercourse of male with female, since it severs semen and casts it into the womb and brings forth man with desire—that is, Aphrodite—within him; that the madness of Cronus is the change of season that brings destruction upon animate and inanimate things; that the bonds and Tartarus are time changing with the seasons and passing away. Our reply is this: if Cronus is time, he changes; if he is a season, he alters; if he is darkness or frost or moisture, none of these is abiding. The divine, however, is immortal, immovable, and unchangeable; so then neither Cronus nor any phantom of him in the mind is a god.

7. As to Zeus, if he, the offspring of Cronus, is air (the male aspect of which is Zeus, the female aspect Hera—and thus she is

---

22. [1] i.e. both combinations of letters, (*H*)*era* and *aer* (air), are heard if the former (or the latter) is repeated in quick succession: *eraeraeraer* etc. (cf. Cicero, *De Natura Deorum* 2. 26. 66).

καὶ γυνή), ἀλλοιοῦται, εἰ δὲ καιρός, τρέπεται· οὔτε δὲ μεταβάλλει
οὔτε μεταπίπτει τὸ θεῖον. 8. τί δὲ¹¹ ⟨δεῖ ὑμῖν ἐπὶ⟩ πλέον λέγοντα
ἐνοχλεῖν, οἳ ἄμεινον τὰ παρ᾽ ἑκάστοις τῶν πεφυσιολογηκότων
οἴδατε, ποῖα¹² περὶ τῆς φύσεως¹³ ἐνόησαν οἱ συγγραψάμενοι ἢ¹⁴
περὶ τῆς Ἀθηνᾶς, ἣν¹⁵ φρόνησιν διὰ πάντων διήκουσάν φασιν, ἢ¹⁶
περὶ τῆς Ἴσιδος, ἣν φύσιν αἰῶνος, ἐξ ἧς πάντες ἔφυσαν καὶ δι᾽ ἧς
πάντες εἰσίν, λέγουσιν, ἢ περὶ τοῦ Ὀσίριδος, οὗ σφαγέντος ὑπὸ
Τυφῶνος τοῦ ἀδελφοῦ †περὶ πελώρου†¹⁷ τοῦ υἱοῦ ἡ Ἶσις ζητοῦσα
τὰ μέλη καὶ εὑροῦσα ἤσκησεν εἰς ταφήν, ἢ ταφὴ ἕως νῦν Ὀσιριακὴ
καλεῖται; 9. ἄνω κάτω γὰρ¹⁸ περὶ τὰ εἴδη τῆς ὕλης στρεφόμενοι
ἀποπίπτουσιν τοῦ¹⁹ λόγῳ θεωρητοῦ θεοῦ, τὰ δὲ στοιχεῖα καὶ τὰ
μόρια αὐτῶν θεοποιοῦσιν, ἄλλοτε ἄλλα ὀνόματα αὐτοῖς τιθέμενοι, τὴν
μὲν τοῦ σίτου σπορὰν Ὄσιριν (ὅθεν φασὶ μυστικῶς ἐπὶ τῇ ἀνευρέσει
τῶν μελῶν ἢ τῶν καρπῶν ἐπιλεχθῆναι τῇ Ἴσιδι "εὑρήκαμεν, συγ-
χαίρομεν"), τὸν δὲ τῆς ἀμπέλου καρπὸν Διόνυσον²⁰ καὶ Σεμέλην
αὐτὴν τὴν ἄμπελον καὶ κεραυνὸν τὴν τοῦ ἡλίου φλόγα. 10. καίτοι
γε²¹ πάντα μᾶλλον ἢ²² θεολογοῦσιν οἱ τοὺς μύθους²³ . . . . θεο-
ποιοῦντες, οὐκ εἰδότες ὅτι οἷς ἀπολογοῦνται ὑπὲρ τῶν θεῶν, τοὺς
ἐπ᾽ αὐτοῖς λόγους βεβαιοῦσιν. 11. τί ἡ Εὐρώπη καὶ ὁ Ταῦρος καὶ ὁ
Κύκνος καὶ ἡ Λήδα πρὸς γῆν καὶ ἀέρα, ἵν᾽ ἡ πρὸς ταύτας²⁴ μιαρὰ
τοῦ Διὸς μῖξις ᾖ γῆς καὶ ἀέρος; 12. ἀλλὰ ἀποπίπτοντες²⁵ τοῦ
μεγέθους τοῦ θεοῦ καὶ ὑπερκύψαι τῷ λόγῳ (οὐ γὰρ ἔχουσιν συμπάθειαν εἰς τὸν οὐράνιον τόπον) οὐ δυνάμενοι, ἐπὶ τὰ εἴδη τῆς ὕλης
συντετήκασιν καὶ καταπίπτοντες τὰς τῶν στοιχείων τροπὰς θεοποιοῦσιν, ὅμοιον εἰ καὶ ναῦν τις, ἐν ᾗ ἔπλευσεν, ἀντὶ τοῦ κυβερνήτου
ἄγοι. ὡς δὲ οὐδὲν πλέον νεώς, κἂν ᾖ πᾶσιν ἠσκημένη, μὴ ἐχούσης
τὸν κυβερνήτην, οὐδὲ τῶν στοιχείων ὄφελος διακεκοσμημένων
δίχα τῆς παρὰ τοῦ θεοῦ προνοίας. ἥ τε γὰρ ναῦς καθ᾽ ἑαυτὴν οὐ
πλευσεῖται τά τε στοιχεῖα χωρὶς τοῦ δημιουργοῦ οὐ κινηθήσεται.

22. ¹¹ post τί δὲ add. δεῖ ὑμῖν (ὑμῖν post ἐνοχλεῖν add. Otto) ἐπὶ Wilamowitz
¹² ποῖα Wilamowitz: ἢ οἷα A   ¹³ περὶ τῆς φύσεως A: περὶ τῆς τῶν θεῶν
φύσεως Wilamowitz, Geffcken   ¹⁴ ἢ A: ἢ ἃ A¹   ¹⁵ ἢν Otto: τὴν A
¹⁶ φασιν ἢ A¹: φασι A   ¹⁷ περὶ πελώρου A: μετ᾽ Ὥρου Gesner: περὶ Πηλού-
σιον μετ᾽ Ὥρου Geffcken: περὶ τὰ ἔλη μετ᾽ Ὥρου Ubaldi   ¹⁸ ἄνω γὰρ κάτω
A: ἄνω κάτω γὰρ Wilamowitz   ¹⁹ τοῦ Maranus: τῷ A   ²⁰ post
Διόνυσον lacunam indicavit Wilamowitz   ²¹ καίτοιγε Gesner: καὶ τί γὰρ A
²² ἢ n: εἰ A   ²³ post μύθους lacunam indicavit Wilamowitz supplens
ἀλληγοροῦντες (ἀλληγοροῦντες καὶ τὰ στοιχεῖα Schwartz)   ²⁴ πρὸς ταύτας A:
corr. Gesner   ²⁵ ἀποπίπτοντας A: corr. p m. rec.

called both sister and wife), he is subject to change; if he is a season, he alters. But the divine neither changes nor decays.

8. Why should I burden you further with such accounts? You know better than I the various views of all who give physical explanations: you know what the writers have thought concerning nature[2] or concerning Athena, who they say is thought pervading all things, or concerning Isis, who they say is the origin of the world from whom all sprang and through whom all exist, or concerning Osiris, who was slain by his brother Typhon and whose limbs Isis with her son Horus sought and found about . . . which she arranged in a tomb that to this day is called the Tomb of Osiris. 9. They twist and turn themselves in every direction about material things and miss the God who is contemplated by reason. They divinize the elements and portions of them, sometimes giving one name to them, sometimes another: the sowing of grain is Osiris (hence they say that in the mysteries, when his limbs—that is, the fruits of the earth—are found, this acclamation is made to Isis: 'we have found, we rejoice together'); at the same time the fruit of the vine is Dionysus, the vine itself Semele, and the flaming heat of the sun Zeus.

10. The fact is that those who divinize . . . the myths do anything but treat of God, since they do not realize that what they use to defend the gods confirms the arguments against them. 11. What have Europa and the Bull or Leda and the Swan to do with earth and air so that the repulsive union of Zeus with these women would signify a union of earth and air?

12. They fail to see the greatness of God and are unable to rise up to it by reason (for they are not attuned to the heavenly realm). They have fixed themselves on material things and falling lower and lower divinize the movements of the elements. It is as if a man were to regard the very ship in which he sailed as performing the work of the pilot. Without a pilot it is nothing more than a ship even though it has been equipped with everything; just so, neither are the elements of any use, no matter how beautifully ordered, without the Providence of God. For the ship will not sail of itself, and the elements will not move without the Artificer.

---

22. [2] There may be a lacuna here ('concerning the nature of the gods'). But problems concerning nature, principles, and elements are not unrelated to the interpretation of the gods in the doxographies. Note that the quotation from Empedocles in 22. 1 is found in just such a context (Aetius, *Plac.* 1. 1. 1–1. 3. 25).

23. Εἴποιτε ἂν οὖν[1] συνέσει πάντας ὑπερέχοντες· τίνι οὖν τῷ λόγῳ ἔνια τῶν εἰδώλων ἐνεργεῖ, εἰ μὴ εἰσὶν θεοί, ἐφ᾽ οἷς ἱδρυόμεθα τὰ ἀγάλματα; οὐ γὰρ εἰκὸς τὰς ἀψύχους καὶ ἀκινήτους εἰκόνας καθ᾽ ἑαυτὰς ἰσχύειν χωρὶς τοῦ κινοῦντος. 2. τὸ μὲν δὴ κατὰ τόπους καὶ πόλεις καὶ ἔθνη γίγνεσθαί τινας ἐπ᾽ ὀνόματι εἰδώλων ἐνεργείας οὐδ᾽ ἡμεῖς ἀντιλέγομεν· οὐ μὴν εἰ ὠφελήθησάν τινες καὶ αὖ ἐλυπήθησαν ἕτεροι, θεοὺς νοοῦμεν τοὺς ἐφ᾽ ἑκάτερα ἐνεργήσαντας, ἀλλὰ καὶ ᾧ λόγῳ νομίζετε ἰσχύειν τὰ εἴδωλα καὶ τίνες οἱ ἐνεργοῦντες ἐπιβατεύοντες αὐτῶν τοῖς ὀνόμασιν, ἐπ᾽ ἀκριβὲς ἐξητάκαμεν. 3. ἀναγκαῖον δέ μοι μέλλοντι δεικνύειν, τίνες οἱ ἐπὶ τοῖς εἰδώλοις ἐνεργοῦντες καὶ ὅτι μὴ θεοί, προσχρήσασθαί τισι καὶ τῶν ἀπὸ φιλοσοφίας μάρτυσιν. 4. πρῶτος Θαλῆς διαιρεῖ, ὡς οἱ τὰ ἐκείνου ἀκριβοῦντες[2] μνημονεύουσιν, εἰς θεόν, εἰς δαίμονας, εἰς ἥρωας. ἀλλὰ "θεὸν" μὲν "τὸν νοῦν τοῦ κόσμου" ἄγει, "δαίμονας" δὲ "οὐσίας" νοεῖ "ψυχικὰς καὶ ἥρωας τὰς κεχωρισμένας ψυχὰς" τῶν ἀνθρώπων, "ἀγαθοὺς μὲν τὰς ἀγαθάς, κακοὺς δὲ τὰς φαύλους".[a] 5. Πλάτων δὲ τὰ ἄλλα ἐπέχων καὶ αὐτὸς εἴς τε τὸν ἀγένητον[3] θεὸν καὶ τοὺς ὑπὸ τοῦ ἀγενήτου[4] εἰς κόσμον τοῦ οὐρανοῦ γεγονότας,[b] τούς τε πλανήτας καὶ τοὺς ἀπλανεῖς ἀστέρας, καὶ εἰς δαίμονας τέμνει· περὶ ὧν δαιμόνων αὐτὸς ἀπαξιῶν λέγειν, τοῖς περὶ αὐτῶν εἰρηκόσιν προσέχειν ἀξιοῖ· "περὶ δὲ τῶν ἄλλων δαιμόνων εἰπεῖν καὶ γνῶναι τὴν γένεσιν μεῖζον ἢ καθ᾽ ἡμᾶς, πειστέον δὲ τοῖς εἰρηκόσιν ἔμπροσθεν, ἐγγόνοις μὲν θεῶν οὖσιν, ὡς ἔφασαν, σαφῶς γέ που τοὺς ἑαυτῶν προγόνους εἰδότων· ἀδύνατον οὖν θεῶν παισὶν ἀπιστεῖν, κἄνπερ ἄνευ εἰκότων καὶ ἀναγκαίων ἀποδείξεων λέγωσιν, ἀλλὰ ὡς οἰκεῖα φασκόντων ἀπαγγέλλειν ἑπομένους τῷ νόμῳ πιστευτέον. 6. οὕτως οὖν κατ᾽ ἐκείνους καὶ ἡμῖν ἡ γένεσις περὶ τούτων τῶν θεῶν ἐχέτω καὶ λεγέσθω. Γῆς τε καὶ Οὐρανοῦ παῖδες Ὠκεανός τε καὶ Τηθὺς ἐγεννήθησαν, τούτων δὲ Φόρκος Κρόνος τε καὶ Ῥέα καὶ ὅσοι μετὰ τούτων, ἐκ δὲ Κρόνου τε καὶ Ῥέας Ζεὺς Ἥρα τε καὶ πάντες, οὓς ἴσμεν πάντας ἀδελφοὺς λεγομένους αὐτῶν ἔτι τε τούτων

---

23. [a] Aetius, Plac. 1. 7. 11; 1. 8. 2   [b] Cf. Tim. 40 a–b

23. [1] αναvoυν A: corr. A[1]   [2] ἀκριβοῦντες Gesner: διαιροῦντες ἀκριβοῦντες A
[3] ἀγένητον A   [4] ἀγεννήτου A

23. Now you, who are wiser than all men, may reply: 'Why is it, then, that some of the images actually effect things if the gods do not exist to whom we erect these statues? For it is not likely that inanimate and motionless images would have such power of themselves if nothing were moving them.' 2. Not even we deny that in some places, cities, and nations certain things are brought about in the name of images; but although some have been benefited and others been harmed, we do not think that gods are responsible for what is brought about in either case; rather we have made a careful examination both as to the reason why you think that the images possess power and who they are who usurp the names of the images and bring these things about.

3. Now that I am about to show who they are who bring these things about by taking possession of the images and to show that they are not gods, I feel that I ought to make use also of certain philosophers as my witnesses.

4. Thales, as those who know his doctrines well record, was the first to distinguish God, demons, and heroes. He presents God as the mind of the world, but regards demons as psychic substances and heroes as souls separated from men—good heroes being good souls, evil heroes evil souls.

5. Even Plato himself, who suspended judgement in regard to all the rest, makes a division between, on the one hand, the uncreated God along with those produced by the uncreated One to beautify the heaven—the planets and fixed stars—and, on the other hand, the demons. Since he does not think it worth discussing these demons, he is satisfied to follow those who have already spoken of them:

> It is beyond our powers to tell of the rest of the demons or to know their origin, but we must put our trust in those who have told the story before, since they were the offspring of the gods (as they said)—gods who clearly know their own ancestors. We cannot, then, distrust the offspring of the gods even though they speak without pertinent and necessary proofs: but we must follow custom and believe them when they claim to be giving information about their family history. 6. On their authority, then, we too are to hold and declare a like view of the origin of these gods: Ocean and Tethys were the offspring of Earth and Heaven, and from these came Phorcus, Cronus, Rhea, and all their company. From Cronus and Rhea came Zeus, Hera, and all the rest whom we know—all those called their brothers and sisters as well as others who are *their* offspring.

ἄλλους ἐκγόνους."[c] 7. ἆρ' οὖν ὁ τὸν ἀΐδιον νῷ[5] καὶ λόγῳ καταλαμβανόμενον περινοήσας θεὸν καὶ τὰ ἐπισυμβεβηκότα αὐτῷ ἐξ-
ειπών,[6] τὸ ὄντως ὄν, τὸ μονοφυές, τὸ ἀγαθὸν ἀπ' αὐτοῦ ἀποχεόμενον,
ὅπερ ἐστὶν ἀλήθεια, καὶ περὶ "πρώτης δυνάμεως".[7] . . . καὶ[8] "περὶ
τὸν[9] πάντων βασιλέα πάντα ἐστὶν καὶ ἐκείνου ἕνεκεν πάντα καὶ
ἐκεῖνο αἴτιον πάντων" καὶ περὶ δευτέρου καὶ τρίτου[10] "δεύτερον
δὲ περὶ τὰ δεύτερα καὶ τρίτον περὶ τὰ τρίτα",[d] περὶ τῶν ἐκ τῶν
αἰσθητῶν, γῆς τε καὶ οὐρανοῦ, λεγομένων γεγονέναι μεῖζον ἢ καθ'
ἑαυτὸν τἀληθὲς μαθεῖν ἐνόμισεν; ἢ οὐκ ἔστιν εἰπεῖν. 8. ἀλλ' ἐπεὶ
ἀδύνατον γεννᾶν καὶ ἀποκυΐσκεσθαι θεοὺς ἐνόμισεν ἑπομένων τοῖς
γιγνομένοις τελῶν καὶ ἔτι[11] τούτου ἀδυνατώτερον μεταπεῖσαι τοὺς
πολλοὺς ἀβασανίστως τοὺς μύθους παραδεχομένους, διὰ ταῦτα
μεῖζον ἢ καθ' ἑαυτὸν γνῶναι καὶ εἰπεῖν ἔφη περὶ τῆς τῶν ἄλλων
δαιμόνων γενέσεως, οὔτε μαθεῖν οὔτε ἐξειπεῖν γεννᾶσθαι θεοὺς
δυνάμενος.[12] 9. καὶ τὸ εἰρημένον αὐτῷ "ὁ δὴ μέγας ἡγεμὼν ἐν
οὐρανῷ Ζεύς, ἐλαύνων πτηνὸν ἅρμα, πρῶτος πορεύεται διακοσμῶν
πάντα καὶ ἐπιμελούμενος, τῷ δὲ ἕπεται στρατιὰ θεῶν τε καὶ
δαιμόνων"[e] οὐκ ἐπὶ τοῦ ἀπὸ Κρόνου λεγομένου ἔχει Διός· ἔστι γὰρ
ἐν τούτῳ ὄνομα τῷ ποιητῇ τῶν ὅλων. 10. δηλοῖ δὲ καὶ αὐτὸς
ὁ Πλάτων· ἑτέρῳ σημαντικῷ προσειπεῖν αὐτὸν οὐκ ἔχων, τῷ
δημώδει ὀνόματι οὐχ ὡς ἰδίῳ τοῦ θεοῦ, ἀλλ' εἰς σαφήνειαν, ὅτι μὴ
δυνατὸν εἰς πάντας φέρειν τὸν θεόν, κατὰ δύναμιν[13] προσεχρήσατο,
ἐπικατηγορήσας τὸ "μέγας", ἵνα διαστείλῃ τὸν οὐράνιον ἀπὸ τοῦ
χαμᾶθεν, τὸν ἀγένητον[14] ἀπὸ τοῦ γενητοῦ,[15] τοῦ νεωτέρου μὲν
οὐρανοῦ καὶ γῆς, νεωτέρου δὲ Κρητῶν, οἳ ἐξέκλεψαν αὐτὸν μὴ
ἀναιρεθῆναι ὑπὸ τοῦ πατρός.

24. Τί δὲ δεῖ πρὸς ὑμᾶς πάντα λόγον κεκινηκότας ἢ ποιητῶν
μνημονεύειν ἢ καὶ ἑτέρας δόξας ἐξετάζειν, τοσοῦτον εἰπεῖν ἔχοντι· εἰ

---

23. [c] Tim. 40 d–e (cf. Clement, Strom. 5. 13. 84; Eusebius, Praep. 2. 7. 1; 13. 1;
13. 14. 5)   [d] Ep. 2, 312 e (cf. Justin, Apol. 1. 60. 7; Origen, Cels. 6. 18)
[e] Phaedr. 246 e

---

23. [5] νοῦν A: corr. Schwartz   [6] ἐξειπεῖν A: corr. Gesner   [7] post
δυνάμεως lacunam indicavit Schwartz   [8] καὶ A: καὶ ὡς A[1]   [9] τὸν p:
τῶν A   [10] δευτέρου καὶ τρίτου Schwartz: δύο καὶ τρία A   [11] ἔτι
Gesner: τὸ A   [12] δυναμένους A: corr. Gesner   [13] κατὰ δύναμιν τὸν
θεόν A: corr. Schwartz   [14] ἀγέννητον A   [15] γεννητοῦ A

7. Did he then who came to understand the eternal God apprehended by mind and reason, who singled out his attributes: true
being, oneness of nature, the good which is truth flowing from
him, and who spoke concerning 'the first power': . . . and 'it is in
relation to the King of all and on his account that all things exist,
and he is the cause of all', and concerning a 'second' and a 'third':
'the second has to do with the second class of things and the third
with the third class'—did he think it beyond his powers to learn
the truth concerning the beings said to have come into existence
from the perceptible realms of earth and heaven? Surely we
cannot say that! 8. But since he thought it impossible for gods to
beget and to be brought forth (for what comes into existence also
comes to an end) and since he thought it still more impossible
than this to persuade the crowd which accepts the myths without
due examination, that is why he said it was beyond his powers to
know and to tell of the birth of the rest of the demons: he could
neither admit nor say that the gods were born. 9. And this
remark of his, 'Zeus, the great Prince in heaven, driving his
winged chariot, proceeds first to order all things and to take care
of them, and a host of gods and demons follows him', does not
have to do with the Zeus called son of Cronus; for in this passage
the name refers to the Maker of all things. 10. Plato himself
shows this: since he could not address him by using any other
designation, he did what he could and employed the popular
name, not because it was proper to God but for the sake of
clarity (since it is not possible to bring God to all men), adding
the epithet 'great' so that he might separate the heavenly from
the earthly Zeus, the uncreated from the created, the latter more
recent than heaven and earth, more recent than the Cretans who
stole him away to prevent him from being destroyed by his
father.

24. What need is there with you who are well versed in everything either to call to mind poets or to examine still other opinions?

καὶ μὴ ποιηταὶ καὶ φιλόσοφοι ἕνα μὲν εἶναι ἐπεγίνωσκον θεόν, περὶ
δὲ τούτων οἱ μὲν ὡς περὶ δαιμόνων, οἱ δὲ ὡς περὶ ὕλης, οἱ δὲ ὡς
περὶ ἀνθρώπων γενομένων ἐφρόνουν, ἡμεῖς [τε]¹ ἂν εἰκότως ἐξεν-
ηλατούμεθα,² διαιρετικῷ λόγῳ καὶ περὶ θεοῦ καὶ ὕλης καὶ περὶ τῆς
τούτων αὐτῶν οὐσίας κεχρημένοι; 2. ὡς γὰρ θεόν φαμεν καὶ υἱὸν
τὸν λόγον αὐτοῦ καὶ πνεῦμα ἅγιον, ἑνούμενα μὲν κατὰ δύναμιν³
⟨διαιρούμενα δὲ κατὰ τάξιν εἰς⟩ τὸν πατέρα, τὸν υἱόν, τὸ πνεῦμα,
ὅτι νοῦς, λόγος, σοφία ὁ υἱὸς⁴ τοῦ πατρὸς καὶ ἀπόρροια ὡς φῶς ἀπὸ
πυρὸς τὸ πνεῦμα, οὕτως καὶ ἑτέρας εἶναι δυνάμεις κατειλήμμεθα
περὶ τὴν ὕλην ἐχούσας καὶ δι' αὐτῆς, μίαν μὲν τὴν ἀντίθεον, οὐχ
ὅτι ἀντιδοξοῦν τί ἐστι τῷ θεῷ ὡς τῇ φιλίᾳ τὸ νεῖκος κατὰ τὸν
Ἐμπεδοκλέα καὶ τῇ ἡμέρᾳ νὺξ κατὰ τὰ φαινόμενα (ἐπεὶ κἂν εἰ
ἀνθειστήκει τι τῷ θεῷ, ἐπαύσατο⁵ τοῦ εἶναι, λυθείσης αὐτοῦ τῇ τοῦ
θεοῦ δυνάμει καὶ ἰσχύι τῆς συστάσεως), ἀλλ' ὅτι τῷ τοῦ θεοῦ
ἀγαθῷ, ὃ κατὰ συμβεβηκός ἐστιν αὐτῷ καὶ συνυπάρχον ὡς χρόα
σώματι, οὗ ἄνευ οὐκ ἔστιν (οὐχ ὡς μέρους ὄντος, ἀλλ' ὡς κατ'
ἀνάγκην συνόντος παρακολουθήματος, ἡνωμένου καὶ συγκεχρωσ-
μένου⁶ ὡς τῷ πυρὶ ξανθῷ εἶναι καὶ τῷ αἰθέρι κυανῷ), ἐναντίον ἐστὶ
τὸ περὶ τὴν ὕλην ἔχον πνεῦμα, γενόμενον μὲν ὑπὸ τοῦ θεοῦ, καθὸ
⟨καὶ⟩⁷ οἱ λοιποὶ ὑπ' αὐτοῦ γεγόνασιν ἄγγελοι, καὶ τὴν ἐπὶ τῇ ὕλῃ
καὶ τοῖς τῆς ὕλης εἴδεσι πεπιστευμένον⁸ διοίκησιν. 3. τούτων⁹ γὰρ
ἡ τῶν ἀγγέλων σύστασις τῷ θεῷ ἐπὶ προνοίᾳ γέγονε τοῖς ὑπ'
αὐτοῦ διακεκοσμημένοις, ἵν' ᾖ¹⁰ τὴν μὲν παντελικὴν καὶ γενικὴν ὁ
θεὸς ⟨ἔχων⟩¹¹ τῶν ὅλων πρόνοιαν, τὴν δὲ ἐπὶ μέρους οἱ ἐπ' αὐτοῖς
ταχθέντες ἄγγελοι. 4. ὡς δὲ καὶ ἐπὶ τῶν ἀνθρώπων αὐθαίρετον καὶ
τὴν ἀρετὴν καὶ τὴν κακίαν ἐχόντων (ἐπεὶ οὐκ ἂν οὔτ' ἐτιμᾶτε τοὺς
ἀγαθοὺς οὔτ' ἐκολάζετε τοὺς πονηρούς, εἰ μὴ ἐπ' αὐτοῖς ἦν καὶ ἡ
κακία καὶ ἡ ἀρετή) [καὶ]¹² οἱ μὲν σπουδαῖοι περὶ ἃ πιστεύονται ὑφ'
ὑμῶν, οἱ δὲ ἄπιστοι εὑρίσκονται, καὶ τὸ κατὰ τοὺς ἀγγέλους ἐν
ὁμοίῳ καθέστηκεν. 5. οἱ μὲν γὰρ ἄλλοι—αὐθαίρετοι δὴ γεγόνασιν

---

24. ¹ τε ἂν A: τε seclusit Geffcken ² ξενηλατούμεθα A: corr. Stephanus
³ διαιρούμενα δὲ κατὰ τάξιν εἰς (cf. 10. 5) add. Schwartz ⁴ υἱὸς A: ὁ
υἱὸς s ⁵ post ἐπαύσατο add. ἂν (ex Method. in Epiph. 64. 20) Schwartz,
Geffcken ⁶ συγκεχρωμένου A ⁷ καὶ add. (ex Method.) Wilamowitz
⁸ πεπιστευμένον (ex Method. in Phot. cod. 234) Schwartz: πιστευσάμενον A
⁹ τούτων (ex Method. in Phot.) Schwartz: τοῦτο A ¹⁰ ἵν' η A: corr.
Wilamowitz ¹¹ ἔχων add. (ex Method.) Wilamowitz ¹² καὶ seclusit
Schwartz

It is sufficient for me to say this: suppose that the poets and philosophers did not recognize that God was one and did not have critical opinions about the other gods, some regarding them as demons, others regarding them as matter, others regarding them as men who once lived, would it make sense to have us banished because we have a doctrine which distinguishes God and matter and their respective substances?

2. We say that there is God and the Son, his Word, and the Holy Spirit, united in power yet distinguished in rank as the Father, the Son, and the Spirit, since the Son is mind, reason [word], and wisdom of the Father and the Spirit an effluence like light from fire. So also we have recognized that there are other powers which are concerned with matter and operate through it. One of them is opposed to God, not because there is a counterpart to God as Strife is a counterpart to Love in Empedocles or as Night is a counterpart to Day in the realm of nature (for if anything had stood opposed to God, it would surely have ceased to exist, its constitution dissolved by the power and might of God), but because the spirit which is concerned with matter is opposed to God's goodness. This goodness belongs to God as an attribute and is coexistent with him as colour is with corporeal substance; without it he does not exist. It is not as though it were a part of him but rather an accompanying quality necessarily associated with him, as united and allied with him as a yellowish-red is with fire and a deep blue with the sky. The spirit opposed to him was in fact created by God just as the rest of the angels were also created by him, and he was entrusted with the administration of matter and material things.

3. These angels were called into being by God to exercise providence over the things set in order by him, so that God would have universal and general providence over all things whereas the angels would be set over particular things.[1] 4. As in the case of men whose virtue and vice is a matter of choice (for you would neither honour the good nor punish the evil if virtue and vice were not in their hands) some take seriously what has been entrusted to them by you whereas others are found untrustworthy, so it is in the case of the angels. 5. Some of them—they were,

---

24. [1] Reminiscent of the teaching of Plato (*Tim.* 41 a). A more Jewish version of this doctrine is preserved in the fragments of Papias (frg. 4).

ὑπὸ τοῦ θεοῦ—ἔμειναν ἐφ᾽ οἷς αὐτοὺς ἐποίησεν καὶ διέταξεν ὁ
θεός, οἱ δὲ ἐνύβρισαν καὶ τῇ τῆς οὐσίας ὑποστάσει καὶ τῇ ἀρχῇ
οὗτός τε ὁ τῆς ὕλης καὶ τῶν ἐν αὐτῇ εἰδῶν ἄρχων καὶ ἕτεροι τῶν
περὶ τὸ πρῶτον τοῦτο στερέωμα (ὥστε δὲ μηδὲν ἡμᾶς ἀμάρτυρον
λέγειν, ἃ δὲ τοῖς προφήταις ἐκπεφώνηται μηνύειν),[a] ἐκεῖνοι μὲν εἰς
ἐπιθυμίαν πεσόντες παρθένων καὶ ἥττους σαρκὸς εὑρεθέντες, οὗτος
δὲ ἀμελήσας καὶ πονηρὸς περὶ τὴν τῶν πεπιστευμένων γενόμενος
διοίκησιν. 6. ἐκ μὲν οὖν τῶν περὶ τὰς παρθένους ἐχόντων οἱ
καλούμενοι ἐγεννήθησαν γίγαντες· εἰ δέ τις ἐκ μέρους εἴρηται περὶ
τῶν γιγάντων καὶ ποιηταῖς λόγος, μὴ θαυμάσητε, τῆς κοσμικῆς[13]
. . . σοφίας ὅσον ἀλήθεια πιθανοῦ διαφέρει διαλλαττουσῶν καὶ τῆς
μὲν οὔσης ἐπουρανίου, τῆς δὲ ἐπιγείου καὶ κατὰ τὸν ἄρχοντα τῆς
ὕλης·

> ἴσμεν ψεύδεα πολλὰ λέγειν ἐτύμοισιν ὁμοῖα.[b]

25. οὗτοι τοίνυν οἱ ἄγγελοι οἱ ἐκπεσόντες τῶν οὐρανῶν, περὶ τὸν
ἀέρα ἔχοντες καὶ τὴν γῆν, οὐκέτι εἰς τὰ ὑπερουράνια ὑπερκύψαι
δυνάμενοι, καὶ αἱ τῶν γιγάντων ψυχαὶ οἱ περὶ τὸν κόσμον εἰσὶ
πλανώμενοι δαίμονες, ὁμοίας κινήσεις, οἱ μὲν αἷς ἔλαβον συστάσεσιν,
οἱ δαίμονες, οἱ δέ, αἷς ἔσχον ἐπιθυμίαις, οἱ ἄγγελοι, ποιούμενοι.
ὁ δὲ τῆς ὕλης ἄρχων, ὡς ἔστιν ἐξ αὐτῶν τῶν γινομένων ἰδεῖν,
ἐναντία τῷ ἀγαθῷ τοῦ θεοῦ ἐπιτροπεύει καὶ διοικεῖ.

> πολλάκι μοι πραπίδων διῆλθε φροντίς,
> εἴτε τύχα εἴτε δαίμων τὰ βρότεια[1] κραίνει,
> παρά τ᾽ ἐλπίδα καὶ παρὰ δίκαν
> †τοὺς μὲν ἀπ᾽ οἴκων δ᾽ ἐναπίπτοντας
> ἀτὰρ θεοῦ,[2] τοὺς δ᾽ εὐτυχοῦντας ἄγει†.[a]

2. ⟨εἰ⟩[3] τὸ παρ᾽ ἐλπίδα καὶ δίκην εὖ πράττειν ἢ κακῶς ἐν ἀφασίᾳ

---

24. [a] Cf. Gen. 6: 1–5; Enoch 6: 2   [b] Hesiod, *Theog.* 27   25. [a] Euripides,
frg. 901 (Nauck²)

---

24. [13] post κοσμικῆς add. καὶ τῆς προφητικῆς Schwartz
25. [1] βιότια A: corr. Dechair   [2] τοὺς μὲν ἀπ᾽ οἴκων καταπίπτοντας (vel
ἀποπίπτοντας) ἄτερ θεοῦ (βίου Grotius) Gesner   [3] εἰ add. Gercke

remember, created free by God—remained true to the task for which God made them and to which he had appointed them. Others violated both their own nature and their office. These include the prince over matter and material things and others who are of those stationed at the first firmament (do realize that we say nothing unsupported by evidence but that we are exponents of what the prophets uttered); the latter are the angels who fell to lusting after maidens and let themselves be conquered by the flesh, the former failed his responsibility and operated wickedly in the administration of what had been entrusted to him.

6. Now from those who went after maidens were born the so-called giants. Do not be surprised that a partial account of the giants has been set forth also by poets. Worldly wisdom and prophetic wisdom differ from one another as truth differs from probability—the one is heavenly, the other earthly and in harmony with the prince of matter:

> We know how to tell many falsehoods which have the form of
> truth.

25. These angels, then, who fell from heaven busy themselves about the air and the earth and are no longer able to rise to the realms above the heavens. The souls of the giants are the demons who wander about the world. Both angels and demons produce movements—demons movements which are akin to the natures they received, and angels movements which are akin to the lusts with which they were possessed. The prince of matter, as may be seen from what happens, directs and administers things in a manner opposed to God's goodness.

> Oft into my heart has come this thought:
> That either chance or demon rules men's lives.
> Against hope and against justice
> It casts some forth from homes
> Apart from God, and others it makes prosper.

2. If faring well or badly against hope and justice left Euripides

τὸν Εὐριπίδην ἐποίησεν, τίνος ἡ τοιαύτη τῶν περιγείων διοίκησις,
ἐν ᾗ εἴποι τις ἄν·

πῶς οὖν τάδ᾽ εἰσορῶντες⁴ ἢ θεῶν γένος
εἶναι λέγωμεν ἤ⁵ νόμοισι χρώμεθα;ᵇ

τοῦτο καὶ τὸν Ἀριστοτέλη ἀπρονόητα εἰπεῖν τὰ κατωτέρω τοῦ
οὐρανοῦ ἐποίησεν, καίτοι τῆς ἀϊδίου ἐπ᾽ ἴσης ἡμῖν μενούσης προνοίας τοῦ θεοῦ,

ἡ γῆ δ᾽ ἀνάγκῃ,⁶ κἂν θέλῃ κἂν μὴ θέλῃ,
φύουσα ποίαν⁷ τἀμὰ πιαίνει βοτά,ᶜ

τῆς δ᾽ ἐπὶ μέρους πρὸς ἀλήθειαν, οὐ πρὸς δόξαν, χωρούσης ἐπὶ τοὺς
ἀξίους καὶ τῶν λοιπῶν κατὰ τὸ κοινὸν συστάσεως νόμῳ λόγου⁸
προνοουμένων. 3. ἀλλ᾽ ἐπεὶ αἱ ἀπὸ τοὐναντίου πνεύματος δαι-
μονικαὶ κινήσεις καὶ ἐνέργειαι τὰς ἀτάκτους ταύτας ἐπιφορὰς
παρέχουσιν, ἤδη καὶ⁹ τοὺς ἀνθρώπους ἄλλον ἄλλως, καὶ καθ᾽ ἕνα καὶ
κατὰ ἔθνη, μερικῶς καὶ κοινῶς, κατὰ τὸν τῆς ὕλης λόγον καὶ τῆς
πρὸς τὰ θεῖα συμπαθείας, ἔνδοθεν καὶ ἔξωθεν κινοῦσαι, διὰ τοῦτό
τινες, ὧν δόξαι οὐ μικραί, ἐνόμισαν οὐ τάξει τινὶ τὸ πᾶν τοῦτο
συνεστάναι, ἀλλ᾽ ἀλόγῳ τύχῃ ἄγεσθαι καὶ φέρεσθαι, οὐκ εἰδότες
ὅτι τῶν μὲν περὶ τὴν τοῦ παντὸς κόσμου σύστασιν οὐδὲν ἄτακτον
οὐδὲ ἀπημελημένον, ἀλλ᾽ ἕκαστον αὐτῶν γεγονὸς λόγῳ, διὸ οὐδὲ
τὴν ὡρισμένην ἐπ᾽ αὐτοῖς παραβαίνουσι τάξιν, 4. ὁ δὲ ἄνθρωπος
κατὰ μὲν τὸν πεποιηκότα καὶ αὐτὸς εὐτάκτως ἔχει καὶ τῇ κατὰ
τὴν γένεσιν φύσει ἕνα καὶ κοινὸν [ἐπ᾽]ἐχούσῃ¹⁰ λόγον καὶ τῇ κατὰ
τὴν πλάσιν διαθέσει οὐ παραβαινούσῃ τὸν ἐπ᾽ αὐτῇ νόμον καὶ τῷ
τοῦ βίου τέλει ἴσῳ καὶ κοινῷ μένοντι, κατὰ δὲ τὸν ἴδιον ἑαυτῷ
λόγον καὶ τὴν τοῦ ἐπέχοντος ἄρχοντος καὶ τῶν παρακολουθούντων
δαιμόνων ἐνέργειαν ἄλλος ἄλλως φέρεται καὶ κινεῖται, κοινὸν
πάντες τὸν ἐν αὐτοῖς ἔχοντες λογισμόν.

25. ᵇ Frg. 99, adesp. (Nauck²)   ᶜ Euripides, Cycl. 332–3

---

25. ⁴ εἰσορῶντος A: εἰσορῶντας A¹   ⁵ λέγομεν εἰ A   ⁶ δὲ ἀνάγκη A
⁷ φύουσαν οἵαν A: τίκτουσα ποίαν Euripides: φύουσα ποίαν Gesner   ⁸ νόμου
λόγου Schwartz: νόμῳ καὶ λόγῳ vel νόμον καὶ λόγον Geffcken   ⁹ ἤδη καὶ A:
textus vix sanus secundum Schwartz, Geffcken   ¹⁰ ἐπέχουσι A: ἐπεχούσῃ
A¹: corr. Schwartz

speechless, to whom belongs the administration of earthly affairs which is of such a nature that a man could say:

> How, then, when we see such things, are we to say
> There is a race of gods, or follow laws obediently?

This is what made Aristotle also say that things below heaven are not guided by Providence, although the eternal providence of God rests equally on us all:

> The earth by necessity, whether it wills or not,
> Makes the grass grow and thus fattens my flocks.

But the particular providence of God which is concerned with truth and not conjecture extends itself to those who are worthy whereas everything else is subject to providence by the law of reason as part of a total system.

3. But since the demonic impulses and activities of the hostile spirit bring these wild attacks—indeed we see them move men from within and from without, one man one way and another man another, some individually and some as nations, one at a time and all together, because of our kinship with matter and our affinity with the divine[1]—in light of this, some men, whose reputations are not small, have thought that our universe did not arise in an orderly fashion but is the random product of irrational chance. They do not recognize that none of the things of which the whole world is composed is disordered and neglected. Each of them is the product of reason, and that is why they do not go beyond their appointed order. 4. Even man himself is a well-ordered creature to the extent that it depends on the One who made him: his nature in its origin has one common reason, his bodily form does not go beyond the law set for it, and the end of life remains common to all alike. But to the extent that it depends on the reason peculiar to each individual and the activity of the ruling prince and his attendant demons, one man is swept along one way, another man another way, even though all have the same rationality within.

---

25. [1] Geffcken thought that here Athenagoras allowed a pagan doctrine of demonic activity (more 'neutral' in character) to overshadow and contradict those elements in his treatment of the subject which he derived from Jewish and Christian sources. But it is not necessary to link the 'affinity with the divine' with the demons. It is more likely, as Puech has noted, that Athenagoras is speaking of a conflict between demonic influence (exercised through matter) and the affinity with the divine which is also proper to man (cf. 7. 2).

26. Καὶ οἱ μὲν περὶ τὰ εἴδωλα αὐτοὺς ἕλκοντες οἱ δαίμονές εἰσιν οἱ προειρημένοι, οἱ προστετηκότες τῷ ἀπὸ τῶν ἱερείων αἵματι καὶ ταῦτα περιλιχμώμενοι· οἱ δὲ τοῖς πολλοῖς ἀρέσκοντες θεοὶ καὶ ταῖς εἰκόσιν ἐπονομαζόμενοι, ὡς ἔστιν ἐκ τῆς κατ᾽ αὐτοὺς ἱστορίας εἰδέναι, ἄνθρωποι γεγόνασιν. 2. καὶ τοὺς μὲν δαίμονας εἶναι τοὺς ἐπιβατεύοντας τοῖς ὀνόμασιν πίστις ἡ ἑκάστου αὐτῶν ἐνέργεια. οἱ μὲν γὰρ¹ ἀποτέμνουσι τὰ αἰδοῖα, οἱ περὶ τὴν Ῥέαν, οἱ δὲ ἐγκόπτουσιν ἢ ἐντέμνουσιν, οἱ περὶ τὴν Ἄρτεμιν. (καὶ ἡ μὲν ἐν Ταύροις φονεύει τοὺς ξένους.) ἐῶ γὰρ τοὺς ταῖς μαχαίραις καὶ τοῖς ἀστραγάλοις αἰκιζομένους αὐτοὺς λέγειν² . . . καὶ ὅσα εἴδη δαιμόνων. οὐ γὰρ θεοῦ κινεῖν ἐπὶ τὰ παρὰ φύσιν· "ὅταν ὁ δαίμων ἀνδρὶ πορσύνῃ κακά, τὸν νοῦν ἔβλαψε πρῶτον",ᵃ ὁ δὲ θεὸς τελείως ἀγαθὸς ὢν ἀϊδίως ἀγαθοποιός ἐστιν. 3. τοῦ τοίνυν ἄλλους μὲν εἶναι τοὺς ἐνεργοῦντας, ἐφ᾽ ἑτέρων δὲ ἀνίστασθαι τὰς εἰκόνας, ἐκεῖνο μέγιστον τεκμήριον, Τρωὰς καὶ Πάριον· ἡ μὲν Νερυλλίνου³ εἰκόνας ἔχει—ὁ⁴ ἀνὴρ τῶν καθ᾽ ἡμᾶς—τὸ δὲ Πάριον Ἀλεξάνδρου καὶ Πρωτέως· τοῦ Ἀλεξάνδρου ἔτι ἐπὶ τῆς ἀγορᾶς καὶ ὁ τάφος καὶ ἡ εἰκών. οἱ μὲν οὖν ἄλλοι ἀνδριάντες τοῦ Νερυλλίνου κόσμημά εἰσι δημόσιον, εἴπερ καὶ τούτοις κοσμεῖται πόλις, εἷς δὲ αὐτῶν καὶ χρηματίζειν καὶ ἰᾶσθαι νοσοῦντας νομίζεται, καὶ θύουσί τε δι᾽ αὐτὰ καὶ χρυσῷ περιαλείφουσιν καὶ στεφανοῦσιν⁵ τὸν ἀνδριάντα οἱ Τρωαδεῖς. 4. ὁ δὲ τοῦ Ἀλεξάνδρου καὶ ὁ τοῦ Πρωτέως (τοῦτον δ᾽ οὐκ ἀγνοεῖτε ῥίψαντα ἑαυτὸν εἰς τὸ πῦρ περὶ τὴν Ὀλυμπίαν), ὁ μὲν καὶ αὐτὸς λέγεται χρηματίζειν, τῷ δὲ τοῦ Ἀλεξάνδρου—"Δύσπαρι, εἶδος ἄριστε, γυναιμανές"ᵇ—δημοτελεῖς ἄγονται θυσίαι καὶ ἑορταὶ ὡς ἐπηκόῳ θεῷ. 5. πότερον οὖν ὁ Νερυλλῖνος καὶ ὁ Πρωτεὺς καὶ ὁ Ἀλέξανδρός εἰσιν οἱ ταῦτα ἐνεργοῦντες περὶ τὰ ἀγάλματα ἢ τῆς ὕλης ἡ σύστασις; ἀλλ᾽ ἡ μὲν ὕλη χαλκός ἐστιν, τί δὲ χαλκὸς δύναται καθ᾽ αὑτόν, ὃν μεταποιῆσαι πάλιν εἰς ἕτερον σχῆμα ἔξεστιν, ὡς τὸν ποδονιπτῆρα ὁ παρὰ τῷ Ἡροδότῳ Ἄμασις;ᶜ ὁ δὲ

---

26. ᵃ Frg. 455, adesp. (Nauck²)   ᵇ Homer, Iliad 3. 39   ᶜ Cf. Herod. 2. 172

26. ¹ post μὲν add. γὰρ Aⁱ
³ Νερυλλίνον A   ⁴ ὁ A: ὃς Aⁱ
witz

² post λέγειν lacunam indicavit Geffcken
⁵ χρυσῷ post στεφανοῦσιν coll. Wilamo-

26. It is these demons who drag men to the images. They engross themselves in the blood from the sacrifices and lick all around them. The gods that satisfy the crowd and give their names to the images, as you can learn from their history, were once men. 2. The activity associated with each of them is your assurance that it is the demons who usurp their names. For some—I mean the devotees of Rhea[1]—castrate themselves; others—I mean the devotees of Artemis[2]—make incisions and gash their genitals. (And the Artemis among the Taurians slaughters strangers!) I shall not discuss those who mutilate themselves with knives and knuckle-bones and what form of demons they have. For it is not God's doing to incite men to things contrary to nature.

> When the demon prepares evil for a man,
> He first perverts his mind.

But God, who is perfectly good, eternally does what is good.
3. Troy and Parium provide the best proof that it is others who operate through the images than those for whom they were erected: Troy has the images of Neryllinus[3] (a man of our own time); Parium has the images of Alexander and Proteus. Both the grave and the image of Alexander[4] are still in the market-place. Almost all of the statues of Neryllinus serve simply as public monuments, since that is how a city is beautified. One of them, however, is thought to give oracles and to heal the sick, and for this reason the Trojans sacrifice to the statue, overlay it with gold, and wreathe it. 4. Then there is the statue of Alexander and that of Proteus. You know about Proteus—the one who threw himself into the fire at Olympia.[5] His statue is also said to give oracles. To the statue of Alexander—'ill-starred Paris, in form most fair, mad for women'[6]—public sacrifices and festivals are celebrated; it is treated as a god who hears men's prayers.
5. Well, then, are Neryllinus, Proteus, and Alexander the ones who are responsible for these phenomena associated with the statues, or is it the nature of the material used for them? The material, however, is bronze, and what can bronze do by itself when it is possible to change it into another shape as the Amasis referred to by Herodotus did with his foot-basin?[7] What more can

---

26. [1] Early identified with Cybele (Rose, *Handbook*, p. 170).

[2] The Ephesian Artemis—that is, Cybele.

[3] Otherwise unknown.

[4] i.e. the infamous Alexander Abonuteichus satirized by Lucian.

[5] i.e. the Peregrinus satirized by Lucian in his *De Morte Peregrini*.

[6] Homer's Paris was also named Alexander.

[7] Amasis had the basin made into an image as a sort of commentary on his own rise from humble circumstances to kingship.

Νερυλλῖνος καὶ ὁ Πρωτεὺς καὶ ὁ Ἀλέξανδρος τί πλέον τοῖς νοσοῦσιν; ἃ γὰρ ἡ εἰκὼν λέγεται νῦν ἐνεργεῖν, ἐνήργει⁶ καὶ ζῶντος καὶ νοσοῦντος Νερυλλίνου.

27. Τί οὖν; πρῶτα μὲν αἱ τῆς ψυχῆς ἄλογοι καὶ ἰνδαλματώδεις περὶ τὰς δόξας κινήσεις ἄλλοτ᾽ ἄλλα εἴδωλα τὰ μὲν ἀπὸ τῆς ὕλης ἕλκουσι, τὰ δὲ αὐταῖς ἀναπλάττουσιν καὶ κυοῦσιν. πάσχει δὲ τοῦτο ψυχὴ μάλιστα τοῦ ὑλικοῦ προσλαβοῦσα καὶ ἐπισυγκραθεῖσα πνεύματος, οὐ πρὸς τὰ οὐράνια καὶ τὸν τούτων ποιητὴν ἀλλὰ κάτω πρὸς τὰ ἐπίγεια βλέπουσα, καθολικῶς εἰπεῖν¹, ὡς μόνον αἷμα καὶ σάρξ, οὐκέτι πνεῦμα καθαρὸν γιγνομένη. 2. αἱ οὖν ἄλογοι αὗται καὶ ἰνδαλματώδεις τῆς ψυχῆς κινήσεις εἰδωλομανεῖς ἀποτίκτουσι φαντασίας· ὅταν δὲ ἀπαλὴ καὶ εὐάγωγος ψυχή, ἀνήκοος μὲν καὶ ἄπειρος λόγων ἐρρωμένων, ἀθεώρητος δὲ τοῦ ἀληθοῦς, ἀπερινόητος δὲ τοῦ πατρὸς καὶ ποιητοῦ τῶν ὅλων, ἐναποσφραγίσηται ψευδεῖς περὶ αὑτῆς δόξας, οἱ περὶ τὴν ὕλην δαίμονες, λίχνοι περὶ τὰς κνίσας καὶ τὸ τῶν ἱερείων αἷμα ὄντες, ἀπατηλοὶ δὲ ἀνθρώπων, προσλαβόντες τὰς ψευδοδόξους ταύτας τῶν πολλῶν τῆς ψυχῆς κινήσεις, φαντασίας αὐτοῖς ὡς ἀπὸ τῶν εἰδώλων καὶ ἀγαλμάτων ἐπιβατεύοντες αὐτῶν τοῖς νοήμασιν εἰσρεῖν παρέχουσιν, καὶ ὅσα καθ᾽ αὑτήν, ὡς ἀθάνατος οὖσα, λογικῶς κινεῖται ψυχὴ ἢ προμηνύουσα τὰ μέλλοντα ἢ θεραπεύουσα τὰ ἐνεστηκότα, τούτων τὴν δόξαν καρποῦνται οἱ δαίμονες.

28. Ἀναγκαῖον δὲ ἴσως κατὰ τὰ προειρημένα περὶ τῶν ὀνομάτων ὀλίγα εἰπεῖν. Ἡρόδοτος μὲν οὖν καὶ Ἀλέξανδρος ὁ¹ τοῦ Φιλίππου ἐν τῇ πρὸς τὴν μητέρα ἐπιστολῇ (ἑκάτεροι δὲ ἐν τῇ Ἡλιουπόλει καὶ ἐν Μέμφιδι² καὶ Θήβαις εἰς λόγους τοῖς ἱερεῦσιν ἀφῖχθαι λέγονται) φασὶ παρ᾽ ἐκείνων ἀνθρώπους αὐτοὺς γενέσθαι μαθεῖν. 2. Ἡρόδοτος· "ἤδη ὧν τῶν αἱ εἰκόνες ἦσαν, τοιούτους ἀπεδείκνυσάν σφεας [αὐτοὺς]³ ἐόντας, θεῶν δὲ πολλὸν ἀπηλλαγμένους. τὸ δὲ πρότερον τῶν ἀνδρῶν τούτων θεοὺς εἶναι τοὺς ἐν Αἰγύπτῳ ἄρχοντας, οἰκέοντας⁴ ἅμα τοῖς ἀνθρώποισιν, καὶ τούτων ἀεὶ ἕνα τὸν κρατέοντα

26. ⁶ ἐνεργεῖ A: corr. Maranus
27. ¹ εἰπεῖν Wilamowitz: εἰς γῆν A
28. ¹ ὁ add. A¹   ² Μέμφι A   ³ αὐτοὺς seclusit Schwartz
⁴ οὐκέοντας A

Neryllinus, Proteus, and Alexander do for the sick? For what the image is said to accomplish now, it did while Neryllinus was alive and ill himself!

27. What is the solution? First, that the movements of the soul not directed by reason but by fantasy in the realm of conjectures derive various images, now one, now another, from matter or simply mould them independently and give birth to them. A soul experiences this especially when it attaches itself to the spirit of matter and blends with it, when it does not look up to heavenly things and their Maker but down to earthly things, or, in general terms, when it becomes mere blood and flesh and is no longer pure spirit.

2. These movements of the soul not directed by reason but by fantasy give birth to illusory images, which bring with them a mad passion for idols. When the soul is weak and docile, ignorant and unacquainted with sound teachings, unable to contemplate the truth, unable to understand who the Father and Maker of all things is—when such a soul has impressed upon it false opinions concerning itself, the demons associated with matter, because they are greedy for the savour of fat and the blood of the sacrifices, and because their business is to delude men, take hold of these deceitful movements in the soul of the many, and by invading their thoughts flood them with illusory images which seem to come from the idols and statues; and the demons harvest the fame of all the remarkable things which the soul, because of its immortal nature, brings about in a rational way of itself, whether it be foretelling the future or healing present ills.

28. After what has been said it is equally necessary to make a few remarks on their names. Herodotus and Alexander the son of Philip in his letter to his mother[1] say that they learned from Egyptian priests that the gods were once men. Both of them are said to have conversed with the priests in Heliopolis, Memphis, and Thebes. 2. Herodotus writes:

> They pointed out, then, that those of whom there were images were of that nature and were far from being gods. Before the time of these men, indeed, those who ruled in Egypt were gods who dwelt among men; and one of them had always ruled.

---

28. [1] This was a forged document actually produced by Leon of Pella (J. Geffcken in *PWK* xii/2 [1925], 2012–14). It dealt with the gods of Egypt from a rationalistic point of view (affinities with Hecataeus of Teos and Euhemerus) and was frequently cited by Christian apologists from Tatian to Augustine.

εἶναι· ὕστερον δὲ αὐτῆς βασιλεῦσαι Ὧρον τὸν Ὀσίρεως παῖδα, τὸν
Ἀπόλλωνα Ἕλληνες ὀνομάζουσιν· τοῦτον καταπαύσαντα Τυφῶνα
βασιλεῦσαι ὕστατον Αἰγύπτου. "Οσιρις δέ ἐστι Διόνυσος κατὰ
Ἑλλάδα γλῶσσαν."ᵃ 3. οἵ τε οὖν ἄλλοι καὶ τελευταῖος βασιλεῖς⁵
Αἰγύπτου· παρὰ δὲ τούτων εἰς Ἕλληνας ἦλθε τὰ ὀνόματα τῶν
θεῶν.ᵇ Ἀπόλλων ὁ Διονύσου καὶ Ἴσιδος· ὁ αὐτὸς Ἡρόδοτος·
"Ἀπόλλωνα δὲ καὶ Ἄρτεμιν Διονύσου καὶ Ἴσιδος λέγουσιν εἶναι
παῖδας, Λητὼ δὲ τροφὸν αὐτοῖσ⟨ι καὶ⟩ σώτειραν⁶ γενέσθαι."ᶜ
4. οὓς οὐρανίους γεγονότας πρώτους βασιλέας⁷ ἔσχον, πῆ μὲν
ἀγνοίᾳ τῆς ἀληθοῦς περὶ τὸ θεῖον εὐσεβείας, πῆ δὲ χάριτι τῆς ἀρχῆς
θεοὺς ὁμοῦ ταῖς γυναιξὶν αὐτῶν ἦγον. "τοὺς μέν νυν καθαροὺς βοῦς
τοὺς ἔρσενας καὶ τοὺς μόσχους οἱ πάντες Αἰγύπτιοι θύουσι, τὰς δὲ
θηλείας οὔ σφιν ἔξεστι θύειν, ἀλλὰ ἱραί εἰσι τῆς Ἴσιδος· ⟨τὸ γὰρ τῆς
Ἴσιδος⟩⁸ ἄγαλμα ἐὸν γυναικήιον βούκερών ἐστι, καθάπερ οἱ
Ἕλληνες τὴν Ἰοῦν γράφουσιν".ᵈ 5. τίνες δ' ἂν μᾶλλον ταῦτα
πιστευθεῖεν λέγοντες ἢ οἱ κατὰ διαδοχὴν γένους παῖς παρὰ πατρός,
ὡς τὴν ἱερωσύνην καὶ τὴν ἱστορίαν διαδεχόμενοι;ᵉ οὐ γὰρ τοὺς
σεμνοποιοῦντας ζακόρους τὰ εἴδωλα εἰκὸς ἀνθρώπους αὐτοὺς
γενέσθαι ψεύδεσθαι. 6. εἰ τοίνυν⁹ Ἡρόδοτος ἔλεγεν περὶ τῶν θεῶν
ὡς περὶ ἀνθρώπων ἱστορεῖν Αἰγυπτίους, καὶ λέγοντι τῷ Ἡροδότῳ
"τὰ μέν νυν θεῖα τῶν ἀφηγημάτων, οἷα ἤκουον, οὐκ εἰμὶ πρόθυμος
διηγεῖσθαι, ἔξω ἢ¹⁰ τὰ ὀνόματα αὐτέων μοῦνα"ᶠ ἐλάχιστα μὴ¹¹
πιστεύειν ὡς μυθοποιῷ ἔδει· ἐπεὶ δὲ Ἀλέξανδρος καὶ Ἑρμῆς ὁ
Τρισμέγιστος ἐπικαλούμενος συνάπτων τὸ ἴδιον¹² αὐτοῖς γένος καὶ
ἄλλοι μυρίοι, ἵνα μὴ καθ' ἕκαστον καταλέγοιμι, οὐδὲ λόγος ἔτι
καταλείπεται βασιλεῖς ὄντας αὐτοὺς μὴ νενομίσθαι θεούς. 7. καὶ
ὅτι μὲν ἄνθρωποι, δηλοῦσιν μὲν καὶ Αἰγυπτίων οἱ λογιώτατοι, οἳ
θεοὺς λέγοντες αἰθέρα, γῆν, ἥλιον, σελήνην, τοὺς ἄλλους ἀνθρώπους
θνητοὺς νομίζουσιν καὶ ἱερὰ τοὺς τάφους αὐτῶν· δηλοῖ δὲ καὶ

---

28. ᵃ Herod. 2. 144   ᵇ Cf. ibid. 2. 50   ᶜ Ibid. 2. 156   ᵈ Ibid. 2. 41
ᵉ Cf. ibid. 2. 143   ᶠ Ibid. 2. 3

---

28. ⁵ βασιλεὺς A : corr. Schwartz   ⁶ αὐτοῖς ὄριαν A : αὐτοῖσι καὶ σώτειραν
Herodotus   ⁷ βασιλῆας A   ⁸ τὸ γὰρ τῆς Ἴσιδος (ex Herod.)
add. Schwartz   ⁹ τοίνυν Wilamowitz : τι μὲν A : τι μὲν οὖν A¹   ¹⁰ ἔξω ἢ
Herodotus : ἐξ ὧν A   ¹¹ ἐλάχιστα μὴ A : μὴ seclusit Schwartz : μηδ'
ἐλάχιστα Geffcken   ¹² ἴδιον Schwartz : ἀίδιον A

Later, Horus, the son of Osiris, whom the Greeks name Apollo, reigned over Egypt. He overthrew Typhon and was the last god to reign over Egypt. Osiris is Dionysus in the Greek language.

3. So, then, all were kings of Egypt including the last. From them the names of the gods came to the Greeks. Apollo is the son of Dionysus and Isis. The same Herodotus says: 'They say that Apollo and Artemis are offspring of Dionysus and Isis and that Leto was their nurse and preserver.' 4. These celestials were their first kings; partly out of ignorance of true piety concerning the divine and partly out of thankfulness for their reign they considered them 'gods' together with their wives.

All the Egyptians sacrifice male cattle and calves which are pure; they are not permitted to sacrifice females, for they are sacred to Isis. For the statue of Isis which is in the form of a woman has the horns of a cow, as the Greeks depict Io.

5. When they talk about these things, who should be believed more readily than those who have received in a natural succession from father to son the account of these stories along with the priesthood? For it is not likely that the personnel of the temple who venerate the images are lying when they say that their gods were once men. 6. If, then, Herodotus said that the Egyptians gave an account of their gods as if they were men, one ought hardly to disbelieve Herodotus as an inventor of fiction even though he says: 'I am not willing to relate things concerning the divine in the stories which I have heard; I will mention only their names.' When Alexander and Hermes who is called Trismegistus[2] link their own family with the gods, and others too numerous to mention individually do likewise, there is no longer any reason left to doubt that they were regarded as gods because they were kings. 7. The most learned of the Egyptians show that these were men; for whereas they call ether, earth, sun, and moon gods, they regard all others as mortal men and their tombs as temples. Apollodorus in his book 'Concerning the Gods' shows

---

28. [2] The supposed author of the *Corpus Hermeticum*. This is the earliest reference to this more than shadowy figure.

Ἀπολλόδωρος ἐν τῷ περὶ θεῶν. 8. Ἡρόδοτος δὲ καὶ τὰ παθήματα¹³ αὐτῶν φησι μυστήρια· "ἐν δὲ Βουσίρι πόλει ὡς ἀνάγουσι¹⁴ τῇ Ἴσι τὴν ἑορτήν, εἴρηται πρότερόν μοι. τύπτονται γὰρ δὴ μετὰ τὴν θυσίην πάντες καὶ πᾶσαι, μυριάδες κάρτα πολλαὶ ἀνθρώπων. τὸν δὲ τύπτονται τρόπον, οὔ μοι ὅσιόν ἐστιν λέγειν."ᵍ εἰ θεοί, καὶ ἀθάνατοι, εἰ δὲ τύπτονται καὶ τὰ πάθη ἐστὶν αὐτῶν μυστήρια, ἄνθρωποι. 9. ὁ αὐτὸς Ἡρόδοτος· "εἰσὶ δὲ καὶ αἱ ταφαὶ τοῦ οὐχ ὅσιον ποιοῦμαι ἐπὶ τοιούτῳ πράγματι ἐξαγορεύειν τὸ ὄνομα, ἐν Σάι ἐν τῷ ἱερῷ τῆς Ἀθηναίης, ὄπισθεν τοῦ νηοῦ, παντὸς τῆς Ἀθηναίης ἐχόμενον τοίχου. λίμνη δ᾽ ἐστὶν ἐχομένη λιθίνη κρηπῖδι κεκοσμημένη ἐν κύκλῳ, μέγεθος, ὡς ἐμοὶ δοκέει, ὅση περ ἐν Δήλῳ ἡ τροχοειδὴς καλεομένη. ἐν δὲ τῇ λίμνῃ ταύτῃ τὰ δείκηλα τῶν παθέων αὐτοῦ νυκτὸς ⟨ποιοῦσι τὰ⟩¹⁵ καλέουσι μυστήρια Αἰγύπτιοι".ʰ 10. καὶ οὐ μόνον ὁ τάφος τοῦ Ὀσίριδος δείκνυται, ἀλλὰ καὶ ταριχεία· "ἐπεάν σφισιν κομισθῇ νεκρός, δεικνύασι τοῖσι κομίσασι παραδείγματα νεκρῶν ξύλινα τῇ γραφῇ μεμιμημένα· καὶ τὴν μὲν σπουδαιοτάτην αὐτέων φασὶν εἶναι τοῦ οὐχ ὅσιον ποιοῦμαι οὔνομα ἐπὶ τοιούτῳ πράγματι ὀνομάζειν."ⁱ

29. Ἀλλὰ καὶ Ἑλλήνων οἱ περὶ ποίησιν καὶ ἱστορίαν σοφοὶ περὶ μὲν Ἡρακλέους¹

> σχέτλιος, οὐδὲ θεῶν ὄπιν ᾐδέσατ᾽ οὐδὲ τράπεζαν
> τὴν ἥν οἱ παρέθηκεν· ἔπειτα δὲ πέφνε καὶ αὐτόν,ᵃ

Ἴφιτον. τοιοῦτος ὢν εἰκότως μὲν ἐμαίνετο, εἰκότως δὲ ἀνάψας πυρὰν κατέκαυσεν αὐτόν. 2. περὶ δὲ Ἀσκληπιοῦ Ἡσίοδος μέν· "πατὴρ ἀνδρῶν τε θεῶν τε

> χώσατ᾽,² ἀπ᾽ Οὐλύμπου δὲ βαλὼν ψολόεντι κεραυνῷ
> ἔκτανε Λητοΐδην †φίλον†³ σὺν θυμὸν ὀρίνων.ᵇ

28. ᵍ Herod. 2. 61   ʰ Ibid. 2. 170   ⁱ Ibid. 2. 86
29. ᵃ Homer, Odyssey 21. 28–9   ᵇ Frg. 125 (Razch³)

---

28. ¹³ παθήματα Otto: μαθήματα A   ¹⁴ ἀνάγωσι A   ¹⁵ ποιοῦσι τὰ
(ex Herod.) add. Schwartz
29. ¹ Ἡρακλεὺς A   ² τε θεῶν τε χώσατ᾽ Dechair: δ᾽ ὅτ᾽ ἐχώσατ᾽ A
³ φίλον: Φοίβῳ Wilamowitz

the same thing.³ 8. Herodotus also calls their sufferings mysteries:

> I have already told how they celebrate the festival of Isis in the city of Busiris. All the men and women, numbering many many thousands, beat their breasts after the sacrifice. I would profane their rites were I to say how they beat their breasts.

If they are gods, they are also immortal; if people beat their breasts for them, and their sufferings are mysteries, they are men. 9. The same Herodotus says:

> At Saïd in the temple of Athena, behind the shrine, attached to the whole length of the wall of the temple there is the tomb of one whose name⁴ I consider it profane to utter on such an occasion. And there is a lake nearby, beautified by a stone margin around it. Its size, I think, equals the so-called wheel-shaped lake in Delos. On this lake they enact by night reproductions of his sufferings which the Egyptians call mysteries.

10. Moreover, not only is the burial of Osiris displayed but also his embalming.

> When a body is brought to them, they show to those who have brought it wooden models of bodies made to look like them by painting. And they say that the most perfect method of embalming was used for him whose name I consider it profane to mention on such an occasion.

29. Greek poets and historians who are informed have similar views. They say of Heracles:

> Wretched indeed, who feared not the vengeance of the gods,
> Respected not the table he set before him, but after the meal
> slew him

—that is, Iphitus. It is only natural that such an individual should go mad, only natural that he should light a pyre and burn himself to death. 2. Concerning Asclepius, Hesiod says:

> The Father of men and gods
> Grew wroth and from Olympus cast his lurid bolt,
> Slew Leto's descendant, and so stirred Phoebus to anger.¹

---

28. ³ Produced by the great scholar in the second century B.C. Despite the number of fragments we possess 'it is very difficult to gain a picture as to how Apollodorus described hellenistic religion' (E. Schwartz in *PWK* i [1894], 2873). It was possibly the source (indirectly, according to Geffcken, through a sceptically oriented manual) of materials called upon by Athenagoras in this chapter and elsewhere. ⁴ Osiris.
29. ¹ Phoebus Apollo, son of Leto, was Asclepius' progenitor.

Πίνδαρος δέ

ἀλλὰ κέρδει καὶ σοφία δέδεται.
ἔτραπε κἀκεῖνον ἀγάνορι μισθῷ⁴ χρυσὸς ἐν χερσὶ φανείς.
χερσὶ δ' ἄρα Κρονίων ῥίψας δι' ἀμφοῖν ἀμπνοὰν στέρνων καθεῖλεν
ὠκέως, αἴθων δὲ κεραυνὸς ἐνέσκηψε μόρον.ᶜ

3. ἢ τοίνυν θεοὶ ἦσαν, καὶ οὔτε αὐτοὺς⁵ πρὸς χρυσὸν εἶχον
   ὦ χρυσέ, δεξίωμα⁶ κάλλιστον βροτοῖς,
   ⟨ὡς⟩⁷ οὔτε μήτηρ ἡδονὰς τοιάσδ'⁸ ἔχει,
   οὐ παῖδεςᵈ

(ἀνεπιδεὲς γὰρ καὶ κρεῖττον ἐπιθυμίας τὸ θεῖον) οὔτε ἀπέθνησκον·
ἢ ἄνθρωποι γεγονότες καὶ πονηροὶ δι' ἀμαθίαν ἦσαν καὶ χρημάτων
ἐλάττους. 4. τί ⟨δεῖ⟩⁹ με πολλὰ λέγειν ἢ Κάστορος ἢ Πολυδεύκους
μνημονεύοντα ἢ Ἀμφιάρεω,¹⁰ οἵ, ὡς εἰπεῖν λόγῳ, χθὲς καὶ πρώην
ἄνθρωποι ἐξ ἀνθρώπων γεγονότες θεοὶ νομίζονται, ὁπότε καὶ Ἰνὼ
μετὰ τὴν μανίαν καὶ τὰ ἐπὶ τῆς μανίας πάθη θεὸν δοξάζουσι
γεγονέναι

πόντου πλάνητες Λευκοθέαν ἐπώνυμονᵉ

καὶ τὸν παῖδα αὐτῆς

σεμνὸς Παλαίμων ναυτίλοις κεκλήσεται;ᶠ

30. εἰ γὰρ καὶ ὡς ἀπόπτυστοι καὶ θεοστυγεῖς δόξαν ἔσχον εἶναι
θεοὶ καὶ ἡ θυγάτηρ τῆς Δερκετοῦς Σεμίραμις, λάγνος γυνὴ καὶ μιαι-
φόνος, ἔδοξε Συρία θεὸς καὶ διὰ τὴν Δερκετὼ ⟨τοὺς ἰχθῦς⟩¹ καὶ τὰς
περιστερὰς διὰ² τὴν Σεμίραμιν σέβουσι Σύροι (τὸ γὰρ ἀδύνατον, εἰς
περιστερὰν μετέβαλεν ἡ γυνή· ὁ μῦθος παρὰ Κτησίᾳ),ᵃ τί θαυμαστὸν

---

29. ᶜ Pyth. 3. 54–5, 57–8   ᵈ Euripides, frg. 324. 1–3 (Nauck²)   ᵉ Frg. 100,
adesp. (Nauck²)   ᶠ Frg. 101, adesp. (Nauck²)
30. ᵃ Cf. F. Jacoby, Die Fragmente der griechischen Historiker, III C (Leiden,
1958), 438

---

29. ⁴ ἄγαν ορμισθωι A   ⁵ αὐτοὺς A: αὐτοὶ A¹: ἀνθρωπίνως Wilamowitz:
αὐτοὺς Geffcken   ⁶ δεξίαμα A   ⁷ ὡς (ex Euripid.) add. Stephanus
⁸ τοιάσδε A: τοιάσδ' Geffcken: τοίας Euripides   ⁹ δεῖ add. Gesner
¹⁰ Ἀμφιάρεως A
30. ¹ τοὺς ἰχθῦς (ex Ps.-Luc. de dea Syr. 14 et Diod. 2. 4) add. Schwartz
² διὰ Schwartz: καὶ A

And Pindar says:

> But even wisdom is entangled by desire for gain.
> When gold lay in his hands, it turned him too with hope of
> rich reward.
> Then did the Son of Cronus hurl with both his hands and swiftly
> crushed the breath of life from his breast;
> The flashing thunderbolt brought doom upon him.

3. Either they are gods, then, and neither would they yield to gold—

> Gold! Fairest gift to mortals!
> Such pleasures no mother provides,
> Nor children—

(for the divine needs nothing and is above all desire), nor would they die. Or they are men, and wicked because of their ignorance and incapable of resisting money.

4. What need is there for me to say very much when I remind you of a Castor or Polydeuces or Amphiareus, who, though men born of men, as one might say, only yesterday or the day before, are considered gods? Or when they think that even Ino became a goddess after her madness and the sufferings which attended it, when she is named by

> Wanderers of the sea Leucothea, 'White Goddess'²—

and her son—

> Revered Palaemon will he be called by sailors.

30. If, despite their detestable and hateful character, these became famed as gods, and if the daughter of Derceto, Semiramis, a licentious and murderous woman, was regarded as the Syrian goddess and the Syrians venerate fish on behalf of Derceto and doves on behalf of Semiramis (for the impossible is related that the woman turned into a dove—the myth is found in Ctesias),

---

29. ² Or 'Runner on the White [Foam]'. At the end of her desperate career she jumped from a cliff into the sea. Dionysus (or Aphrodite) transformed her into a goddess of the sea (Rose, *Handbook*, p. 151).

τοὺς μὲν ἐπὶ ἀρχῇ καὶ τυραννίδι ὑπὸ τῶν κατ' αὐτοὺς κληθῆναι
θεούς — Σίβυλλα (μέμηνται δ' αὐτῆς καὶ Πλάτων)·

> δὴ τότε δὴ δεκάτη γενεὴ μερόπων ἀνθρώπων,
> ἐξ οὗ δὴ κατακλυσμὸς ἐπὶ προτέρους γένετ' ἄνδρας,
> καὶ βασίλευσε[3] Κρόνος καὶ Τιτὰν Ἰαπετός τε,
> Γαίης τέκνα φέριστα καὶ Οὐρανοῦ, οὓς[4] ἐκάλεσσαν[5]
> ἄνθρωποι Γαῖάν τε καὶ Οὐρανὸν οὔνομα θέντες,
> οὔνεκα οἱ πρώτιστοι ἔσαν μερόπων ἀνθρώπων[b] —

τοὺς δ' ἐπ' ἰσχύι, ὡς Ἡρακλέα καὶ Περσέα, τοὺς δ' ἐπὶ τέχνῃ, ὡς
Ἀσκληπιόν; 2. οἷς μὲν οὖν ἢ αὐτοὶ[6] οἱ ἀρχόμενοι τιμῆς μετε-
δίδοσαν ἢ αὐτοὶ οἱ ἄρχοντες, οἱ μὲν φόβῳ, οἱ δὲ καὶ αἰδοῖ μετεῖχον
τοῦ ὀνόματος (καὶ Ἀντίνους φιλανθρωπίᾳ τῶν ὑμετέρων προγόνων
πρὸς τοὺς ὑπηκόους ἔτυχε νομίζεσθαι θεός)· οἱ δὲ μετ' αὐτοὺς
ἀβασανίστως παρεδέξαντο.

> Κρῆτες ἀεὶ ψεῦσται· καὶ γὰρ τάφον, ὦ ἄνα, σεῖο
> Κρῆτες ἐτεκτήναντο· σὺ δ' οὐ θάνες.[c]

πιστεύων, Καλλίμαχε, ταῖς γοναῖς τοῦ Διὸς ἀπιστεῖς αὐτοῦ τῷ
τάφῳ καὶ νομίζων ἐπισκιάσειν τἀληθὲς καὶ τοῖς ἀγνοοῦσι κηρύσσεις
τὸν τεθνηκότα κἂν μὲν τὸ ἄντρον[7] βλέπῃς, τὸν Ῥέας ὑπομιμνήσκῃ
τόκον, ἂν δὲ τὴν σορὸν ἴδῃς, ἐπισκοτεῖς τῷ τεθνηκότι, οὐκ εἰδὼς
ὅτι μόνος ἀίδιος ὁ ἀγένητος[8] θεός. 4. ἢ γὰρ ἄπιστοι οἱ ὑπὸ τῶν
πολλῶν καὶ ποιητῶν λεγόμενοι μῦθοι περὶ τῶν θεῶν καὶ περισσὴ ἡ
περὶ αὐτοὺς εὐσέβεια (οὐ γὰρ εἰσὶν ὧν ψευδεῖς οἱ λόγοι), ἢ εἰ
ἀληθεῖς αἱ γενήσεις, οἱ ἔρωτες,[9] αἱ μιαιφονίαι, αἱ κλοπαί, αἱ
ἐκτομαί, οἱ κεραυνοί, οὐκέτ' εἰσίν, παυσάμενοι εἶναι, ἐπεὶ καὶ
ἐγένοντο οὐκ ὄντες. 5. τίς γὰρ τοῖς μὲν πιστεύειν λόγος, τοῖς δὲ
ἀπιστεῖν, ἐπὶ τὸ σεμνότερον περὶ αὐτῶν τῶν ποιητῶν ἱστορηκότων;

---

30. [b] Orac. Sibyll. 3. 108–13   [c] Callimachus, *Hymn. in Iov.* 8–9

---

30. [3] βασιλεύς A   [4] Οὐρανοῦ οὓς Maranus: Οὐρανοὺς A   [5] ἐκά-
λεσεν A   [6] αὐτοὶ ante οἱ ἀρχόμενοι del. Schwartz, Geffcken   [7] ἄντρον
p corr.: ἄντλον A   [8] ἀγέννητος A   [9] ἔρωντες A: corr. p m. rec.

what wonder is it that those exercising a despotic rule were called
gods by their contemporaries? As the Sibyl, whom Plato also
mentions, says:

Then was the tenth generation of mortal men
Since the time the flood had come upon men of old.
And Cronus and Titan and Iapetus ruled,
Mighty offspring of earth and heaven, whom men called
'Earth' and 'Heaven' when they gave them names,
Since they were the first of mortal men.[1]

Some were called gods because of their strength, such as Heracles
and Perseus; others because of their skill, such as Asclepius.
    2. Either their subjects honoured them as gods of their own
accord or the rulers themselves—some out of fear, others out
of a genuine sense of reverence—obtained the title (thus even
Antinous[2] had the good fortune to be thought a god because of
the humane affection shown by your ancestors to their subjects).
But those who came after them accepted the claim without further
examination.

    3. The Cretans are ever liars! For thy tomb, O King,
    Have the Cretans contrived; and yet have you not died!

Although you believe, Callimachus, in the birth of Zeus, you do
not believe in his tomb. Although you think that you will obscure
the truth, you proclaim him even to the ignorant as one who has
died. Thus if you look upon his cave, you call to mind his birth
from Rhea; but if you view his tomb, you cast a shadow over the
one who has died. You do not know that the uncreated God is
alone eternal. 4. For either the popular myths about the gods
recounted by poets are untrustworthy and the piety shown the
gods useless (for they do not exist if the stories about them are
false), or if these births, loves, murders, thefts, castrations, and
thunderbolts are true, then they no longer exist, they have ceased
to be, since from non-existence they came into being.
    5. What reason is there to believe some stories and not to
believe others, seeing that the poets have given such lofty accounts
of them? For these men who caused the gods to be acknowledged

---

30. [1] The 'Sibylline Oracles' contain many Jewish and Christian inter-
polations. Geffcken, however, considers this passage to be of pagan origin (cf.
Lactantius, *Div. Inst.* 1. 14).
    [2] A favourite of Hadrian in whose honour the latter erected a temple in
Mantinea and founded the city of Antinoöpolis in Egypt. Athenagoras' treat-
ment of the matter is in striking contrast to the virulence of the attack of Justin
(*Ap.* 1. 29. 4) and other apologists.

οὐ γὰρ ἂν δι' οὓς ἐνομίσθησαν θεοὶ σεμνοποιήσαντας τὴν κατ'
αὐτοὺς ἱστορίαν, οὗτοι τὰ πάθη τὰ αὐτῶν ἐψεύσαντο.

6. Ὡς μὲν οὖν οὐκ ἐσμὲν ἄθεοι θεὸν ἄγοντες τὸν ποιητὴν τοῦδε
τοῦ παντὸς καὶ τὸν παρ' αὐτοῦ λόγον, κατὰ δύναμιν τὴν ἐμήν, εἰ
καὶ μὴ πρὸς ἀξίαν, ἐλήλεγκται.

31. Ἔτι δὲ καὶ τροφὰς καὶ μίξεις λογοποιοῦσιν ἀθέους καθ'
ἡμῶν, ἵνα τε μισεῖν νομίζοιεν μετὰ λόγου καὶ οἰόμενοι τῷ δεδίτ-
τεσθαι ἢ τῆς ἐνστάσεως ἀπάξειν ἡμᾶς τοῦ βίου ἢ πικροὺς καὶ
ἀπαραιτήτους τῇ τῶν αἰτιῶν ὑπερβολῇ τοὺς ἄρχοντας παρασκευά-
σειν, πρὸς εἰδότας παίζοντες, ὅτι ἄνωθέν πως ἔθος καὶ οὐκ ἐφ'
ἡμῶν μόνον κατά τινα θεῖον νόμον καὶ λόγον παρηκολούθηκε
προσπολεμεῖν τὴν κακίαν τῇ ἀρετῇ. 2. οὕτω καὶ Πυθαγόρας
μὲν ἅμα τριακοσίοις ἑταίροις κατεφλέχθη πυρί, Ἡράκλειτος δὲ
καὶ Δημόκριτος, ὁ μὲν τῆς Ἐφεσίων πόλεως ἠλαύνετο, ὁ δὲ τῆς
Ἀβδηριτῶν ἐπικατηγορούμενος μεμηνέναι, καὶ Σωκράτους Ἀθηναῖοι
θάνατον κατέγνωσαν. ἀλλ' ὡς ἐκεῖνοι οὐδὲν χείρους εἰς ἀρετῆς
λόγον διὰ τὴν τῶν πολλῶν δόξαν, οὐδ' ἡμῖν οὐδὲν ἐπισκοτεῖ πρὸς
ὀρθότητα βίου ἡ παρά τινων ἄκριτος βλασφημία· εὐδοξοῦμεν γὰρ
παρὰ τῷ θεῷ. πλὴν ἀλλὰ καὶ πρὸς ταῦτα ἀπαντήσω τὰ ἐγκλήματα.
3. ὑμῖν[1] μὲν οὖν καὶ δι' ὧν εἴρηκα εὖ οἶδα ἀπολελογῆσθαι ἐμαυτόν.
συνέσει γὰρ πάντας ὑπερφρονοῦντες, οἷς ὁ βίος ὡς πρὸς στάθμην
τὸν θεὸν κανονίζεται, ὅπως ἀνυπαίτιος καὶ ἀνεπίληπτος ἕκαστος
ἡμῶν ἄνθρωπος[2] αὐτῷ γένοιτο,[3] ἴστε τούτους μηδ' εἰς ἔννοιάν ποτε
τοῦ βραχυτάτου ἐλευσομένους ἁμαρτήματος. 4. εἰ μὲν γὰρ ἕνα
τὸν ἐνταῦθα βίον βιώσεσθαι ἐπεπείσμεθα,[4] κἂν ὑποπτεύειν ἐνῆν
δουλεύοντας σαρκὶ καὶ αἵματι ἢ κέρδους ἢ ἐπιθυμίας ἐλάττους
γενομένους ἁμαρτεῖν· ἐπεὶ δὲ ἐφεστηκέναι μὲν οἷς ἐννοοῦμεν, οἷς
λαλοῦμεν καὶ νύκτωρ καὶ μεθ' ἡμέραν τὸν θεὸν οἴδαμεν, πάντα δὲ
φῶς αὐτὸν ὄντα καὶ τὰ ἐν τῇ καρδίᾳ ἡμῶν ὁρᾶν, πεπείσμεθα ⟨δὲ⟩[5]
τοῦ ἐνταῦθα ἀπαλλαγέντες βίου βίον ἕτερον βιώσεσθαι ἀμείνονα ἢ
κατὰ τὸν ἐνθάδε καὶ ἐπουράνιον, οὐκ ἐπίγειον, ὡς ἂν μετὰ θεοῦ καὶ
σὺν θεῷ ἀκλινεῖς καὶ ἀπαθεῖς τὴν ψυχὴν οὐχ ὡς σάρκες κἂν ἔχωμεν,

31. [1] ὑμεῖς Α: corr. Stephanus   [2] ἕκαστος ἡμῶν ἄνθρωπος Gesner : ἑκάστου
ἡμῶν ἀ͞ν͞ο͞ς Α   [3] γένοιτε Α: corr. p   [4] πεπείσμεθα Α: corr. Schwartz
[5] δὲ add. Wilamowitz

by the lofty treatment of the stories about them would not have
lied about their weaknesses and afflictions.

6. Proof has now been offered to show to the best of my
ability, if not as it deserves, that we are not atheists when we
recognize the Maker of the universe and the Word proceeding
from him as God.

31. They go on to charge us, however, with godless banquets
and sexual unions. They do so that they may believe their hatred
reasonable, and because they think that by frightening people
they can draw us away from the strictness of our way of life or
make our rulers harsh and unyielding with their fantastic charges.
They are wasting their time with men who know that from time
immemorial, and not only in our own day, evil has habitually
opposed virtue by some divine law or principle. 2. That is why
Pythagoras, too, with three hundred companions was burned to
death; Heraclitus and Democritus were driven out, the one from
the city of Ephesus, the other, accused of being mad, from the
city of Abdera; and the Athenians condemned Socrates to death.
But just as they were no worse in the scale of virtue because of
the opinion of the crowd, neither does the indiscriminate slander
of a few cast any shadow upon the uprightness of our life. For we
have our good reputation with God. Still I shall also meet these
complaints.

3. I am well aware that as far as you are concerned I have
made my case by what I have already said. For you, whose
wisdom is greater than that of all others, know that men whose
life is regulated, so to speak, by God as their measure, so that each
one of us may be blameless and faultless before him, have no
intention of doing the least wrong. 4. If we were persuaded that
our life here below was the only one we would live, there would
be reason to suspect us of wrong-doing in serving flesh and blood
and yielding to the temptations of gain or lust. But since we are
aware that God knows what we think and say both night and day
and that he who is totally light sees also what is in our hearts; and
since we are persuaded that when we depart this present life we
shall live another life better than that here, a heavenly one, not
earthly, so that we may then abide with God and with his help
remain changeless and impassible in soul as though we were not
body, even if we have one, but heavenly spirit; and, alternatively,

ἀλλ' ὡς οὐράνιον πνεῦμα μένωμεν,⁶ ἢ συγκαταπίπτοντες τοῖς
λοιποῖς χείρονα καὶ διὰ πυρὸς (οὐ γὰρ καὶ ἡμᾶς ὡς πρόβατα ἢ
ὑποζύγια, πάρεργον καὶ ἵνα ἀπολοίμεθα καὶ ἀφανισθείημεν, ἔπλασεν
ὁ θεός), ἐπὶ τούτοις οὐκ εἰκὸς ἡμᾶς ἐθελοκακεῖν οὐδ' αὐτοὺς τῷ
μεγάλῳ παραδιδόναι κολασθησομένους δικαστῇ.

32. Τοὺς μὲν οὖν θαυμαστὸν οὐδὲν λογοποιεῖν περὶ ἡμῶν ἃ περὶ τῶν
σφετέρων λέγουσι θεῶν (καὶ ⟨γὰρ⟩¹ τὰ πάθη αὐτῶν δεικνύουσι
μυστήρια· χρῆν δ' αὐτούς, εἰ δεινὸν τὸ ἐπ' ἀδείας καὶ ἀδιαφόρως
μίγνυσθαι κρίνειν ἔμελλον, ἢ τὸν Δία μεμισηκέναι, ἐκ μητρὸς μὲν
'Ρέας θυγατρὸς δὲ Κόρης πεπαιδοποιημένον, γυναικὶ δὲ τῇ ἰδίᾳ
ἀδελφῇ² χρώμενον, ἢ τὸν τούτων ποιητὴν 'Ορφέα, ὅτι καὶ ἀνόσιον
ὑπὲρ τὸν Θυέστην καὶ μιαρὸν ἐποίησεν τὸν Δία· καὶ γὰρ οὗτος τῇ
θυγατρὶ κατὰ χρησμὸν ἐμίγη, βασιλεῦσαι θέλων καὶ [Θυέστης]³
ἐκδικηθῆναι)· 2. ἡμεῖς δὲ τοσοῦτον ⟨τοῦ⟩⁴ ἀδιάφοροι⁵ εἶναι
ἀπέχομεν, ὡς μηδὲ ἰδεῖν ἡμῖν πρὸς ἐπιθυμίαν ἐξεῖναι. "ὃ" γὰρ
"βλέπων", φησί, "γυναῖκα πρὸς τὸ ἐπιθυμῆσαι αὐτῆς ἤδη μεμοί-
χευκεν ἐν τῇ καρδίᾳ αὐτοῦ".ᵃ 3. οἷς οὖν μηδὲν πλέον ἔξεστιν
ὁρᾶν ἢ ἐφ' ἃ ἔπλασεν τοὺς ὀφθαλμοὺς ὁ θεός, ἡμῖν φῶς αὐτοὺς
εἶναι, καὶ οἷς τὸ ἰδεῖν ἡδέως μοιχεία, ἐφ' ἕτερα τῶν ὀφθαλμῶν
γεγονότων, μέχρις ἐννοίας κριθησομένοις, πῶς ἂν οὗτοι ἀπιστη-
θεῖεν σωφρονεῖν; 4. οὐ γὰρ πρὸς ἀνθρωπικοὺς νόμους ὁ λόγος
ἡμῖν, οὓς ἄν τις γενόμενος πονηρὸς καὶ λάθοι (ἐν ἀρχῇ δὲ ὑμῖν,
δεσπόται,⁶ θεοδίδακτον εἶναι τὸν καθ' ἡμᾶς λόγον ἐπιστούμην),
ἀλλ' ἔστιν ἡμῖν νόμος⁷ * * * ἢ δικαιοσύνης μέτρον ἐποίησεν
αὐτοὺς καὶ τοὺς πέλας ἔχειν.ᵇ 5. διὰ τοῦτο καὶ καθ' ἡλικίαν τοὺς
μὲν υἱοὺς καὶ θυγατέρας νοοῦμεν, τοὺς δὲ ἀδελφοὺς ἔχομεν καὶ
ἀδελφὰς καὶ τοῖς προβεβηκόσι τὴν τῶν πατέρων καὶ μητέρων
τιμὴν ἀπονέμομεν. οὓς οὖν ἀδελφοὺς καὶ ἀδελφὰς καὶ τὰ λοιπὰ τοῦ

32. ᵃ Matt. 5: 28   ᵇ Cf. Matt. 7: 12, 22: 39

31. ⁶ μενοῦμεν A: corr. Schwartz
32. ¹ γὰρ add. Wilamowitz   ² γυναικι διαδελφῆ (ῇ A¹) A: corr. Schwartz
³ Θυέστης seclusit Dechair   ⁴ post τοσοῦτον add. τοῦ περὶ τὰς μίξεις
Wilamowitz: τοῦ add. Ubaldi   ⁵ ἀδιάφοροι A¹: διάφοροι A   ⁶ δεσπότης
A: δεσπόται Gesner: seclusit Schwartz   ⁷ post νόμος lacunam indicavit
Schwartz: καὶ ἐντολὴ add. Bardy

since we are convinced that, if we fall with the rest of men, we shall live another life worse than that here in realms of fire (for God did not create us like sheep or beasts of burden, and it would not be incidental if we were to be destroyed and disappear); since all this is so, it is not likely that we should want to do evil and deliver ourselves up to the great Judge to be punished.

32. It is not at all remarkable that they fabricate stories about us such as they tell of their own gods. They present the sufferings of their deities as mysteries; but if they are about to condemn promiscuous and licentious unions, then they ought to hate either Zeus, who begot children by his mother Rhea and his daughter Core[1] and had his own sister to wife, or Orpheus, the creator of these stories, because he made Zeus even more irreligious and abominable than Thyestes. For it was in fulfilment of an oracle that the latter had intercourse with his daughter, because he wanted to gain a kingdom and be avenged.[2]

2. But we are so far from promiscuity that it is not even permissible for us to look with lust: for 'he who looks at a woman to lust after her', it says, 'has already committed adultery in his heart.' 3. What doubt could there be of the chastity of such men? They are not permitted to look at anything other than that for which God has created the eyes, so that these may be a light for us. For them to look with pleasure is adultery since the eyes were created for other purposes; and they will be judged for nothing more tangible than a thought!

4. For our teaching is not set forth with a view to human laws whose surveillance an evil man may well escape. At the beginning I assured you, my masters, that our doctrine is taught by God.[3] We have a law, then, . . . which prompts us to consider ourselves and our neighbours the measure for justice. 5. For this reason we regard some, depending on their age, as our sons and daughters, others we consider our brothers and sisters, and to those advanced in years we give the honour due to fathers and mothers. But we are profoundly concerned that the bodies of

---

32. [1] Cf. 20. 3.

[2] The point of this statement depends on the following information: Thyestes had seduced and intrigued with the wife of his elder brother Atreus and was banished by the latter. Atreus afterwards pretended reconciliation and set before Thyestes the famous banquet in which Thyestes' own sons were served up. 'But when Thyestes after learning of the villainy sought revenge, Apollo replied that it was possible for an avenger of this villainy to be born through another crime—that is, if he would sleep with his daughter Pelopia' (Servius, *Comm. in Aen.* 11. 262). The offspring was Aegisthus, who carried on the feud.

[3] Cf. 11. 1.

γένους νοοῦμεν ὀνόματα, περὶ πολλοῦ ἡμῖν ἀνύβριστα καὶ ἀδιάφθορα
αὐτῶν τὰ σώματα μένειν, πάλιν ἡμῖν λέγοντος τοῦ λόγου· "ἐάν
τις διὰ τοῦτο ἐκ δευτέρου καταφιλήσῃ, ὅτι ἤρεσεν αὐτῷ" καὶ
ἐπιφέροντος⁸ οὕτως οὖν ἀκριβώσασθαι τὸ φίλημα μᾶλλον δὲ τὸ
προσκύνημα δεῖ, ὡς, εἴ που μικρὸν τῇ διανοίᾳ παραθολωθείη, ἔξω
ἡμᾶς τῆς αἰωνίου τιθέντος ζωῆς.⁹

33. Ἐλπίδα οὖν ζωῆς αἰωνίου ἔχοντες, τῶν ἐν τούτῳ τῷ βίῳ
καταφρονοῦμεν μέχρι καὶ τῶν τῆς ψυχῆς ἡδέων, γυναῖκα μὲν
ἕκαστος ἡμῶν ἣν ἠγάγετο κατὰ τοὺς ὑφ' ἡμῶν τεθειμένους νόμους
νομίζων καὶ ταύτην μέχρι τοῦ παιδοποιήσασθαι. 2. ὡς γὰρ ὁ
γεωργὸς καταβαλὼν εἰς γῆν τὰ σπέρματα ἄμητον περιμένει οὐκ
ἐπισπείρων, καὶ ἡμῖν μέτρον ἐπιθυμίας ἡ παιδοποιία. εὕροις δ' ἂν
πολλοὺς τῶν παρ' ἡμῖν καὶ ἄνδρας καὶ γυναῖκας καταγηράσκοντας
ἀγάμους ἐλπίδι τοῦ μᾶλλον συνέσεσθαι τῷ θεῷ. 3. εἰ δὲ τὸ ἐν
παρθενίᾳ καὶ ἐν εὐνουχίᾳ μεῖναι μᾶλλον παρίστησι τῷ θεῷ, τὸ
δὲ μέχρις ἐννοίας καὶ ἐπιθυμίας ἐλθεῖν ἀπάγει, ὧν τὰς ἐννοίας
φεύγομεν, πολὺ πρότερον τὰ ἔργα παραιτούμεθα. 4. οὐ γὰρ ⟨ἐν⟩
μελέτῃ¹ λόγων ἀλλ' ἐπιδείξει καὶ διδασκαλίᾳ ἔργων τὰ ἡμέτερα² ἢ
οἷός τις ἐτέχθη μένειν ἢ ἐφ' ἑνὶ γάμῳ· ὁ γὰρ δεύτερος εὐπρεπής ἐστι
μοιχεία.³ 5. "ὃς" γὰρ "ἂν ἀπολύσῃ", φησί, "τὴν γυναῖκα αὐτοῦ
καὶ γαμήσῃ ἄλλην, μοιχᾶται",ᵃ οὔτε ἀπολύειν ἐπιτρέπων ἧς ἔπαυσέ
τις τὴν παρθενίαν οὔτε ἐπιγαμεῖν. 6. ὁ γὰρ ἀποστερῶν ἑαυτὸν τῆς
προτέρας γυναικός, καὶ εἰ τέθνηκεν, μοιχός ἐστιν παρακεκαλυμ-
μένος, παραβαίνων μὲν τὴν χεῖρα τοῦ θεοῦ, ὅτι ἐν ἀρχῇ ὁ θεὸς ἕνα
ἄνδρα ἔπλασεν καὶ μίαν γυναῖκα, λύων δὲ τὴν †σάρκα πρὸς σάρκα
κατὰ τὴν ἕνωσιν πρὸς μῖξιν τοῦ γένους κοινωνίαν.†

34. Ἀλλ' οἱ¹ τοιοῦτοι (ὦ, τί² ἂν εἴποιμι τὰ ἀπόρρητα;) ἀκούομεν

---

33. ᵃ Matt. 19: 9, Mark 10: 11

32. ⁸ post ἤρεσεν αὐτῷ lacunam indicavit Otto: post ἐπιφέροντος lacunam
indicavit Schwartz   ⁹ ζωῆς add. A¹
33. ¹ ἐν μελέτῃ Gesner: μελέτη A   ² post τὰ ἡμέτερα lacunam indicavit
Schwartz   ³ μοιχείαι A
34. ¹ ἀλλ' οἱ A¹: ἄλλου A   ² ὦ, τί A¹: ὅτι A: καὶ τί Wilamowitz

those whom we consider brothers and sisters and who are known
by all the other terms applied to kin remain inviolate and un-
sullied. Again our teaching has it: 'If anyone kisses twice because
it was pleasurable, . . .', and it adds: 'So then one must be
scrupulous about the kiss, or more precisely, the reverential
greeting', since it places us outside eternal life if our thoughts are
the least bit stirred by it.[4]

33. Since we hope for eternal life, we despise the things of this
life, including even the pleasures of the soul. Thus each of us
thinks of his wife, whom he married according to the laws that
we have laid down, with a view to nothing more than procreation.[1] 2. For as the farmer casts seed into the ground and
awaits the harvest without further planting, so also procreation
is the limit that we set for the indulgence of our lust. You could
find many among us, both men and women, growing old un-
married in the hope of being united more closely with God.

3. If to remain a virgin and abstain from sexual intercourse
brings us closer to God, and if to allow ourselves nothing more
tangible than a lustful thought leads us away from God, then,
since we flee the thought, much more will we refuse to commit the
deed. 4. We are not concerned with the exercise of eloquence
but with the performance and teaching of deeds—either to stay
in the state in which a man was born or to remain satisfied with
one marriage; for a second marriage is gilded adultery. 5. For
'whoever divorces his wife', it says, 'and marries another, com-
mits adultery.' Neither does it allow a man to divorce a woman
whose maidenhead he has taken, nor does it allow him to marry
again. 6. For he who detaches himself from his previous wife,
even if she has died, is a covert adulterer. He thwarts the hand of
God (because in the beginning God formed one man and one
woman), and he destroys the communion of flesh with flesh in
the unity characteristic of the intercourse of the sexes.[2]

34. Since we are so oriented (indeed how can I even recount
such abominations?),[1] there rings in our ears the words of the

32. 4 It is uncertain as to how much of this is the 'teaching' and how much
Athenagoras' commentary on it. Some editors place the lacuna after 'and it
adds'.
33. 1 In its origin a Stoic teaching and a corollary of Stoic opposition to
the arch-vice 'pleasure' (see *C. Musonii Rufi Reliquiae*, ed. O. Hense [Leipzig,
Teubner, 1905], pp. 63–81; cf. Justin, *Ap.* 1. 29. 1).
2 This is at best an approximation of the last clause, the text of which is
corrupt.
34. 1 See Euripides, *Orestes* 14, where a similar expression occurs alluding to

τὰ τῆς παροιμίας "ἡ πόρνη τὴν σώφρονα". 2. οἱ γὰρ ἀγορὰν
στήσαντες πορνείας καὶ καταγωγὰς ἀθέσμους πεποιημένοι τοῖς
νέοις πάσης αἰσχρᾶς ἡδονῆς καὶ μηδὲ τῶν ἀρσένων φειδόμενοι,
ἄρσενες ἐν ἄρσεσι τὰ δεινὰ κατεργαζόμενοι,ᵃ ὅσων σεμνότερα καὶ
εὐειδέστερα σώματα, παντοίως αὐτὰ ὑβρίζοντες, ἀτιμοῦντες καὶ τὸ
ποιητὸν τοῦ θεοῦ καλόν (οὐ γὰρ αὐτοποίητον ἐπὶ γῆς τὸ κάλλος,
ἀλλὰ ὑπὸ χειρὸς καὶ γνώμης πεμπόμενον τοῦ θεοῦ), οὗτοι δὲ³ ἃ
συνίσασιν αὐτοῖς καὶ τοὺς σφετέρους λέγουσι θεούς, ἐπ' αὐτῶν
ὡς σεμνὰ καὶ τῶν θεῶν ἄξια⁴ αὐχοῦντες, ταῦτα ἡμᾶς λοιδοροῦνται,
3. κακίζοντες οἱ μοιχοὶ καὶ παιδερασταὶ τοὺς εὐνούχους καὶ μονο-
γάμους, οἱ δίκην ἰχθύωνᵇ ζῶντες (καὶ γὰρ οὗτοι καταπίνουσι τὸν
ἐμπεσόντα, ἐλαύνοντες ὁ ἰσχυρότερος τὸν ἀσθενέστερον, καὶ τοῦτό
ἐστι σαρκῶν ἅπτεσθαι ἀνθρωπικῶν, τὸ κειμένων νόμων, οὓς ὑμεῖς
καὶ οἱ ὑμέτεροι πρόγονοι πρὸς πᾶσαν δικαιοσύνην ἐξετάσαντες
ἐθήκατε, παρὰ τούτους αὐτοὺς⁵ βιάζεσθαι, ὡς μηδὲ τοὺς ὑφ' ὑμῶν
καταπεμπομένους ἡγεμόνας τῶν ἐθνῶν ἐξαρκεῖν ταῖς δίκαις)⁶ οἷς
οὐδὲ παιομένοις μὴ παρέχειν ἑαυτοὺς οὐδὲ κακῶς ἀκούουσιν μὴ
εὐλογεῖν ἔξεστιν· οὐ γὰρ ἀπαρκεῖ δίκαιον εἶναι (ἔστι δὲ δικαιοσύνη
ἴσα ἴσοις ἀμείβειν), ἀλλ' ἀγαθοῖς καὶ ἀνεξικάκοις εἶναι πρόκειται.

35. Τίς ἂν οὖν¹ εὖ φρονῶν εἴποι τοιούτους ὄντας ἡμᾶς ἀνδρο-
φόνους εἶναι; οὐ γὰρ ἔστι πάσασθαι κρεῶν ἀνθρωπικῶν μὴ πρότερον ἀποκτείνασί τινα. 2. τὸ πρότερον οὖν ψευδόμενοι² . . . τὸ
δεύτερον, κἂν μέν τις αὐτοὺς ἔρηται,³ εἰ ἑωράκασιν ἃ λέγουσιν,
οὐδείς ἐστιν οὕτως ἀπηρυθριασμένος ὡς εἰπεῖν ἰδεῖν. 3. καίτοι καὶ
δοῦλοί εἰσιν ἡμῖν, τοῖς μὲν καί πλείους τοῖς δὲ ἐλάττους, οὓς⁴ οὐκ
ἔστι λαθεῖν· ἀλλὰ καὶ τούτων οὐδεὶς καθ' ἡμῶν τὰ τηλικαῦτα οὐδὲ

---

34. ᵃ Cf. Rom. 1: 27   ᵇ Cf. Hesiod, Op. 276–8

34. ³ οὗτοι δὲ: δὲ seclusit Schwartz   ⁴ ἄξια Schwartz: αὐτὰ A
⁵ τούτοις αὐτοὺς A: corr. A¹   ⁶ parenthesin indicavit Wilamowitz
35. ¹ ἂν οὖν Schwartz: αν A: οὖν A¹   ² post ψευδόμενοι lacunam indicavit
Gesner   ³ εἴρηται A: corr. A¹   ⁴ οὓς A¹: οἷς A

proverb, 'The harlot presumes to teach her who is chaste!'[2]
2. For it is they who have made a business of harlotry and have
established immoral houses of every base pleasure for the young.
Nor have they neglected male prostitution. Men work their
frightful deeds with men; they violate in every way those whose
bodies are especially noble or comely; thus they dishonour even
the beauty created by God (for there is no self-made beauty on
earth; it comes from the hand and mind of God). They, of all
people, revile us for vices which they have on their own consciences
and which they attribute to their own gods, boasting of them as
noble deeds and worthy of the gods.

3. These adulterers and pederasts reproach men who abstain
from intercourse or are satisfied with a single marriage, whereas
they themselves live like fish. For they swallow up whoever comes
their way, the stronger driving out the weaker. And this is what
it really means to feed on human flesh: that when laws have been
established which you and your ancestors promulgated to further
every form of justice, they violate these very ordinances so that
the governors of the provinces which you have sent out cannot
even handle all the lawsuits. Yet it is they who reproach us
though we are not even premitted to draw back when struck nor
to refuse to bless when ill spoken of; for it is not enough to be just
(justice is to return measure for measure); but it is required of us
to be good and long-suffering.

35. What reasonable person, then, could say that we who are
so oriented are murderers? It is impossible to devour human
flesh without having previously killed someone! 2. First, then,
they lie; second, if someone asks them whether they have seen
what they report, none has the hardihood to say that they have.
3. Further, we have slaves, some many, some few, and it is impossible to escape their observation. Yet not one of them has ever
told such monstrous lies about us.[1]

the story of Atreus and Thyestes. There it reflects the speaker's unhappiness in
recalling the terrible deeds associated with their names. 'Such abominations',
then, probably refer to both illicit sexual practices and cannibalism (cf. 32. 1).
The Christian has difficulty even recounting such deeds; but pagans, as the
sequel shows, are guilty both of perverse sexual practices and a sort of cannibalism. Hence the proverb.

34. [2] The proverb in form and content is much like the famous *sus Minervam*.
The inferior ignorantly and impudently take it upon themselves to instruct
the superior—that is, pagan pimps with gods to match (see the next lines) cry
out against non-existent Christian licentiousness.

35. [1] The contrary is indicated by Justin (*Ap.* 2. 12. 4).

κατεψεύσατο. 4. οὓς γὰρ ἴσασιν οὐδ' ἰδεῖν κἂν δικαίως φονευόμενον ὑπομένοντας, τούτων τίς ἂν κατείποι ἢ ἀνδροφονίαν ἢ
ἀνθρωποβορίαν; τίς †οὐχ ἡ τῶν περὶ σπουδῆς†⁵ τὰς δι' ὅπλων
ἀγωνίας καὶ διὰ θηρίων καὶ μάλιστα τὰς ὑφ' ὑμῶν ἀγομένας
ἔχει; 5. ἀλλ' ἡμεῖς πλησίον εἶναι τὸ ἰδεῖν [τὸ]⁶ φονευόμενον τοῦ⁷
ἀποκτεῖναι νομίζοντες, ἀπηγορεύσαμεν τὰς τοιαύτας θέας. πῶς οὖν
οἱ μηδὲ ὁρῶντες ἵνα μὴ ἑαυτοῖς ἄγος καὶ μίασμα προστριψαίμεθα,
φονεύειν δυνάμεθα; 6. καὶ οἱ τὰς τοῖς ἀμβλωθριδίοις χρωμένας
ἀνδροφονεῖν τε καὶ λόγον ὑφέξειν τῆς ἐξαμβλώσεως τῷ θεῷ φαμεν,
κατὰ ποῖον ἀνδροφονοῦμεν λόγον; οὐ γὰρ τοῦ αὐτοῦ νομίζειν μὲν⁸
καὶ τὸ κατὰ γαστρὸς ζῷον εἶναι καὶ διὰ τοῦτο αὐτοῦ μέλειν τῷ θεῷ,
καὶ παρεληλυθότα⁹ εἰς τὸν βίον φονεύειν, καὶ μὴ ἐκτιθέναι μὲν τὸ
γεννηθέν, ὡς τῶν ἐκτιθέντων τεκνοκτονούντων, πάλιν δὲ τὸ τραφὲν
ἀναιρεῖν· ἀλλ' ἐσμὲν πάντα πανταχοῦ ὅμοιοι καὶ ἴσοι, δουλεύοντες
τῷ λόγῳ καὶ οὐ κρατοῦντες¹⁰ αὐτοῦ.

36. Τίς ἂν οὖν ἀνάστασιν πεπιστευκὼς [ἐπὶ]¹ σώμασιν ἀναστη-
σομένοις ἑαυτὸν παράσχοι τάφον; οὐ γὰρ τῶν αὐτῶν καὶ ἀνα-
στήσεσθαι ἡμῶν πεπεῖσθαι τὰ σώματα καὶ ἐσθίειν αὐτὰ ὡς οὐκ
ἀναστησόμενα, καὶ ἀποδώσειν μὲν νομίζειν τὴν γῆν τοὺς ἰδίους
νεκρούς, οὓς δέ τις αὐτὸς ἐγκατέθαψεν αὐτῷ, μὴ² ἀπαιτήσεσθαι.³
2. τοὐναντίον μὲν οὖν εἰκὸς τοὺς μὲν μήτε⁴ λόγον ὑφέξειν τοῦ
ἐνταῦθα ἢ πονηροῦ ἢ χρηστοῦ βίου μήτε ἀνάστασιν εἶναι οἰομένους,
συναπόλλυσθαι δὲ τῷ σώματι καὶ τὴν ψυχὴν καὶ οἷον ἐναποσβέν-
νυσθαι λογιζομένους, μηδενὸς ἂν ἀποσχέσθαι τολμήματος· τοὺς δὲ
μηδὲν ἀνεξέταστον ἔσεσθαι παρὰ τῷ θεῷ, συγκολασθήσεσθαι δὲ
καὶ τὸ ὑπουργῆσαν σῶμα ταῖς ἀλόγοις ὁρμαῖς τῆς ψυχῆς καὶ
ἐπιθυμίαις πεπεισμένους, οὐδεὶς λόγος ἔχει οὐδὲ τῶν βραχυτάτων

35. ⁵ τίς οὐχ ὑμῶν περισπούδαστος Gesner   ⁶ τὸ seclusit Schwartz
⁷ τοῦ A¹ : τὸ A   ⁸ μὲν del. Wilamowitz, Schwartz, Geffcken   ⁹ τὰ
παρεληλυθότα Wilamowitz, Schwartz, Geffcken   ¹⁰ κρατοῦντες p : καρτες
A : καταμαρτυροῦντες Schwartz
36. ¹ ἐπὶ seclusit Wilamowitz   ² μὴ Schwartz : μήτε A   ³ ἀπαιτηθή-
σεσθαι A¹   ⁴ μὲν μήτε : μὲν A : μὴ A¹

4. Who can charge people with murder and cannibalism who are known not to allow themselves to be spectators at the slaying of a man even when he has been justly condemned? Who among you does not enthusiastically follow the gladiatorial contests or animal fights especially those which you yourselves sponsor? 5. But since we regard seeing a man slain as next thing to murdering him, we have renounced such spectacles.[2] How, then, can we be capable of murder when we will not even look at such sights to avoid being polluted and defiled?

6. Again, what sense does it make to think of us as murderers when we say that women who practice abortion are murderers and will render account to God for abortion?[3] The same man cannot regard that which is in the womb as a living being and for that reason an object of God's concern and then murder it when it has come into the light. Neither can the same man forbid exposing a child that has been born[4] on the grounds that those who do so are murderers and then slay one that has been nourished. On the contrary, we remain the same and unchanging in every way at all times: we are servants of reason and not its masters.

36. What man who believes in a resurrection would offer himself as a tomb for bodies destined to arise? For it is impossible at one and the same time to believe that our bodies will arise and then eat them as though they will not arise, or to think that the earth will yield up its dead and then suppose that those whom a man had buried within himself will not reclaim their bodies. 2. On the contrary, the likelihood is that those who would not shrink from any outrage are men who think that they will not render an account of their present life, whether bad or good, and that there is no resurrection, but who believe that the soul also perishes along with the body and is, so to speak, snuffed out. On the other hand there is no reason for those to commit the slightest wrong who believe that nothing will remain unexamined in the presence of God and that the body too will be punished which promotes the irrational impulses and lusts of the soul.

35. [2] For a full discussion see Tertullian, *De Spectaculis* (cf. Seneca, *Ep.* 7. 2; 90. 45).

[3] A Jewish and Christian point of view (Philo, *De Spec. Leg.* 3. 108–15; Josephus, *C. Ap.* 2. 202; *Didache* 2. 2; Barnabas 19. 5; Clement, *Paed.* 2. 96. 1; cf. J. H. Waszink, 'Abtreibung', *RAC* i [1950], 55–60).

[4] See in addition to some of the sources cited in the previous note Justin, *Ap.* 1. 27. 1; 1. 29. 1; *Ad Diog.* 5. 6. A rare pagan sentiment (*C. Musonii Rufi Reliquiae*, ed. O. Hense, pp. 77–81).

τι ἁμαρτεῖν. 3. εἰ δέ τῳ λῆρος πολὺς δοκεῖ τὸ σαπὲν καὶ διαλυθὲν
καὶ ἀφανισθὲν σῶμα συστῆναι πάλιν, κακίας μὲν οὐκ ἂν εἰκότως
δόξαν ἀποφεροίμεθα διὰ τοὺς οὐ πιστεύοντας, ἀλλ᾽ εὐηθείας· οἷς γὰρ
ἀπατῶμεν ἑαυτοὺς λόγοις ἀδικοῦμεν οὐδένα· ὅτι μέντοι οὐ καθ᾽
ἡμᾶς μόνον ἀναστήσεται τὰ σώματα, ἀλλὰ καὶ κατὰ πολλοὺς τῶν
φιλοσόφων, περίεργον ἐπὶ τοῦ παρόντος δεικνύειν, ἵνα μὴ ἐξαγω-
νίους τοῖς προκειμένοις ἐπεισάγειν δοκῶμεν λόγους, ἢ περὶ νοητῶν
καὶ αἰσθητῶν καὶ τῆς τοιούτων συστάσεως λέγοντες ἢ ὅτι πρεσ-
βύτερα τὰ ἀσώματα τῶν σωμάτων καὶ τὰ νοητὰ προάγει τῶν
αἰσθητῶν κἂν πρώτοις περιπίπτωμεν τοῖς αἰσθητοῖς, συνισταμένων
ἐκ μὲν τῶν ἀσωμάτων κατὰ τὴν ἐπισύνθεσιν τῶν νοητῶν σωμάτων,
ἐκ δὲ τῶν νοητῶν ⟨τῶν αἰσθητῶν⟩·⁵ οὐ γὰρ κωλύει κατὰ τὸν
Πυθαγόραν καὶ τὸν Πλάτωνα γενομένης τῆς διαλύσεως τῶν
σωμάτων ἐξ ὧν τὴν ἀρχὴν συνέστη, ἀπὸ τῶν αὐτῶν αὐτὰ καὶ πάλιν
συστῆναι.

37. Ἀλλ᾽ ἀνακείσθω μὲν ὁ περὶ τῆς ἀναστάσεως λόγος. ὑμεῖς δέ,
ὦ πάντα ἐν πᾶσι φύσει καὶ παιδείᾳ χρηστοὶ καὶ μέτριοι καὶ φιλ-
άνθρωποι καὶ τῆς βασιλείας ἄξιοι, διαλελυμένῳ μὲν τὰ ἐγκλήματα
ἐπιδεδειχότι δὲ ὅτι καὶ θεοσεβεῖς καὶ ἐπιεικεῖς καὶ τὰς ψυχὰς
κεκολασμένοι, τὴν βασιλικὴν κεφαλὴν ἐπινεύσατε. 2. τίνες γὰρ καὶ
δικαιότεροι ὧν δέονται τυχεῖν ἢ οἵτινες περὶ μὲν τῆς ἀρχῆς τῆς
ὑμετέρας εὐχόμεθα,[a] ἵνα παῖς μὲν παρὰ πατρὸς κατὰ τὸ δικαιότατον
διαδέχησθε τὴν βασιλείαν, αὔξην δὲ καὶ ἐπίδοσιν καὶ ἡ ἀρχὴ ὑμῶν,
πάντων ὑποχειρίων γιγνομένων, λαμβάνῃ; 3. τοῦτο δ᾽ ἐστὶ καὶ πρὸς
ἡμῶν, ὅπως ἤρεμον καὶ ἡσύχιον βίον διάγοιμεν,[a] αὐτοὶ δὲ πάντα τὰ
κεκελευσμένα προθύμως ὑπηρετοῖμεν.

37. [a] Cf. 1 Tim. 2: 2

36. ⁵ τῶν αἰσθητῶν add. Suffridius Petrus   Subscriptio: ΑΘΗΝΑΓΟΡΟΥ
ΠΡΕΣΒΕΙΑ

3. If it seems the height of folly to anyone that the body should be reconstituted after it has rotted, decayed, and disappeared, then we may reasonably be regarded not as evil but as foolish by those who do not believe it; for we harm no man with the doctrines by which we delude ourselves. To show that in fact it is not only we who teach that bodies will arise but also many of the philosophers is superfluous for the present; it is beside the point to try to counter the impression that we bring forward views irrelevant to our present argument,[1] either when we talk about intelligible and perceptible things and their structure, or when we observe that incorporeal things are more important than corporeal things and that intelligible things excel perceptible things (even though we first encounter perceptible things), seeing that bodies arise from incorporeal things by the compounding of intelligible things[2] and that perceptible things arise from intelligible things. For nothing in the teachings of Pythagoras or Plato stands in the way of bodies' being reconstituted from the same elements once their dissolution to that from which they arose has taken place.[3]

37. Let our teaching concerning the resurrection be set aside for the present; but do you, who by nature and learning are in every way good, moderate, humane, and worthy of your royal office, nod your royal heads in assent now that I have destroyed the accusations advanced and have shown that we are godly, mild, and chastened in soul. 2. Who ought more justly to receive what they request than men like ourselves, who pray for your reign that the succession to the kingdom may proceed from father to son, as is most just, and that your reign may grow and increase as all men become subject to you? 3. This is also to our advantage that we may lead a quiet and peaceable life and at the same time may willingly do all that is commanded.

---

36. [1] i.e. about resurrected bodies.

[2] i.e. bodies have as their exemplars Platonic ideas.

[3] According to the doxographies (Aetius, *Plac.* 1. 17. 4; 1. 24. 3) Pythagoras and Plato taught that the elements could be changed into one another. This may be the aspect of their teaching which Athenagoras had in mind.

ΤΟΥ ΑΥΤΟΥ ΠΕΡΙ ΑΝΑΣΤΑΣΕΩΣ ΝΕΚΡΩΝ

1. Παντὶ δόγματι καὶ λόγῳ τῆς ἐν τούτοις ἀληθείας ἐχομένῳ παραφύεταί τι ψεῦδος· παραφύεται δὲ οὐκ ἐξ ὑποκειμένης τινός ἀρχῆς κατὰ φύσιν ὁρμώμενον ἢ τῆς κατ᾽ αὐτὸ ὅπερ ἐστὶν ἕκαστον αἰτίας, ἀλλ᾽ ὑπὸ τῶν τὴν ἔκθεσμον σπορὰν ἐπὶ διαφθορᾷ τῆς ἀληθείας τετιμηκότων σπουδαζόμενον. 2. τοῦτο δ᾽ ἔστιν εὑρεῖν πρῶτον μὲν ἐκ τῶν πάλαι ταῖς περὶ τούτων φροντίσιν ἐσχολακότων καὶ τῆς ἐκείνων πρός τε τοὺς ἑαυτῶν[1] πρεσβυτέρους καὶ τοὺς ὁμοχρόνους γενομένης διαφορᾶς, οὐχ ἥκιστα δὲ ἐξ αὐτῆς τῆς τῶν ἐν μέσῳ στρεφομένων ταραχῆς. οὐδὲν γὰρ τῶν ἀληθῶν οἱ τοιοῦτοι κατέλιπον ἀσυκοφάντητον, οὐ τὴν οὐσίαν τοῦ θεοῦ, οὐ τὴν γνῶσιν, οὐ τὴν ἐνέργειαν, οὐ τὰ τούτοις ἐφεξῆς καθ᾽ εἱρμὸν ἑπόμενα καὶ τὸν τῆς εὐσεβείας ἡμῖν ὑπογράφοντα λόγον· ἀλλ᾽ οἱ μὲν πάντῃ καὶ καθάπαξ ἀπογινώσκουσιν τὴν περὶ τούτων ἀλήθειαν, οἱ δὲ πρὸς τὸ δοκοῦν αὐτοῖς διαστρέφουσιν, οἱ δὲ καὶ περὶ τῶν ἐμφανῶν ἀπορεῖν ἐπιτηδεύουσιν. 3. ὅθεν οἶμαι δεῖν τοῖς περὶ ταῦτα πονουμένοις λόγων διττῶν, τῶν μὲν ὑπὲρ τῆς ἀληθείας, τῶν δὲ περὶ τῆς ἀληθείας· καὶ τῶν μὲν ὑπὲρ τῆς ἀληθείας πρὸς τοὺς ἀπιστοῦντας ἢ τοὺς ἀμφιβάλλοντας, τῶν δὲ περὶ τῆς ἀληθείας πρὸς τοὺς εὐγνωμονοῦντας καὶ μετ᾽ εὐνοίας δεχομένους τὴν ἀλήθειαν.[a] ὧν ἕνεκεν χρὴ τοὺς περὶ τούτων ἐξετάζειν ἐθέλοντας τὴν ἑκάστοτε προκειμένην χρείαν σκοπεῖν καὶ ταύτῃ τοὺς λόγους μετρεῖν τήν τε περὶ τούτων τάξιν μεθαρμόζειν πρὸς τὸ δέον καὶ μὴ τῷ δοκεῖν τὴν αὐτὴν πάντοτε φυλάττειν ἀρχὴν ἀμελεῖν τοῦ προσήκοντος καὶ τῆς ἐπιβαλλούσης ἑκάστῳ χώρας. 4. ὡς μὲν γὰρ πρὸς ἀπόδειξιν καὶ τὴν φυσικὴν ἀκολουθίαν, πάντοτε πρωτοστατοῦσιν οἱ περὶ αὐτῆς λόγοι τῶν ὑπὲρ αὐτῆς, ὡς δὲ πρὸς τὸ χρειωδέστερον, ἀνεστραμμένως οἱ ὑπὲρ αὐτῆς τῶν περὶ αὐτῆς. οὔτε γὰρ γεωργὸς δύναιτ᾽ ἂν προσηκόντως καταβάλλειν τῇ γῇ τὰ σπέρματα, μὴ προεξελὼν τὰ τῆς ἀγρίας ὕλης

---

1. [a] Cf. Luke 8: 13

1. [1] post ἑαυτῶν erasa sunt καὶ τῆς ἐκείνων πρὸς τοὺς ἑαυτῶν A

BY THE SAME AUTHOR
CONCERNING THE RESURRECTION
OF THE DEAD

1. Some falsehood grows up alongside of every doctrine and teaching which abides by the truth that it contains. It grows, not because it springs up naturally from some underlying source or cause inherent in the various teachings themselves, but because it is fostered by those who honour the sowing of spurious seed to the destruction of the truth. 2. This may be gathered first from those who long ago concerned themselves with reflections on these matters and the discord which arose between them and their predecessors and contemporaries; but also, and by no means least of all, from the confusion which characterizes the discussion of matters currently debated. Such men have left no truth free from misrepresentation—not the nature of God, not his knowledge, not his activity, nor all that logically flows from these and follows the lines of our religious teaching. Some of them simply despair of knowing the truth concerning these things; others are concerned with what seems likely to themselves; others exercise themselves in doubting even what is obvious.

3. Consequently I think that those who are occupied in these matters need to adopt two lines of argument—the one *on behalf of* the truth, the other *concerning* the truth. That on behalf of the truth is directed to those who disbelieve or dispute it. That concerning the truth is directed to those who are well disposed and receive the truth gladly. Those who desire to investigate these problems ought then to consider what is needed at any particular point, to measure their words accordingly, and as far as necessary to adapt the usual order of treating such issues; they ought not to neglect the argument that fits the occasion nor the place that is suitable for each point in a desire to adhere to the same basic method throughout. 4. For just as it is normal in offering proof and working out logical consequences to reason concerning them first and then on behalf of them, so, when it comes to the more practical side, the opposite is true—reasoning on behalf of them precedes that concerning them. Thus a farmer could not cast seeds into the ground with any hope of success if he did not first root up wild growth and anything that damages the cultivated

καὶ ⟨τὰ⟩² τοῖς καταβαλλομένοις ἡμέροις σπέρμασιν λυμαινόμενα,
οὔτε ἰατρὸς ἐνεῖναί τι τῶν ὑγιεινῶν³ φαρμάκων τῷ δεομένῳ
θεραπείας σώματι, μὴ τὴν ἐνοῦσαν κακίαν προκαθήρας ἢ τὴν
ἐπιρρέουσαν ἐπισχών· οὔτε μὴν ὁ τὴν ἀλήθειαν διδάσκειν ἐθέλων
περὶ τῆς ἀληθείας λέγων πεῖσαι δύναιτ᾽ ἄν τινα ψευδοδοξίας τινὸς
ὑποικουρούσης τῇ τῶν ἀκουόντων διανοίᾳ καὶ τοῖς λόγοις ἀντι-
στατούσης. 5. διὸ πρὸς τὸ χρειωδέστερον ἀφορῶντες καὶ ἡμεῖς
προτάσσομεν ἔσθ᾽ ὅτε τοὺς ὑπὲρ τῆς ἀληθείας λόγους τῶν περὶ τῆς
ἀληθείας· κατὰ τὸν αὐτὸν δὲ τρόπον ποιῆσαι καὶ νῦν ἐπὶ τῶν τῆς
ἀναστάσεως λόγων οὐκ ἀχρεῖον φαίνεται σκοποῦσι τὸ δέον. καὶ
γὰρ ἐν τούτοις εὑρίσκομεν τοὺς μὲν ἀπιστοῦντας πάντῃ, τινὰς δὲ
ἀμφιβάλλοντας καὶ τῶν γε τὰς πρώτας ὑποθέσεις δεξαμένων τινὰς
ἐπ᾽ ἴσης τοῖς ἀμφιβάλλουσιν ἀποροῦντας· τὸ δὲ πάντων παραλογώτατον ὅτι ταῦτα πάσχουσιν οὐδ᾽ ἡντιναοῦν ἔχοντες ἐκ τῶν πραγμάτων ἀπιστίας ἀφορμὴν οὐδ᾽ αἰτίαν εὑρίσκοντες εἰπεῖν εὔλογον, δι᾽
ἣν ἀπιστοῦσιν ἢ διαποροῦσιν.

2. Σκοπῶμεν δὲ οὑτωσί.¹ πᾶσα ἀπιστία μὴ προχείρως καὶ κατά
τινα δόξαν ἄκριτον ἐγγινομένη τισὶν ἀλλὰ μετά τινος αἰτίας ἰσχυρᾶς
καὶ τῆς κατὰ τὴν ἀλήθειαν ἀσφαλείας τότε² τὸν εἰκότα σῴζει λόγον,
ὅταν αὐτὸ τὸ πρᾶγμα περὶ οὗ ἀπιστοῦσιν ἄπιστον εἶναι δοκῇ· τὸ γάρ
τοι τοῖς οὐκ οὖσιν ἀπίστοις ἀπιστεῖν ἀνθρώπων ἔργον οὐχ ὑγιαι-
νούσῃ κρίσει περὶ τὴν ἀλήθειαν χρωμένων. 2. οὐκοῦν χρὴ καὶ τοὺς
περὶ τῆς ἀναστάσεως ἀπιστοῦντας ἢ διαποροῦντας μὴ πρὸς τὸ
δοκοῦν αὑτοῖς ἀκρίτως καὶ τὸ τοῖς ἀκολάστοις κεχαρισμένον τὴν
περὶ ταύτης ἐκφέρειν γνώμην, ἀλλ᾽ ἢ μηδεμιᾶς αἰτίας ἐξάπτειν τὴν
τῶν ἀνθρώπων γένεσιν (ὃ δὴ καὶ λίαν ἐστὶν εὐεξέλεγκτον) ἢ τῷ
θεῷ τὴν τῶν ὄντων ἀνατιθέντας αἰτίαν εἰς τὴν τοῦδε τοῦ δόγματος
ἀποβλέπειν ὑπόθεσιν καὶ διὰ ταύτης δεικνύναι τὴν ἀνάστασιν
οὐδαμόθεν ἔχουσαν τὸ πιστόν. 3. τοῦτο δὲ ποιήσουσιν, ἐὰν δεῖξαι
δυνηθῶσιν ἢ ἀδύνατον ὂν τῷ θεῷ ἢ ἀβούλητον τὰ νεκρωθέντα τῶν
σωμάτων ἢ καὶ πάντῃ διαλυθέντα πάλιν ἑνῶσαι καὶ συναγαγεῖν πρὸς
τὴν τῶν αὐτῶν ἀνθρώπων σύστασιν. ἐὰν δὲ τοῦτο μὴ δύνωνται,

---

1. ² τὰ add. Wilamowitz   ³ ὑγιεινῶν Α
2. ¹ οὗτως εἰ Α: corr. Schwartz   ² post τότε add. γὰρ Α¹

strains of seeds that are sown. Nor could a physician introduce health-giving medicines into an ailing body if he did not first purge the infection already there or prevent it from spreading. Nor, surely, could the man who wishes to teach the truth persuade anyone with his presentation if some false opinion lurks in the mind of his hearers and opposes his teachings.

5. That is why we too, as we look to the more practical side, sometimes present arguments on behalf of the truth before we present those concerning the truth. It does not seem inappropriate for us also now in discussing the resurrection to proceed in the same way in light of the present need: for in this matter we find men who simply do not believe it, others who dispute it, and others who, although they are among those who accept our basic assumptions, are as doubtful as those who dispute it; and the height of absurdity is that they suffer this delusion without having the least foundation in the facts for their disbelief and without being able to present any plausible reason because of which they disbelieve or doubt.

2. Let us make the following observations. Every attitude of disbelief which men adopt, not in a rash spirit or on some unexamined grounds, but for a strong reason and out of the security provided by the truth, remains a probable account whenever the matter which they challenge appears in fact unworthy of belief;[1] but surely not to believe things which have no such character is the mark of men who exercise unsound judgement concerning the truth. 2. That is why those who do not believe in the resurrection, or have doubts, ought not to bring forward their opinion on the issue if it is a matter of what merely seems likely to themselves, without critical investigation, or what would give comfort to the immoral; but they should either make the creation of men dependent on no cause (which can very easily be refuted) or, if they ascribe the cause of existing things to God, examine closely the presupposition of this doctrine and in elaborating its significance show that the resurrection is not in any way a trustworthy doctrine.

3. This they will be able to do if they can show that God either is not able, or is unwilling, to knit together again dead bodies (or even those entirely decomposed) and restore them so as to constitute the very men they once were. If they cannot do this, let

---

2. [1] For the Platonic phrase 'probable account' in discussions not unlike those which follow here (2. 5) see Plato's *Timaeus* 57 d and Theophrastus' *Opinions* (Diels, *Doxographi Graeci*, p. 525).

παυσάσθωσαν τῆς ἀθέου ταύτης ἀπιστίας καὶ τοῦ βλασφημεῖν ἃ
μὴ θέμις· ὅτι γὰρ οὔτε τὸ ἀδύνατον λέγοντες ἀληθεύουσιν οὔτε τὸ
ἀβούλητον, ἐκ τῶν ῥηθησομένων γενήσεται φανερόν. 4. Τὸ ἀδύνατόν τινι γινώσκεται κατ' ἀλήθειαν τοιοῦτον ἢ ἐκ τοῦ
μὴ γινώσκειν τὸ γενησόμενον ἢ ἐκ τοῦ δύναμιν ἀρκοῦσαν μὴ ἔχειν
πρὸς τὸ ποιῆσαι καλῶς τὸ ἐγνωσμένον. ὅ τε γὰρ ἀγνοῶν τι τῶν
γενέσθαι δεόντων οὐκ ἂν οὔτ' ἐγχειρῆσαι οὔτε ποιῆσαι δυνηθείη τὸ
παράπαν ὅπερ ἀγνοεῖ, ὅ τε γινώσκων καλῶς τὸ ποιηθησόμενον καὶ
πόθεν γένοιτ' ἂν καὶ πῶς, δύναμιν δὲ ἢ μηδ' ὅλως ἔχων πρὸς τὸ
ποιῆσαι τὸ γινωσκόμενον ἢ μὴ ἀρκοῦσαν ἔχων, οὐκ ἂν ἐγχειρήσειεν
τὴν ἀρχήν, εἰ σωφρονοῖ καὶ τὴν ἰδίαν ἐπισκέψαιτο δύναμιν, ἐγχειρή-
σας δὲ ἀπερισκέπτως οὐκ ἂν ἐπιτελέσειεν τὸ δόξαν. 5. ἀλλ' οὔτε
ἀγνοεῖν τὸν θεὸν δυνατὸν τῶν ἀναστησομένων σωμάτων τὴν φύσιν
κατά τε[3] μέρος ὅλον[4] καὶ μόριον οὔτε μὴν ὅποι χωρεῖ τῶν λυομένων
ἕκαστον καὶ ποῖον τοῦ στοιχείου μέρος δέδεκται τὸ λυθὲν καὶ
χωρῆσαν πρὸς τὸ συγγενές, κἂν πάνυ παρ' ἀνθρώποις ἀδιάκριτον
εἶναι δοκῇ τὸ τῷ παντὶ πάλιν προσφυῶς ἡνωμένον. ᾧ γὰρ οὐκ
ἠγνόητο πρὸ τῆς οἰκείας ἑκάστου συστάσεως οὔτε τῶν γενησομένων
στοιχείων ἡ φύσις, ἐξ ὧν τὰ τῶν ἀνθρώπων σώματα, οὔτε τὰ μέρη
τούτων, ἐξ ὧν ἔμελλεν λήψεσθαι τὸ δόξαν πρὸς τὴν τοῦ ἀνθρωπείου
σώματος σύστασιν, εὔδηλον ὡς οὐδὲ μετὰ τὸ διαλυθῆναι τὸ πᾶν
ἀγνοηθήσεται ποῦ κεχώρηκεν ἕκαστον ὧν εἴληφεν πρὸς τὴν ἑκάστου
συμπλήρωσιν. 6. ὅσον μὲν γὰρ κατὰ τὴν νῦν κρατοῦσαν παρ' ἡμῖν
τῶν πραγμάτων τάξιν καὶ τὴν ἐφ' ἑτέρων κρίσιν, μεῖζον τὸ τὰ μὴ
γενόμενα προγινώσκειν· ὅσον δὲ πρὸς τὴν ἀξίαν τοῦ θεοῦ καὶ τὴν

2. ³ τε seclusit Schwartz   ⁴ ὅλον seclusit Schwartz

them give up this godless disbelief and their impious blasphemy. It will become clear from the following arguments that they do not have the truth when they speak of God's inability or unwillingness to do this.[2]

4. One knows inability to be what it really is either when there is a lack of knowledge of what will happen or a lack of sufficient power effectively to accomplish what is determined upon. For he who knows nothing of what is to happen can in no way undertake or accomplish what he does not know; and he who knows well what is to be accomplished—what would give rise to it and how it would come about—and yet either has no power at all, or insufficient power, to accomplish it would not undertake the task if he were sober and considered his limitations; if he rashly attempted to do so, he would not accomplish his purpose.

5. It is impossible for God, however, to be ignorant of the nature of our bodies which are destined to arise; he knows every part and member in their entirety. Nor indeed can he be ignorant as to where everything goes that decomposes and what part of the appropriate element receives what is decomposed and dissolved into its own kind.[3] This is the case in spite of the fact that men are very much inclined to think that what has been intimately reunited with everything else of its kind has become indistinguishable from it. Before the particular formation of individual things, God knew the nature of the elements yet to be created from which men's bodies arise; and he knew the parts of the elements from which he planned to select in order to form the human body. When all has been dissolved, it is clear that such a God will also know where everything has gone—everything which he had selected that he might give substance to individual things.

6. It is to be expected in reflecting on the order of circumstances which now determines our lives, and in considering our judgement as to other possibilities, that foreknowledge of what has not yet happened is more highly regarded; it is likewise to be expected in view of God's majesty and wisdom that both

2. [2] Methodius' Origenist (*De Res.* 1. 20–2) complained of believers in the resurrection of the whole body who retreated to the statements that 'God does what he wills' and that 'all things are possible with God', without realizing that they were speaking of things both 'impossible' and 'unworthy of God'.

[3] For the language and ideas reflected here see Plato's discussion of the elements and their dissolution in the *Timaeus* (especially 57 b; cf. 81 a). That the elements are 'compounds' was commonly held (Aetius, *Plac.* 1. 1. 2). Plato himself speaks of the 'parts' of elements which drift about as the result of 'dissolution' and which recombine in various ways (*Tim.* 56 d–57 c). Our author refers to the 'parts of elements' being brought together 'into one' shortly (2. 5 below; 3. 2).

τούτου σοφίαν, ἀμφότερα κατὰ φύσιν καὶ ῥᾴδιον ἐπ' ἴσης τῷ τὰ μὴ γενόμενα προγινώσκειν τὸ καὶ διαλυθέντα γινώσκειν.

3. Καὶ μὴν καὶ τὴν δύναμιν ὡς ἔστιν ἀρκοῦσα πρὸς τὴν τῶν σωμάτων ἀνάστασιν, δείκνυσιν ἡ τούτων αὐτῶν γένεσις. εἰ γὰρ μὴ ὄντα κατὰ τὴν πρώτην σύστασιν ἐποίησεν τὰ τῶν ἀνθρώπων σώματα καὶ τὰς τούτων ἀρχάς, καὶ διαλυθέντα καθ' ὃν ἂν τύχῃ τρόπον, ἀναστήσει μετὰ τῆς ἴσης εὐμαρείας· ἐπ' ἴσης γὰρ αὐτῷ καὶ τοῦτο δυνατόν. 2. καὶ τῷ λόγῳ βλάβος οὐδέν, κἂν ἐξ ὕλης ὑπο-θῶνταί τινες τὰς πρώτας ἀρχάς, κἂν ἐκ τῶν στοιχείων ὡς πρώτων τὰ σώματα τῶν ἀνθρώπων, κἂν ἐκ σπερμάτων. ἧς γάρ ἐστι δυνά-μεως καὶ τὴν παρ' αὐτοῖς[1] νενομισμένην ἄμορφον οὐσίαν[2] μορφῶσαι καὶ τὴν ἀνείδεον καὶ ἀδιακόσμητον πολλοῖς καὶ διαφόροις εἴδεσιν κοσμῆσαι καὶ τὰ μέρη τῶν στοιχείων εἰς ἓν συναγαγεῖν καὶ τὸ σπέρμα ἓν ὂν καὶ ἁπλοῦν εἰς πολλὰ διελεῖν καὶ τὸ ἀδιάρθρωτον διαρθρῶσαι καὶ τῷ μὴ ζῶντι δοῦναι ζωήν, τῆς αὐτῆς ἐστιν καὶ τὸ διαλελυμένον ἑνῶσαι καὶ τὸ κείμενον ἀναστῆσαι καὶ τὸ τεθνηκὸς ζωοποιῆσαι πάλιν καὶ τὸ φθαρτὸν μεταβαλεῖν εἰς ἀφθαρσίαν.[a] 3. τοῦ αὐτοῦ δ' ἂν εἴη καὶ τῆς αὐτῆς δυνάμεως καὶ σοφίας καὶ τὸ διατεθρυμμένον ⟨εἰς⟩[3] πλήθη ζῴων παντοδαπῶν ὁπόσα τοῖς τοιούτοις σώμασιν ἐπιτρέχειν εἴωθεν καὶ τὸν ἐκ τούτων ἀγείρειν κόρον, διακρῖναι μὲν ἐκεῖθεν, ἑνῶσαι δὲ πάλιν τοῖς οἰκείοις μέρεσι καὶ μορίοις, κἂν εἰς ἓν[4] ἐξ ἐκείνων χωρήσῃ ζῷον, κἂν εἰς πολλά, κἂν ἐντεῦθεν εἰς ἕτερα, κἂν αὐτοῖς ἐκείνοις συνδιαλυθὲν ἐπὶ τὰς

---

3. ᵃ Cf. 1 Cor. 15: 53

---

things—his knowledge of what has been dissolved as much as his foreknowledge of what has not yet happened—are natural and easy for him.

3. As to power, the creation of our bodies shows that God's power suffices for their resurrection. For if when he first gave them form, he made the bodies of men and their principal constituents from nothing, he will just as easily raise them up again after their dissolution, however it may have taken place. For this is equally possible for him. 2. And our argument loses none of its force whether men suppose that the principal constituents arise from matter or that human bodies have the elements as their basic ingredients or that they are made up of seeds.[1] For the power which can give shape to substance regarded by these thinkers[2] as shapeless, can arrange in many different patterns that which is unstructured and disordered, can gather into one the parts of the elements, can divide seed which is one and simple into many, can make an articulated organism of that which is undifferentiated,[3] and can give life to that which is not alive—such a power can also unite what has been dissolved, can raise up what has fallen, can restore the dead to life, and can change the corruptible into incorruption.

3. The same God and the same wisdom and power can also separate out what has been torn apart and devoured by numerous animals of every kind which are accustomed to attack bodies like our own and satisfy their wants with them; and he can reunite the fragments with their own parts and members whether they have gone into one such animal or into many, or whether they have passed in turn from them into others and after decomposition

---

3. [1] Athenagoras may be referring to (a) the pre-Socratics (matter), (b) Plato and Aristotle (elements), (c) Anaxagoras (seeds). The term 'matter' (in the sense of 'body') was used to describe the first principle of the Milesian philosophers (Aetius, *Plac.* 1. 9. 6). Plato and Aristotle (as well as the Stoics), on the other hand, were known to have distinguished 'first principles'—such as 'matter' (*Plac.* 1. 3. 21)—from the 'elements' (*Plac.* 1. 2. 1; 1. 3. 25); and Plato's theories would perhaps have been uppermost in the minds of those who regarded the elements as the constituents of physical reality (*Tim.* 48 e–53 c; cf. Aristotle, *De Gen. et Corr.* 2. 1, 328^{b}25). The doxographies also discuss the *homoeomeriae* of Anaxagoras as first principles (Aetius, *Plac.* 1. 3. 5); apparently these were actually called 'seeds' by Anaxagoras (G. S. Kirk and J. E. Raven, *The Presocratic Philosophers* [Cambridge, 1957], pp. 378, 387).

[2] Particularly Platonists (Plato, *Tim.* 30 a, 51 a; cf. Aetius, *Plac.* 1. 9. 4–5; Wisdom of Solomon 11: 17; Justin, *Ap.* 1. 10. 2).

[3] Biological language having to do with the 'articulation' of the embryo (Aetius, *Plac.* 5. 20. 1–2).

πρώτας ἀρχὰς ἐνεχθῇ κατὰ τὴν φυσικὴν εἰς ταύτας ἀνάλυσιν· ὃ δὴ

καὶ μάλιστα ταράττειν ἔδοξέν τινας καὶ τῶν ἐπὶ σοφίᾳ θαυμαζομένων,

ἰσχυρὰς οὐκ οἶδ᾽ ὅπως ἡγησαμένων τὰς παρὰ τῶν πολλῶν φερομένας

διαπορήσεις.

4. Οὗτοι δέ γέ φασιν πολλὰ μὲν σώματα τῶν ἐν ναυαγίοις ἢ

ποταμοῖς δυσθανάτων ἰχθύσιν γενέσθαι τροφήν, πολλὰ δὲ τῶν

ἐν πολέμοις θνησκόντων ἢ κατ᾽ ἄλλην τινὰ τραχυτέραν αἰτίαν καὶ

πραγμάτων περίστασιν ταφῆς ἀμοιρούντων τοῖς προστυγχάνουσιν

ζῴοις προκεῖσθαι βοράν. 2. τῶν οὖν οὕτως ἀναλισκομένων σωμάτων

καὶ τῶν ταῦτα συμπληρούντων μερῶν καὶ μορίων εἰς πολὺ πλῆθος

ζῴων διαθρυπτομένων καὶ διὰ τῆς τροφῆς τοῖς τῶν τρεφομένων

σώμασιν ἑνουμένων, πρῶτον μὲν τὴν διάκρισιν τούτων φασὶν

ἀδύνατον, πρὸς δὲ ταύτῃ τὸ δεύτερον ἀπορώτερον. 3. τῶν γὰρ τὰ

σώματα τῶν ἀνθρώπων ἐκβοσκηθέντων ζῴων, ὁπόσα πρὸς τροφὴν

ἀνθρώποις ἐπιτήδεια, διὰ τῆς τούτων γαστρὸς ἰόντων καὶ τοῖς τῶν

μετειληφότων σώμασιν ἑνουμένων, ἀνάγκην εἶναι πᾶσαν τὰ μέρη

τῶν ἀνθρώπων, ὁπόσα τροφὴ γέγονεν τοῖς μετειληφόσι ζῴοις, πρὸς

ἕτερα τῶν ἀνθρώπων μεταχωρεῖν σώματα, τῶν μεταξὺ τούτοις

τραφέντων ζῴων τὴν ἐξ ὧν ἐτράφησαν τροφὴν διαπορθμευόντων

εἰς ἐκείνους τοὺς ἀνθρώπους ὧν ἐγένετο τροφή. 4. εἶτα τούτοις

ἐπιτραγῳδοῦσιν τὰς ἐν λιμοῖς καὶ μανίαις τολμηθείσας τεκνοφαγίας

been resolved along with their destroyers into their principal constituents and so followed the natural course of dissolution back into them. This view seems to have greatly upset some people even among those admired for their wisdom, because for some reason which I cannot grasp they regarded the doubts voiced by the crowd as strong arguments.[4]

4. This in any event is what they say:[1] The bodies of many who die in shipwrecks or who drown in rivers become food for fish; and the bodies of many who die in wars or who are deprived of burial by some other calamity or turn of events lie exposed as food for any animal that happens by. 2. Their first point is that since bodies are destroyed in this way and the parts and limbs which make them up are torn apart and devoured by a large number of animals and in being digested are united with the bodies of the creatures so nourished, any separation of them is impossible. In addition, however, they bring forward an even greater difficulty.

3. For there are creatures[2] which feed on human bodies but are themselves also fit nourishment for men. These creatures are digested by humans and so are united with the bodies of those who have eaten them. It is inevitable, then, that the parts of men that served as food for the creatures which devoured them should pass over into other human bodies; for the creatures who in their quest for food served as intermediaries have transmitted the nourishment derived from their victims to those men whose food they in turn became.

4. Our disputants go on to dramatize their case with reports of children whose parents dared to devour them in times of famine[3]

3. [4] The reference may well be to Origenists who stressed the fact of the dissolution of the body and the difficulty in recovering the elements once they have been dispersed (Methodius, *De Res.* 1. 20. 4; 2. 26. 2–5).

4. [1] The following remarks are similar to those of Methodius' Origenist (*De Res.* 1. 20. 4–5) and especially those of the (Origenist) opponents of Gregory of Nyssa as reported in his discussion of the resurrection (*De Hom. Opif.* 26. 1). Both make a special point of the problem raised by the union of human flesh with the body of other men through the eating of animals that had themselves fed on human flesh.   [2] e.g. fish or birds.

[3] Probably a reference to the grisly story in Josephus, *B.J.* 6. 199–219—'a deed which had been recorded in the history neither of the Greeks nor of the barbarians.' Gregory of Nyssa (*De Hom. Opif.* 25. 3) treats the account of 'her who devoured her child' as fulfilment of Christ's prophecy in Luke 23: 27–9; and he concludes that such confirmation of Christ's authority also permits us to trust his teaching on the resurrection. The passage shows that Josephus' tale had become commonplace in some Christian circles and that it hovered about reflections on the resurrection. The context shows that Gregory had gained his knowledge of Josephus from Eusebius (*H.E.* 3. 6. 1–7. 6).

καὶ τοὺς κατ' ἐπιβουλὴν ἐχθρῶν ὑπὸ τῶν γεννησαμένων[1] ἐδηδε-
μένους παῖδας καὶ τὴν Μηδικὴν τράπεζαν ἐκείνην καὶ τὰ τρα-
γικὰ δεῖπνα Θυέστου καὶ τοιαύτας δή τινας ἐπισυνείρουσι παρ'
Ἕλλησιν καὶ βαρβάροις καινουργηθείσας συμφορὰς ἔκ τε τούτων
κατασκευάζουσιν, ὡς νομίζουσιν, ἀδύνατον τὴν ἀνάστασιν, ὡς οὐ
δυναμένων τῶν αὐτῶν μερῶν ἑτέροις τε καὶ ἑτέροις συναναστῆναι
σώμασιν, ἀλλ' ἤτοι τὰ τῶν προτέρων συστῆναι μὴ δύνασθαι, μετ-
εληλυθότων τῶν ταῦτα συμπληρούντων μερῶν πρὸς ἑτέρους, ἢ
τούτων ἀποδοθέντων τοῖς προτέροις ἐνδεῶς ἕξειν τὰ τῶν ὑστέρων.

5. Ἐμοὶ δὲ δοκοῦσιν οἱ τοιοῦτοι πρῶτον μὲν τὴν τοῦ δημιουργήσαντος καὶ διοικοῦντος τόδε τὸ πᾶν ἀγνοεῖν δύναμίν τε καὶ σοφίαν,
ἑκάστου ζῴου φύσει καὶ γένει τὴν προσφυῆ καὶ κατάλληλον
συναρμόσαντος τροφὴν καὶ μήτε πᾶσαν φύσιν πρὸς ἕνωσιν ἢ κρᾶσιν
παντὸς σώματος ἰέναι δικαιώσαντος μήτε πρὸς διάκρισιν τῶν
ἑνωθέντων ἀπόρως ἔχοντος, ἀλλὰ καὶ τῇ καθ' ἕκαστον φύσει τῶν
γενομένων τὸ δρᾶν ἢ πάσχειν ἃ πέφυκεν ἐπιτρέποντος ἄλλο δὲ[1]
κωλύοντος καὶ πᾶν ὃ βούλεται καὶ πρὸς ὃ βούλεται συγχωροῦντος ἢ
μεταστρέφοντος, πρὸς δὲ τοῖς εἰρημένοις μηδὲ τὴν ἑκάστου τῶν
τρεφόντων ἢ τρεφομένων ἐπεσκέφθαι δύναμίν τε καὶ φύσιν. 2. ἢ
γὰρ ἂν ἔγνωσαν ὅτι μὴ πᾶν ὃ προσφέρεταί τις ὑπενδόσει τῆς
ἔξωθεν ἀνάγκης,[2] τοῦτο γίνεται τῷ ζῴῳ τροφὴ προσφυής· ἀλλὰ τὰ
μὲν ἅμα τῷ προσομιλῆσαι τοῖς περιπτυσσομένοις τῆς κοιλίας μέρεσι

4. [1] γενησαμένων A
5. [1] ἄλλοτε A : corr. Wilamowitz   [2] ἂν ἀνάγκης A

or in fits of madness[4] and with stories of others who were eaten by their progenitors through the plotting of enemies, including the famous account of the Median feast and the lamentable banquet of Thyestes; and they gather together a whole series of such horrors perpetrated among Greeks and barbarians. On this basis they think that they establish the thesis that the resurrection is an impossibility, for the reason that the same parts cannot rise again in both sets of individuals. Either the bodies of the first set could not be reconstituted, since the parts of which they were made up had passed over into the second set; or if these parts were restored to the first set, the bodies of the second set would be incomplete.

5. Those who argue in this way seem to me in the first place to be ignorant of the power and wisdom of him who created and guides the universe. He adapted to the nature and species of each animal a suitable and appropriate food.[1] He did not think it right that every species should be united or fused with every kind of body, nor is he at a loss when it comes to the separation of things that have been united. On the contrary he permits the individual species of created beings the active and passive functions which are natural;[2] he prevents anything else, while furthering everything that proceeds in accordance with his will and purpose or turning it in that direction.

Our disputants, moreover, do not seem to me to have considered the capacity and nature of each of the creatures which give or receive nourishment. 2. Otherwise they would have known that not everything that one of them eats under the pressure of external necessity becomes suitable food for that animal. On the contrary some food as soon as it meets the folds of

4. [4] For some examples from Greek mythology see Apollodorus 2. 2. 2; 3. 5. 2.
5. [1] Analogous ideas are to be found already in the pre-Socratics (Aetius, *Plac.* 1. 3. 5; 5. 27. 1). But in view of the close resemblance between the following arguments and those of Galen on digestion, there can be little doubt that these views are derived from a medical source. See Galen, *De Nat. Fac.* 1. 10 (Kühn, ii. 20): '. . . therefore in the first place it is natural that not every animal can gain nourishment from the same food; moreover, not every animal can gain nourishment immediately from that which it is able to absorb' (cf. Gregory of Nyssa, *Or. Catech.* 37). Athenagoras, to be sure, applies these doctrines in a somewhat special way.
[2] The reference to active and passive functions which make combination possible suggests the influence of Aristotle (*De Gen. et Corr.* 1. 6–10, 315[b]2–328[b]22). But Galen also uses the same terminology in discussing the body's reception of what is suitable and its rejection of what is foreign to it (e.g. *De Nat. Fac.* 1. 2, 1. 3, 1. 14, 2. 8; Kühn, ii. 7, 8, 46, 111).

φθείρεσθαι πέφυκεν ἐμούμενά τε καὶ διαχωρούμενα ἢ³ τρόπον
ἕτερον διαφορούμενα, ὡς μηδὲ κατὰ βραχὺ τὴν πρώτην καὶ κατὰ
φύσιν ὑπομεῖναι πέψιν, ἢ που γε τὴν εἰς τὸ τρεφόμενον σύγκρασιν,
3. ὥσπερ οὖν οὐδὲ πᾶν τὸ πεφθὲν καὶ τὴν πρώτην δεξάμενον
μεταβολὴν τοῖς τρεφομένοις μορίοις προσπελάζει πάντως, τινῶν μὲν
κατ' αὐτὴν τὴν γαστέρα τῆς θρεπτικῆς δυνάμεως ἀποκρινομένων,
τῶν δὲ κατὰ τὴν δευτέραν μεταβολὴν καὶ τὴν ἐν ἥπατι γινομένην
πέψιν διακρινομένων καὶ πρὸς ἕτερόν τι μεταχωρούντων ὃ τὴν τοῦ
τρέφειν ἐκβέβηκεν δύναμιν, καὶ αὐτῆς γε τῆς ἐν ἥπατι γινομένης
μεταβολῆς οὐ πάσης εἰς τροφὴν ἀνθρώποις χωρούσης, ἀλλ' εἰς
ἃ πέφυκεν περιττώματα διακρινομένης τῆς τε καταλειφθείσης
τροφῆς ἐν αὐτοῖς ἔσθ' ὅτε τοῖς τρεφομένοις μέρεσι καὶ μορίοις πρὸς
ἕτερόν τι μεταβαλλούσης κατὰ τὴν ἐπικράτειαν τοῦ πλεονάζοντος ἢ
περιττεύοντος καὶ φθείρειν πως ἢ πρὸς ἑαυτὸ τρέπειν τὸ πλησιάσαν
εἰωθότος.

6. Πολλῆς οὖν οὔσης ἐν πᾶσι τοῖς ζῴοις τῆς φυσικῆς διαφορᾶς
καὶ αὐτῆς γε τῆς κατὰ φύσιν τροφῆς ἑκάστῳ γένει ζῴων¹ καὶ
τῷ τρεφομένῳ σώματι συνεξαλλαττομένης, τριττῆς δὲ κατὰ τὴν
ἑκάστου ζῴου τροφὴν γινομένης καθάρσεως καὶ διακρίσεως, δεῖ
πάντως φθείρεσθαι μὲν καὶ διαχωρεῖν ᾗ πέφυκεν ἢ πρὸς ἕτερόν τι
μεταβάλλειν πᾶν ὁπόσον ἀλλότριον εἰς τὴν τοῦ ζῴου τροφὴν ὡς
συγκραθῆναι μὴ δυνάμενον, συμβαίνουσαν δὲ καὶ κατὰ φύσιν εἶναι
τὴν τοῦ τρέφοντος σώματος δύναμιν ταῖς τοῦ τρεφομένου ζῴου
δυνάμεσιν καὶ ταύτην ἐλθοῦσαν δι' ὧν πέφυκεν κριτηρίων καὶ

5. ³ ἢ Wilamowitz: καὶ A
6. ¹ ζῴων Wilamowitz: ζῴου A

the belly is inevitably spoiled and is eliminated as vomit or excretion or in some other form[3] since it cannot even for a short time endure the first natural digestive process, much less organic union with the recipient of such food. 3. So too not even all that is digested and capable of the first transformation is entirely assimilated by the organs which are being nourished. Some of it loses its nourishing power in the stomach itself; some of it is secreted in its second transformation—the digestive process that takes place in the liver—and changes into something else which has lost the power to nourish. As a matter of fact, even the change which takes place in the liver is not bound to have products all of which become food for men; rather some of them are naturally secreted as waste products, and the food that then remains undergoes transformation from time to time[4] in the parts and members which are being nourished; this occurs when what predominates is that which causes growth or increase and whose nature it is somehow to break down or convert into itself what comes into contact with it.[5]

6. There is, then, a great natural variety among all the animals. And the same natural food undergoes a transformation corresponding to each species of animal and the body that is being nourished. And a threefold purification and secretion attends the nourishing of each animal.[1] Consequently all food that is so foreign to an animal that it cannot be assimilated must be entirely spoiled and evacuated in the way one would expect, or it must change into something else; so too the property of the body that provides nourishment must have a natural affinity with the properties of the animal receiving nourishment; and this element

5. [3] For these other forms of elimination see Galen, *De Nat. Fac.* 3. 13 (Kühn, ii. 193), *De Aliment.* 3. 17 (Kühn, xv. 320–1); but Galen does not attach the same significance to these symptoms.

[4] Not always, since members or organs, according to Galen, like the stomach itself, have a 'limit to nourishment' required (*De Nat. Fac.* 3. 13, Kühn, ii. 198–9).

[5] The whole section is clearly dependent on the theory of Galen that there are three points at which digestive processes take place—the stomach, the liver, and the various organs of the body (*De Prob. Prav. Aliment. Succ.* 5, Kühn, vi. 786–7; *De Aliment.* 2. 2, Kühn, xv. 232–3)—and that waste products may be expected at any of these points. For the important role of the liver in digestion see especially Galen, *De Usu Part. Corp.* 4. 3 (Kühn, iii. 269), *De Symp. Caus.* 1. 3 (Kühn, vii. 221), *De Aliment.* 4. 5 (Kühn, xv. 385–6). Similar theories are known also to Gregory of Nyssa (*De Opif. Hom.* 30. 1–2; cf. Methodius, *De Res.* 2. 9. 1–3).

6. [1] For the 'purification' and 'secretion' of waste products see Galen, *De Nat. Fac.* 2. 8 (Kühn, ii. 113–14), 3. 13 (Kühn, ii. 192–3, cf. 200). This takes place in the stomach, the liver, and the organs.

καθαρθεῖσαν ἀκριβῶς τοῖς φυσικοῖς καθαρσίοις εἰλικρινεστάτην γενέσθαι πρόσληψιν εἰς οὐσίαν· 2. ἣν δὴ καὶ μόνην ἐπαληθεύων ἄν τις τοῖς πράγμασιν ὀνομάσειεν τροφὴν ὡς ἀποβάλλουσαν² πᾶν ὁπόσον ἀλλότριον καὶ βλαβερὸν εἰς τὴν τοῦ τρεφομένου ζῴου σύστασιν καὶ τὸν πολὺν ἐκεῖνον ὄγκον ἐπεισαχθέντα³ πρὸς τὴν τῆς γαστρὸς ἀποπλήρωσιν καὶ τὴν τῆς ὀρέξεως θεραπείαν. 3. ἀλλὰ ταύτην⁴ μὲν οὐκ ἄν τις ἀμφισβητήσειεν ἐνοῦσθαι τῷ τρεφομένῳ σώματι συνδιαπλεκομένην τε καὶ περιπλαττομένην πᾶσι τοῖς τούτου μέρεσιν καὶ μορίοις· τὴν δ' ἑτέρως ἔχουσαν καὶ παρὰ φύσιν φθείρεσθαι μὲν ταχέως, ἢν ἐρρωμενεστέρᾳ⁵ συμμίξῃ δυνάμει, φθείρειν δὲ σὺν εὐμαρείᾳ τὴν κρατηθεῖσαν εἴς τε μοχθηροὺς ἐκτρέπεσθαι χυμοὺς καὶ φαρμακώδεις ποιότητας ὡς μηδὲν οἰκεῖον ἢ φίλον τῷ τρεφομένῳ σώματι φέρουσαν. 4. καὶ τούτου τεκμήριον μέγιστον τὸ πολλοῖς τῶν τρεφομένων ζῴων ἐκ τούτων ἐπακολουθεῖν ἄλγος ἢ κίνδυνον ἢ θάνατον, ἢν ὑπὸ σφοδροτέρας ὀρέξεως τῇ τροφῇ καταμεμιγμένον συνεφελκύσηταί τι φαρμακῶδες καὶ παρὰ φύσιν· ὃ δὴ καὶ πάντως φθαρτικὸν ἂν εἴη τοῦ τρεφομένου σώματος, εἴ γε τρέφεται μὲν τὰ τρεφόμενα τοῖς οἰκείοις καὶ κατὰ φύσιν, φθείρεται δὲ τοῖς ἐναντίοις. 5. εἴπερ οὖν τῇ διαφορᾷ τῶν τῇ φύσει διαφερόντων ζῴων ἡ κατὰ φύσιν συνδιήρηται τροφὴ καὶ ταύτης γε αὐτῆς οὔτε πᾶν ὅπερ ἂν προσενέγκηται τὸ ζῷον οὔτε τὸ τυχὸν ἐκ τούτου τὴν πρὸς τὸ τρεφόμενον σῶμα δέχεται σύγκρασιν, ἀλλ' αὐτὸ μόνον τὸ διὰ πάσης πέψεως κεκαθαρμένον καὶ μεταβεβληκὸς εἰλικρινῶς πρὸς τὴν τοῦ ποιοῦ σώματος ἕνωσιν καὶ τοῖς τρεφομένοις μέρεσιν εὐάρμοστον, εὔδηλον ὡς οὐδὲν τῶν παρὰ φύσιν ἑνωθείη ποτ' ἂν τούτοις οἷς οὐκ ἔστιν τροφὴ προσφυὴς καὶ κατάλληλος, ἀλλ' ἤτοι κατ' αὐτὴν τὴν κοιλίαν διαχωρεῖ πρὶν ἕτερόν τινα γεννῆσαι χυμὸν ὠμὸν καὶ⁶ διεφθαρμένον, ἢ συστὰν ἐπὶ πλεῖον τίκτει πάθος ἢ νόσον δυσίατον, συνδιαφθείρουσαν καὶ τὴν κατὰ φύσιν τροφὴν ἢ καὶ αὐτὴν τὴν τῆς τροφῆς δεομένην σάρκα. 6. ἀλλὰ κἂν ἀπωσθῇ ποτε φαρμάκοις τισὶν ἢ σιτίοις βελτίοσιν ἢ ταῖς φυσικαῖς δυνάμεσι νικηθέν, μετ' οὐκ ὀλίγης ἐξερρύη τῆς βλάβης ὡς μηδὲν φέρον τοῖς κατὰ φύσιν εἰρηνικὸν διὰ τὸ πρὸς τὴν φύσιν ἀσύγκρατον.

6. ² ἀποβαλοῦσαν Wilamowitz, Schwartz   ³ ἐπεισαχθέντα Α¹ (σαχθέντα in ras.) : ἐπισαχθέντα Α¹ in mg.   ⁴ ταύτην Α¹ : ταύτῃ Α   ⁵ ἐρρωμενεστέρα Α   ⁶ ὠμὸν ἢ Wilamowitz, Schwartz

must also pass through the appropriate channels and be subjected to a rigorous process of natural purifications; only then does it contribute additional nourishment of the purest kind to the substance of an animal.

2. This nourishment alone genuinely deserves the name 'food', since it eliminates everything foreign and hurtful to the constitution of the animal which is being nourished and frees it from the urge to stuff down the enormous bulk which serves only to fill the belly and cater to the appetite.

3. No one, then, can doubt that such food unites with the body which is being nourished, as it is interwoven and intermingled with the body's parts and members. No one can doubt that food of a different sort, contrary to nature, is quickly spoiled if it meets a force more powerful, but that it easily spoils what it overpowers and is turned into harmful humours and poisonous qualities, since it brings nothing fitting or suitable to the body which is being nourished.

4. The greatest proof of this is the fact that pain, illness, or death afflict many animals so nourished if in yielding to great hunger they swallow something mixed in with the food they eat which is poisonous and contrary to nature. This would be utterly ruinous to the body which is being nourished, since organisms absorbing food are nourished by things fitting and according to nature but destroyed by the opposite.

5. There are, then, different kinds of natural food corresponding to the various kinds of naturally distinct animals; and even of such food neither all, nor any random part, that is set before the animal admits of fusion with the body which is being nourished, except that which has been purified at every stage of digestion and entirely transformed, with a view to its union with a body of a particular kind, and is well adapted to the parts which are being nourished; consequently it is clear that nothing contrary to nature can ever be united with anything for which it is not a fitting and proper food; either it is evacuated from the belly before it produces some strange raw and rotten humour, or it remains longer and gives rise to a sickness or disease hard to cure, spoiling along with itself the natural food or even the very flesh which requires the food. 6. But even if it is at length overpowered and dislodged by certain medicines, by better kinds of food, or by the powers of nature, it is drained off only after having caused much harm, because it brought nothing suited to the natural requirements of its host, incapable as it is of fusing with its nature.

7. Ὅλως δὲ κἂν συγχωρήσῃ τις τὴν ἐκ τούτων εἰσιοῦσαν τροφὴν
(προσειρήσθω δὲ τοῦτο συνηθέστερον), καίπερ οὖσαν παρὰ φύσιν,
διακρίνεσθαι καὶ μεταβάλλειν εἰς ἕν τι τῶν ὑγραινόντων ἢ ξηραι-
νόντων ἢ θερμαινόντων ἢ ψυχόντων, οὐδ᾽ οὕτως ἐκ τῶν συγ-
χωρηθέντων αὐτοῖς γενήσεταί τι προὔργου, τῶν μὲν ἀνισταμένων
σωμάτων ἐκ τῶν οἰκείων μερῶν πάλιν συνισταμένων, οὐδενὸς δὲ
τῶν εἰρημένων μέρους ὄντος οὐδὲ τὴν ὡς μέρους ἐπέχοντος σχέσιν
ἢ τάξιν, οὐ μὴν οὐδὲ παραμένοντος πάντοτε τοῖς τρεφομένοις
τοῦ σώματος μέρεσιν ἢ συνανισταμένου τοῖς ἀνισταμένοις, οὐδὲν
συντελοῦντος ἔτι πρὸς τὸ ζῆν οὐχ αἵματος οὐ φλέγματος οὐ χολῆς
οὐ πνεύματος.[1] οὐδὲ γὰρ ὧν ἐδεήθη ποτὲ τὰ τρεφόμενα σώματα,
δεηθήσεται καὶ τότε, συνανῃρημένης τῇ τῶν τρεφομένων ἐνδείᾳ καὶ
φθορᾷ τῆς ἐξ ὧν ἐτρέφετο χρείας. 2. ἔπειτ᾽ εἰ καὶ[2] μέχρι σαρκὸς
φθάνειν τὴν ἐκ τῆς τοιαύτης τροφῆς μεταβολὴν ὑποθοῖτό τις, οὐδ᾽
οὕτως ἀνάγκη τις ἔσται τὴν νεωστὶ μεταβληθεῖσαν ἐκ τῆς τοιᾶσδε
τροφῆς σάρκα προσπελάσασαν ἑτέρου τινὸς ἀνθρώπου σώματι
πάλιν ὡς μέρος εἰς τὴν ἐκείνου τελεῖν συμπλήρωσιν, τῷ μήτε αὐτὴν
τὴν προσλαμβάνουσαν σάρκα πάντοτε φυλάττειν ἣν προσείληφεν,
μήτε τὴν ἑνωθεῖσαν ταύτην μόνιμον εἶναι καὶ παραμένειν ᾗ προσ-
ετέθη, πολλὴν δὲ καὶ τὴν ἐπὶ θάτερα δέχεσθαι μεταβολήν, ποτὲ μὲν
πόνοις ἢ φροντίσιν διαφορουμένην, ἄλλοτε δὲ λύπαις ἢ καμάτοις
ἢ νόσοις συντηκομένην,[3] καὶ ταῖς ἐξ ἐγκαύσεως ἢ περιψύξεως
ἐπιγινομέναις δυσκρασίαις, μὴ συμμεταβαλλομένων σαρκὶ καὶ
πιμελῇ τῶν [δημῶν][4] ἐν τῷ μένειν ἅπερ ἐστὶ τὴν τροφὴν δεχομένων.
3. τοιούτων δὲ γενομένων ἐπὶ τῆς[5] σαρκὸς παθημάτων, πολύ γ᾽ ἔτι
μᾶλλον εὕροι τις ἂν ταῦτα πάσχουσαν τὴν ἐξ ἀνοικείων τρεφομένην
σάρκα, νῦν μὲν εἰς ὄγκον προϊοῦσαν καὶ πιαινομένην ἐξ ὧν προσείληφεν, εἶτα πάλιν ἀποπτύουσαν ὃν ἂν τύχῃ τρόπον καὶ μειουμένην ἢ
μιᾷ τινι τῶν ἔμπροσθεν ῥηθεισῶν ἢ πλείοσιν· μόνην[6] δὲ παραμένειν
τοῖς μέρεσιν ἃ συνδεῖν ἢ στέγειν ἢ θάλπειν πέφυκεν, τὴν ὑπὸ τῆς

---

7. [1] οὐ χολῆς οὐ πῦς A in mg.: fortasse οὐ ξανθῆς χολῆς, οὐ χολῆς μελαίνης
[2] ἔπειτ᾽ εἰ καὶ Schwartz: ἔπειθ᾽ ὅτι κἂν A   [3] post συντηκομένην add. ἢ
Wilamowitz, πολλάκις δὲ Schwartz   [4] δημῶν seclusit Wilamowitz
[5] τῆς: πάσης Wilamowitz, Schwartz   [6] μόνην Maranus: μόνα (α in ras.) A

7. In fact, even if one admits that food from such sources—let us
use the normal term 'food'—, though contrary to nature, is
broken up and transformed into one of the substances which are
wet or dry or hot or cold,[1] even so our opponents can gain no
advantage from such concessions. Bodies which arise are reconstituted from their own parts. None of the things to which we
have referred is such a part nor does it possess anything like the
nature or function of a part. Moreover it will not remain per-
manently in the parts of the body now being nourished nor will it
arise with the parts that arise, since in that state blood, phlegm,
bile, or breath[2] will make no further contribution to life. For then
bodies will not need the nourishment they once needed, since the
usefulness of what nourished them will disappear when these
organisms have no further need of nourishment and have undergone dissolution.

2. Moreover, even if one were to grant that transformation
from food of that kind will result in its being turned into flesh,
still it will not necessarily be the case that the flesh which is so
recent a transformation from such food and which has attached
itself to the body of another man will again form an essential part
of that individual. Neither does the flesh which has received some
addition always retain what it has received, nor is the assimilated
flesh stable and capable of remaining with its recipient. It is
susceptible of profound transformation, and in two ways: sometimes it is dissipated through exertions or preoccupations; at
other times it wastes away through suffering, fatigue, or disease,
as well as through the disturbances that affect us because of heat-
strokes or chills, since the members which receive food and remain
what they were do not change along with alterations in bulk of
flesh or fat.

3. If flesh in general is subject to such things, how much more
would this be found true of flesh that has been nourished with
unsuitable foods. Sometimes it swells up and grows fat from what
it has taken in; and then again it rejects such nourishment one
way or the other, and it diminishes in bulk for one or more of the
reasons mentioned above. Only that flesh stays with our members,
remaining naturally united with them by bonds of intimacy and

---

7. [1] For the important role that these opposites play in Galen's system see his
De Aliment. 1 (Kühn, xv. 226), *De Nat. Fac.* 1. 5 (Kühn, ii. 11–12). They are also
referred to by Methodius (*De Res.* 2. 10. 2); and arguments somewhat similar
to what follows are advanced by Methodius in this context (*De Res.* 2. 10–14).
    [2] Perhaps we had here originally (see textual apparatus) a reference to the
four humours: blood, phlegm, yellow bile, black bile (Galen, *De Nat. Hom.*
1. 18, Kühn, xv. 59).

φύσεως ἐξειλεγμένην καὶ τούτοις προσπεφυκυῖαν οἷς τὴν κατὰ
φύσιν συνεξέπλησεν ζωὴν καὶ τοὺς ἐν τῇ ζωῇ πόνους. 4. ἀλλ᾽
(οὔτε γὰρ καθ᾽ ὃ δεῖ κρινομένων τῶν ἔναγχος ἐξητασμένων οὔτε
κατὰ συγχώρησιν παραδεχθέντων τῶν ἐπ᾽ ἐκείνοις γεγυμνασμένων
ἀληθὲς δεικνύναι δυνατὸν τὸ πρὸς αὐτῶν λεγόμενον) οὐκ⁷ ἂν
συγκραθείη ποτὲ τὰ τῶν ἀνθρώπων σώματα τοῖς τῆς αὐτῆς οὖσι
φύσεως, κἂν ὑπ᾽ ἀγνοίας ποτὲ κλαπῶσι τὴν αἴσθησιν δι᾽ ἑτέρου τινὸς
μετασχόντες τοιούτου σώματος, κἂν αὐτόθεν ὑπ᾽ ἐνδείας ἢ μανίας
ὁμοειδοῦς τινος μιανθῶσιν σώματι· εἴ γε μὴ λελήθασιν ἡμᾶς
ἀνθρωποειδεῖς τινες ὄντες θῆρες ἢ μικτὴν ἔχοντες φύσιν ἐξ ἀνθρώπων καὶ θηρίων, οἵους πλάττειν εἰώθασιν οἱ τολμηρότεροι τῶν
ποιητῶν.

8. Καὶ τί δεῖ λέγειν περὶ τῶν μηδενὶ ζῴῳ πρὸς τροφὴν ἀποκληρω-
θέντων σωμάτων μόνην δὲ τὴν εἰς γῆν ταφὴν ἐπὶ τιμῇ τῆς φύσεως
μεμοιραμένων, ὅπου γε μηδ᾽ ἄλλο τι τῶν ζῴων τοῖς ἐκ ταὐτοῦ
εἴδους εἰς τροφὴν ἀπεκλήρωσεν ὁ ποιήσας, κἂν [ἐν]¹ ἄλλοις τισὶ
τῶν ἑτερογενῶν τροφὴ γίνηται κατὰ φύσιν; 2. εἰ μὲν οὖν ἔχουσιν
δεικνύναι σάρκας ἀνθρώπων ἀνθρώποις εἰς βρῶσιν ἀποκληρωθείσας,
οὐδὲν κωλύσει τὰς ἀλληλοφαγίας εἶναι κατὰ φύσιν ὥσπερ ἄλλο τι
τῶν τῇ φύσει συγκεχωρημένων καὶ τούς γε τὰ τοιαῦτα λέγειν
τολμῶντας τοῖς τῶν φιλτάτων ἐντρυφᾶν σώμασιν ὡς οἰκειοτέροις
ἢ καὶ τοὺς εὐνουστάτους σφίσιν τούτοις αὐτοῖς ἑστιᾶν. 3. εἰ δὲ
τοῦτο μὲν οὐδ᾽² εἰπεῖν εὐαγές, τὸ δὲ σαρκῶν ἀνθρώπων ἀνθρώπους
μετασχεῖν ἔχθιστόν τι καὶ παμμίαρον καὶ πάσης ἐκθέσμου καὶ παρὰ
φύσιν βρώσεως ἢ πράξεως ἐναγέστερον, τὸ δὲ παρὰ φύσιν οὐκ ἂν
ποτε χωρήσειεν εἰς τροφὴν τοῖς ταύτης δεομένοις μέρεσιν καὶ
μορίοις, τὸ δὲ μὴ χωροῦν εἰς τροφὴν οὐκ ἂν ἑνωθείη τούτοις ἃ
μηδὲ τρέφειν πέφυκεν, οὐδὲ τὰ τῶν ἀνθρώπων σώματα συγκραθείη³
ποτ᾽ ἂν τοῖς ὁμοίοις σώμασιν, οἷς ἐστιν εἰς τροφὴν παρὰ φύσιν, κἂν
πολλάκις διὰ τῆς τούτων ἴῃ γαστρὸς κατά τινα πικροτάτην συμ-
φοράν· 4. ἀποχωροῦντα δὲ τῆς θρεπτικῆς δυνάμεως καὶ σκιδ-
νάμενα πρὸς ἐκεῖνα πάλιν ἐξ ὧν τὴν πρώτην ἔσχεν σύστασιν,

7. ⁷ οὐκ Schwartz : οὔτ᾽ A
8. ¹ ἐν seclusit Schwartz   ² οὔτ᾽ A   ³ συγκριθείη A : corr. Wilamowitz

familiarity, which has been selected by nature and joined to those parts along with which it contributes to life according to nature and sustains life's labours.

4. It is impossible, then, for our opponents to demonstrate the truth of what they say, either when the points just examined are judged on their own merits, or when arguments worked out on behalf of our adversaries are granted for the sake of argument; consequently, human bodies can never be fused with others of the same nature, even if it happens that men ever eat of such a body out of ignorance, when deprived of an awareness of their deed by someone else,[3] or if of their own accord they become defiled with a body of the same kind through hunger or madness.[4] I assume that we have not overlooked certain man-like beasts or creatures with natures partly human and partly bestial, such as the bolder poets like to fabricate!

8. What need is there to discuss bodies which have not been destined as food for any animal but have simply been allotted burial in the earth as befits the dignity of their nature? There at least the Maker has destined no creature, human or other, to serve as food for its own kind, even though it may naturally become food for other creatures of different species.

2. If they really can show that human flesh is destined to serve as food for humans, then nothing stands in the way of saying that cannibalism is according to nature, like anything else in harmony with nature; and those who dare to say such things can enjoy themselves feasting on the bodies of their nearest and dearest as being more suitable nourishment for them, or they can entertain their intimate friends with the same sort of fare. 3. But even to say such a thing is sacrilegious. For men to eat human flesh is the most hateful and defiling act. It is more sacrilegious than the eating of any other food or the doing of any other deed which is lawless and contrary to nature. What is unnatural can never become food for the parts and members which require it; what does not become food cannot be assimilated by organisms which it was not even intended to nourish. If this is so, then neither can human bodies ever become fused with bodies of a similar kind. It is contrary to nature for them to serve as food in this capacity, even though they often pass through the belly of like bodies in times of dire distress.

4. Such parts of the body lose their nourishing power and are dispersed again to the elements out of which they first arose, and

7.   [3] As in the case of Thyestes.
     [4] As in the cases discussed in 4. 4 above.

ἐνοῦται μὲν τούτοις ἐφ' ὅσον ἂν ἕκαστον τύχῃ χρόνον, ἐκεῖθεν δὲ
διακριθέντα πάλιν σοφίᾳ καὶ δυνάμει τοῦ πᾶσαν ζῴου φύσιν σὺν
ταῖς οἰκείαις δυνάμεσι συγκρίναντος ἐνοῦται προσφυῶς ἕκαστον
ἑκάστῳ, κἂν πυρὶ καυθῇ, κἂν ὕδατι κατασαπῇ, κἂν ὑπὸ θηρίων ἢ
τῶν ἐπιτυχόντων ζῴων καταδαπανηθῇ, κἂν τοῦ παντὸς σώματος
ἐκκοπὲν προδιαλυθῇ τῶν ἄλλων μερῶν· ἐνωθέντα δὲ πάλιν ἀλλήλοις
τὴν αὐτὴν ἴσχει χώραν πρὸς τὴν τοῦ αὐτοῦ σώματος ἁρμονίαν τε
καὶ σύστασιν καὶ τὴν τοῦ νεκρωθέντος ἢ καὶ πάντῃ διαλυθέντος
ἀνάστασιν καὶ ζωήν.[a] 5. ταῦτα μὲν οὖν ἐπὶ πλεῖον μηκύνειν οὐκ
εὔκαιρον· ὁμολογουμένην γὰρ ἔχει τὴν ἐπίκρισιν τοῖς γε μὴ μιξο-
θήροις.

9. Πολλῶν δὲ ὄντων τῶν εἰς τὴν προκειμένην ἐξέτασιν χρησι-
μωτέρων, παραιτοῦμαι δὴ νῦν τοὺς καταφεύγοντας ἐπὶ τὰ τῶν
ἀνθρώπων ἔργα καὶ τοὺς τούτων δημιουργοὺς ἀνθρώπους, οἵ τὰ
συντριβέντα τῶν ἔργων ἢ χρόνῳ παλαιωθέντα ἢ καὶ ἄλλως δια-
φθαρέντα καινουργεῖν ἀδυνατοῦσιν, εἶτα ἐξ ὁμοίου τοῖς κεραμεῦσι
καὶ τέκτοσι δεικνύναι πειρωμένους τὸ καὶ τὸν θεὸν μήτ' ἂν βουλη-
θῆναι μήτε βουληθέντα δυνηθῆναι νεκρωθὲν ἢ καὶ διαλυθὲν ἀναστῆσαι σῶμα, καὶ μὴ λογιζομένους ὅτι διὰ τούτων ⟨ἐπ' ἴσης⟩[1] τοῖς
χειρίστοις ἐξυβρίζουσιν εἰς θεόν, συνεξισοῦντες τῶν πάντῃ διεστη-
κότων τὰς δυνάμεις, μᾶλλον δὲ καὶ τῶν ταύταις χρωμένων τὰς
οὐσίας καὶ τὰ τεχνητὰ τοῖς φυσικοῖς. 2. περὶ μὲν οὖν τούτων
σπουδάζειν οὐκ ἀνεπιτίμητον· ἠλίθιον γὰρ ὡς ἀληθῶς τὸ τοῖς ἐπι-
πολαίοις καὶ ματαίοις ἀντιλέγειν. μακρῷ γε μὴν ἐνδοξότερον καὶ
πάντων ἀληθέστατον τὸ φῆσαι τὸ παρ' ἀνθρώποις ἀδύνατον παρὰ θεῷ
δυνατόν.[a] εἰ δὲ δι' αὐτῶν τούτων ὡς ἐνδόξων καὶ διὰ πάντων τῶν

---

8. [a] Cf. John 11: 25   9. [a] Cf. Luke 18: 27

9. [1] ἐπ' ἴσης add. Schwartz

remain united with them for whatever length of time it turns out
to be in each case. After they have been separated again from the
elements by the wisdom and power of him who links every kind of
animal with its appropriate properties, they reunite intimately,
one part with the other, even though they may be consumed
by fire, rotted away by water, devoured by wild beasts or any
animal that comes along, or have one part which has been cut off
from the whole body and has decomposed before the others. They
are united again to one another and occupy the same place as
before so as to restore the harmonious composition of the body and
effect the resurrection and the life of the body that has died and
has totally decomposed.

5. This is not the time to dwell on these things any longer; for
they gain ready assent at least from those who are not half beast.

9. Since there are many points more pertinent to the present
investigation, I do not intend to occupy myself now with those
who take refuge in parallels provided by the works of men and
their human creators. Men cannot recreate works of their own
that have been shattered, worn out by time, or destroyed in some
other way. Yet out opponents try to show from the analogy of
potters and carpenters that God would not even want to raise a
dead body or one already decomposed and that if he did want to,
he would not be able.[1] They do not reflect that they mock God
in this way as much as the most unprincipled do. They equate the
powers of those[2] who are in every way disparate, or rather, they
equate the *natures* of those[2] who make use of these diverse powers,
setting the contrivances of art on a level with the products of
nature.[3]

2. One would deserve censure to take such arguments seriously;
for it would be downright foolish to dispute what is superficial
and vain. It is far more plausible and is most in harmony with the
truth to say: 'What is impossible with men is possible with God.'[4]
If our discussion shows by these very appeals, plausible as they

---

9. [1] Traces of a similar debate (between orthodox and radically Origenist
thinkers) can be found in Gregory of Nyssa (*De Hom. Opif.* 25. 1, 26. 1).

[2] i.e. God and man.

[3] Man's work and God's work are related as art is to nature. The former is
regarded as having to do with what is artificial and derived, the latter with
what is uncontrived and original.

[4] Precisely the language of the Gospels in which simple Christians mindlessly
took refuge according to Methodius' Origenist (*De Res.* 1. 21. 1). Celsus,
however, had already criticized such language (Origen, *Contra Celsum* 5. 14;
cf. R. Walzer, *Galen on Jews and Christians* [1949], pp. 23–37).

μικρῷ πρόσθεν ἐξητασμένων δείκνυσιν ὁ λόγος δυνατόν, εὔδηλον ὡς
οὐκ ἀδύνατον. ἀλλὰ μὴν οὐδ᾽ ἀβούλητον.

10. Τὸ γὰρ ἀβούλητον ἢ ὡς ἄδικον αὐτῷ[1] ἐστιν ἀβούλητον ἢ ὡς
ἀνάξιον. καὶ πάλιν τὸ ἄδικον ἢ περὶ αὐτὸν θεωρεῖται τὸν ἀναστη-
σόμενον ἢ περὶ ἄλλον τινὰ παρ᾽ αὐτόν.[2] ἀλλ᾽ ὅτι μὲν οὐδεὶς ἀδικεῖται
τῶν ἔξωθεν καὶ τῶν ἐν τοῖς οὖσιν ἀριθμουμένων, πρόδηλον. 2. οὔτε
γὰρ αἱ νοηταὶ φύσεις ἐκ τῆς τῶν ἀνθρώπων ἀναστάσεως ἀδικη-
θεῖεν ἄν· οὐδὲ γὰρ ἐμπόδιόν τι ταύταις πρὸς τὸ εἶναι, οὐ βλάβος,
οὐχ ὕβρις ἡ τῶν ἀνθρώπων ἀνάστασις· οὐ μὴν οὐδὲ τῶν ἀλόγων ἡ
φύσις οὐδὲ τῶν ἀψύχων· οὐδὲ γὰρ ἔσται μετὰ τὴν ἀνάστασιν, περὶ
δὲ τὸ μὴ ὂν οὐδὲν ἄδικον. 3. εἰ δὲ καὶ εἶναί τις ὑποθοῖτο διὰ παντός,
οὐκ ἂν ἀδικηθείη ταῦτα τῶν ἀνθρωπίνων σωμάτων ἀνανεωθέντων·
εἰ γὰρ νῦν ὑπείκοντα τῇ φύσει τῶν ἀνθρώπων [καὶ][3] τῆς τούτων
χρείας[4] ὄντων ἐνδεῶν ὑπό τε ζυγὸν ἠγμένα καὶ δουλείαν παντοίαν
οὐδὲν ἀδικεῖται, πολὺ μᾶλλον, ἀφθάρτων καὶ ἀνενδεῶν γενομένων
καὶ μηκέτι δεομένων τῆς τούτων χρείας, ἐλευθερωθέντα δὲ πάσης
δουλείας, οὐκ ἀδικηθήσεται. 4. οὐδὲ γὰρ, εἰ φωνῆς μετεῖχεν,
ᾐτιάσατο ἂν τὸν δημιουργὸν ὡς παρὰ τὸ δίκαιον ἐλαττούμενα τῶν
ἀνθρώπων, ὅτι μὴ τῆς αὐτῆς τούτοις τετύχηκεν ἀναστάσεως. ὧν
γὰρ ἡ φύσις οὐκ ἴση, τούτοις οὐδὲ τὸ τέλος ἴσον ὁ δίκαιος ἐπιμετρεῖ.
χωρὶς δὲ τούτων, παρ᾽ οἷς οὐδεμία τοῦ δικαίου κρίσις, οὐδὲ μέμψις
ἀδικίας. 5. οὐ μὴν οὐδ᾽ ἐκεῖνο φῆσαι δυνατὸν ὡς περὶ αὐτὸν
θεωρεῖταί τις ἀδικία τὸν ἀνιστάμενον ἄνθρωπον. ἔστι μὲν γὰρ
οὗτος ἐκ ψυχῆς καὶ σώματος, οὔτε δὲ εἰς ψυχὴν οὔτε εἰς σῶμα
δέχεται τὴν ἀδικίαν. οὔτε γὰρ τὴν ψυχὴν ἀδικεῖσθαι φήσει τις
σωφρονῶν· λήσεται γὰρ[5] ταύτῃ συνεκβάλλων καὶ τὴν παροῦσαν
ζωήν· εἰ γὰρ νῦν ἐν φθαρτῷ καὶ παθητῷ κατοικοῦσα σώματι
μηδὲν ἠδίκηται, πολὺ μᾶλλον ἀφθάρτῳ καὶ ἀπαθεῖ συζῶσα οὐκ
ἀδικηθήσεται. ἀλλ᾽ οὐδὲ τὸ σῶμα ἀδικεῖταί τι· εἰ γὰρ νῦν φθαρτὸν
ἀφθάρτῳ συνὸν† ⟨ἀδικηθή⟩σεται.[6] 6. οὐ μὴν οὐδ᾽ ἐκεῖνο φαίη τις

---

10. [1] αὐτῷ n: αὐτό A : seclusit Wilamowitz   [2] αὐτόν p: αὐτοῖς A
[3] καὶ seclusit Wilamowitz   [4] ταῖς τούτων χρείαις A : corr. Schwartz
[5] λήσεται γὰρ Schwartz: λήσεται γε A : ὅτι in mg. add. A[1]   [6] συνὸν / / / / / / /
/ / / / / σεται A : οὐδ᾽ ἀφθάρτῳ ἀδικηθή in ras. add. A[1]: τὸ ὁλόκληρον οὕτως· εἰ γὰρ
νῦν φθαρτῷ συνὸν οὐκ ἀδικεῖται, δῆλον ὅτι οὐδὲ ἀφθάρτῳ συνὸν οὐκ ἀδικηθήσεται in
mg. add. A[1]: suppleverim ex. gr. μηδὲν ἠδίκηται, πολὺ μᾶλλον ἄφθαρτον ἀφθάρτῳ
συνὸν οὐκ ἀδικηθή...

are, and by all the arguments examined shortly before, that the thing is possible, clearly it is not impossible; then, certainly, neither is it foreign to the will of God.

10. What is foreign to the will of God is so because he regards it either as unjust or as unworthy[1] of him. Injustice may in turn be seen in regard to either the one who will arise or some other being. It is clear, however, that no being distinct from man and numbered among created things is thereby wronged. 2. The resurrection of men could not wrong purely rational natures;[2] for it surely is no impediment, no injury, no affront to their existence. And it surely could not wrong those creatures who have no reason or soul;[3] for they will not exist after the resurrection, and there can be no injustice in the case of that which does not exist. 3. Even if one supposed that they in fact exist for ever, they would not be wronged by the renewal of human bodies. For if they are not wronged now, when they are subjected to mankind (which requires their services) and are placed under the yoke and endure every kind of slavery, much less will they be wronged when they are freed from all slavery, because mankind has become incorruptible and in need of nothing and no longer requires their services. 4. Even if they had a voice, then, they would not have complained to the Creator that it was unjust for them to have been made inferior to men by not having a share in the resurrection with them. For a just appraiser does not assign the same destiny to beings whose nature is not the same. Apart from animals, who cannot discern justice, there are no creatures on whose behalf a charge of injustice can be brought.

5. And it certainly cannot be said that any injustice is to be seen in regard to the man himself who is resurrected. For he consists of soul and body, and no wrong is inflicted on either his soul or his body. No sensible person will say that man's soul is wronged, for otherwise he will unwittingly reject also our present life along with the resurrection; if the soul is not wronged now when it dwells in a corruptible and passible body, much less will it be wronged when it lives with an incorruptible and impassible one. Neither is the body wronged in any way; for if the corruptible body has not been wronged now when linked with an incorruptible soul, much less will the incorruptible body be wronged when linked with an incorruptible soul.

6. Moreover one cannot say that it is a work unworthy of God

---

10. [1] Cf. 2. 3 above.
[2] Such as angels.
[3] Animals.

ἂν ὡς ἀνάξιον ἔργον τοῦ θεοῦ τὸ διαλυθὲν ἀναστῆσαι σῶμα καὶ
συναγαγεῖν· εἰ γὰρ τὸ χεῖρον οὐκ ἀνάξιον, τοῦτ' ἔστι τὸ φθαρτὸν
ποιῆσαι σῶμα καὶ παθητόν, πολὺ μᾶλλον τὸ κρεῖττον οὐκ ἀνάξιον,
ὅπερ ἐστὶν ἄφθαρτον καὶ ἀπαθές.

11. Εἰ δὲ διὰ τῶν κατὰ φύσιν πρώτων καὶ τῶν τούτοις ἑπομένων
δέδεικται τῶν ἐξητασμένων ἕκαστον, εὔδηλον ὅτι καὶ δυνατὸν καὶ
βουλητὸν καὶ ἄξιον τοῦ δημιουργήσαντος ἔργον ἡ τῶν διαλυθέντων
σωμάτων ἀνάστασις· διὰ γὰρ τούτων ἐδείχθη ψεῦδος τὸ τούτοις
ἀντικείμενον καὶ τὸ τῶν ἀπιστούντων παράλογον. 2. τί γὰρ δεῖ
λέγειν[1] περὶ τῆς ἑκάστου τούτων[2] πρὸς ἕκαστον ἀντιστροφῆς καὶ
τῆς πρὸς ἄλληλα συναφείας, εἴ γε δεῖ καὶ συνάφειαν εἰπεῖν ὡς
ἑτερότητί τινι κεχωρισμένων, οὐχὶ δὲ καὶ τὸ δυνατὸν λέγειν
βουλητὸν καὶ τὸ τῷ θεῷ βουλητὸν πάντως εἶναι δυνατὸν καὶ κατὰ
τὴν τοῦ βουληθέντος ἀξίαν;

3. Καὶ ὅτι μὲν ἕτερος ὁ περὶ τῆς ἀληθείας λόγος, ἕτερος δὲ ὁ
ὑπὲρ τῆς ἀληθείας, εἴρηται διὰ τῶν προλαβόντων μετρίως οἷς τε
διενήνοχεν ἑκάτερος καὶ πότε καὶ πρὸς τίνας ἔχει τὸ χρήσιμον·
κωλύει δὲ ἴσως οὐδὲν τῆς τε κοινῆς ἀσφαλείας ἕνεκεν καὶ τῆς τῶν
εἰρημένων πρὸς τὰ λειπόμενα συναφείας ἀπ' αὐτῶν τούτων καὶ τῶν
τούτοις προσηκόντων πάλιν ποιήσασθαι τὴν ἀρχήν. προσῆκεν δὲ
τῷ μὲν τὸ πρωτεύειν κατὰ φύσιν, τῷ δὲ τὸ δορυφορεῖν τὸν πρῶτον
ὁδοποιεῖν τε καὶ προανείργειν πᾶν ὁπόσον ἐμποδὼν καὶ πρόσαντες.
4. ὁ μὲν γὰρ περὶ τῆς ἀληθείας λόγος ἀναγκαῖος ὢν πᾶσιν ἀνθρώποις πρὸς ἀσφάλειαν καὶ σωτηρίαν πρωτοστατεῖ καὶ τῇ φύσει καὶ
τῇ τάξει καὶ τῇ χρείᾳ· τῇ φύσει μὲν, ὡς τὴν τῶν πραγμάτων γνῶσιν
παρεχόμενος, τῇ τάξει δὲ, ὡς ἐν τούτοις καὶ ἅμα τούτοις ὑπάρχων
ὧν γίνεται μηνυτής, τῇ χρείᾳ δὲ, ὡς τῆς ἀσφαλείας καὶ τῆς σωτηρίας
τοῖς γινώσκουσι γινόμενος πρόξενος. 5. ὁ δ' ὑπὲρ τῆς ἀληθείας
φύσει τε καὶ δυνάμει καταδεέστερος, ἔλαττον γὰρ τὸ τὸ ψεῦδος
ἐλέγχειν τοῦ τὴν ἀλήθειαν κρατύνειν· καὶ τάξει δεύτερος, κατὰ γὰρ
τῶν ψευδοδοξούντων ἔχει τὴν ἰσχύν· ψευδοδοξία δὲ ἐξ ἐπισπορᾶς
ἐπεφύη καὶ παραφθορᾶς· ἀλλὰ δὴ καὶ τούτων οὕτως ἐχόντων
προτάττεται πολλάκις καὶ γίνεταί ποτε χρειωδέστερος ὡς ἀναιρῶν

11. [1] λέγει A: corr. n   [2] τούτων Schwartz: τῶν A

to raise up and reconstitute a decomposed body; for if the lesser work—the making of a corruptible and passible body—is not unworthy of God, how much more is the greater work—the making of an incorruptible and impassible body—not unworthy of God.

11. If then each point of the inquiry has been demonstrated from the first natural principles and what flows from them logically, clearly the resurrection of decomposed bodies is a work that is possible for the Creator, willed by him, and worthy of him. For with these arguments it has been shown that the objections to them and the absurd opinions of unbelievers are false. 2. What need, then, is there to speak concerning the relation of each of these points to the other and the intimate connection between them—if indeed one can even use the term 'connection', as though they were marked off from one another by some difference, rather than simply say that what is 'possible' is 'willed' and what is 'willed' by God is assuredly 'possible' and 'worthy' of the one who willed it?

3. Some attention has been given above to the fact that debate *concerning* the truth is one thing and debate *on behalf of* the truth another; and we have indicated in what way the two approaches differ as well as when and against whom they are useful.[1] Still nothing, I think, prevents us from making a fresh start on the basis of points already made and consequences derived from them, thereby giving certainty to everyone and exploiting the connection between the matters already discussed and what remains to be said. Of the two approaches, one is naturally foremost; the other naturally stands guard over the former, paves the road for it, and removes in advance any barrier or obstacle in its path. 4. Debate concerning the truth has primacy by its nature, rank, and usefulness since it is necessary for the security and deliverance of all men. It has primacy by its nature because it supplies knowledge of reality; by its rank because it remains bound up with the realities of which it is the exponent; by its usefulness because it serves as patron to provide security and deliverance to those who know it. 5. Debate on behalf of the truth is inferior by its nature and function, for it is a less significant thing to refute falsehood than to confirm truth. And it is second in rank since it exercises its power against adherents to error. Error is an aftergrowth produced by a second sowing and an adulteration of the first.[2] Since this is the situation, the second mode of argumentation is often placed first and is sometimes more useful, because it destroys and purges away the unbelief which disturbs some men

11. [1] Cf. 1. 3–5 above.　　　　[2] Cf. 1. 1 above.

καὶ προδιακαθαίρων τὴν ἐνοχλοῦσάν τισιν ἀπιστίαν καὶ τοῖς ἄρτι
προσιοῦσι τὴν ἀμφιβολίαν ἢ ψευδοδοξίαν. 6. καὶ πρὸς ἓν μὲν
ἑκάτερος ἀναφέρεται τέλος· εἰς γὰρ τὴν εὐσέβειαν ἔχει τὴν ἀνα-
φορὰν ὅ τε τὸ ψεῦδος ἐλέγχων καὶ ὁ τὴν ἀλήθειαν κρατύνων· οὐ
μὴν καὶ καθάπαξ ἕν εἰσιν, ἀλλ' ὁ μὲν ἀναγκαῖος, ὡς ἔφην, πᾶσι τοῖς
πιστεύουσι καὶ τοῖς τῆς ἀληθείας καὶ τῆς ἰδίας σωτηρίας φροντί-
ζουσιν, ὁ δὲ ἔστιν ὅτε καί τισιν καὶ πρός τινας γίνεται χρειωδέστερος. 7. καὶ ταῦτα μὲν ἡμῖν κεφαλαιωδῶς προειρήσθω πρὸς
ὑπόμνησιν τῶν ἤδη λεχθέντων· ἰτέον δὲ ἐπὶ τὸ προκείμενον, καὶ
δεικτέον ἀληθῆ τὸν περὶ τῆς ἀναστάσεως λόγον ἀπό τε τῆς αἰτίας
αὐτῆς, καθ' ἣν καὶ δι' ἣν ὁ πρῶτος γέγονεν ἄνθρωπος οἵ τε μετ'
ἐκεῖνον, εἰ καὶ μὴ κατὰ τὸν ὅμοιον γεγόνασι τρόπον, ἀπό τε τῆς
κοινῆς πάντων ἀνθρώπων ὡς ἀνθρώπων φύσεως, ἔτι δὲ ἀπὸ τῆς τοῦ
ποιήσαντος ἐπὶ τούτοις κρίσεως, καθ' ὅσον ἕκαστος ἔζησε χρόνον
καὶ καθ' οὓς ἐπολιτεύσατο νόμους, ἣν οὐκ ἄν τις ἀμφισβητήσειεν
εἶναι δικαίαν.

12. Ἔστι δὲ ὁ μὲν ἀπὸ τῆς αἰτίας λόγος, ἐὰν ἐπισκοπῶμεν πότερον
ἁπλῶς καὶ μάτην γέγονεν ἄνθρωπος ἢ τινὸς ἕνεκεν· εἰ δὲ τινὸς
ἕνεκεν, πότερον ἐπὶ τῷ[1] γενόμενον αὐτὸν[2] ζῆν καὶ διαμένειν καθ'
ἣν ἐγένετο φύσιν ἢ διὰ χρείαν τινός· εἰ δὲ κατὰ χρείαν, ἤτοι τὴν
αὐτοῦ τοῦ ποιήσαντος ἢ ἄλλου τινὸς τῶν αὐτῷ προσηκόντων καὶ
πλείονος φροντίδος ἠξιωμένων. 2. ὃ δὴ καὶ κοινότερον σκοποῦντες
εὑρίσκομεν ὅτι πᾶς εὖ φρονῶν καὶ λογικῇ κρίσει πρὸς τὸ ποιεῖν τι
κινούμενος οὐδὲν ὧν κατὰ πρόθεσιν ἐνεργεῖ ποιεῖ μάτην, ἀλλ' ἤτοι
τῆς ἰδίας ἕνεκεν χρήσεως ἢ διὰ χρείαν ἄλλου τινὸς ὧν πεφρόντικεν
ἢ δι' αὐτὸ τὸ γινόμενον, ὁλκῇ τινι φυσικῇ καὶ στοργῇ πρὸς τὴν
αὐτοῦ[3] γένεσιν κινούμενος· οἷον (λεγέσθω γὰρ δι' εἰκόνος τινός, ἵνα
σαφὲς γένηται τὸ προκείμενον) ἄνθρωπος ποιεῖ μὲν οἶκον διὰ τὴν
ἰδίαν χρείαν, ποιεῖ δὲ βουσὶ καὶ καμήλοις ἢ τοῖς ἄλλοις ζώοις, ὧν
ἐστιν ἐνδεής, τὴν ἑκάστῳ τούτων ἁρμόζουσαν σκέπην οὐκ ἰδίας
ἕνεκεν χρήσεως κατὰ τὸ φαινόμενον, ἀλλὰ κατὰ μὲν τὸ τέλος διὰ
τοῦτο, κατὰ δὲ τὸ προσεχὲς διὰ τὴν τούτων ὧν πεφρόντικεν ἐπιμέ-
λειαν· ποιεῖται δὲ καὶ παῖδας οὔτε διὰ χρείαν ἰδίαν οὔτε δι' ἕτερόν τι

---

12. [1] τῷ Schwartz: τὸ A: τοῦτο A¹   [2] αὐτὸν c: αὐτὸ A: αὐτὸ τὸ A¹
[3] αὐτοῦ Wilamowitz, Schwartz

and the doubt or error which troubles those who now are coming forward. 6. Both modes of argumentation have one goal; for that which refutes falsehood and that which confirms truth have in view true piety. Certainly they are not absolutely one and the same thing. The one is necessary, as I said, to all who believe and have a concern for the truth and their own deliverance. The other is sometimes more useful both for and against certain people.

7. This is what we have to say by way of summary, as a reminder of what has already been discussed. Now let us proceed to the task before us and show the truth of the argument concerning the resurrection: (a) by investigating the fundamental reason in accordance with which and because of which the first man came into existence and those after him (even though they did not come into existence in the same way), and (b) by examining the common nature of all men simply as men, and, we may add, (c) by considering the judgement of their Maker upon them, a judgement which takes into account the whole time each man lives and the laws by which he governed himself, a judgement the justice of which no man can doubt.

12. The argument which investigates the reason is a consideration on our part whether man came into being by chance, and for no purpose, or with some end in view; and if it was with some end in view, was it that after his creation he should live and perdure in accordance with the nature with which he was created or should exist for the use of another; and if he was created for the use of another, was it for the use of the Maker himself or some other being about whom God is concerned and who is considered worthy of higher regard than men.

2. When we examine this matter more broadly, we find that no one who is in his right mind and who is moved by rational judgement to make something makes anything in vain which he undertakes with a purpose in mind. He is moved by some natural inclination and yearning to produce it either (a) for his own use or (b) for the use of some other being for whom he has regard or (c) for the sake of the thing itself which he produces. Let us resort to analogy to clarify the issue: (a) A man makes a house for his own use but (b) makes for his cattle and camels or other animals on which he depends the shelter suitable for each. To all appearances he does not make such a shelter for his own use; but in terms of his ultimate object it is precisely for that purpose that he does so and only secondarily on behalf of those animals for which he shows his regard. He also (c) begets children, not (a) for his

τῶν αὐτῷ προσηκόντων, ἀλλ' ἐπὶ τῷ⁴ εἶναί τε καὶ διαμένειν καθόσον
οἷόν τε⁵ τοὺς ὑπ' αὐτοῦ γεννωμένους, τῇ τῶν παίδων καὶ τῶν
ἐγγόνων διαδοχῇ τὴν ἑαυτοῦ τελευτὴν παραμυθούμενος καὶ ταύτῃ
τὸ θνητὸν ἀπαθανατίζειν οἰόμενος. 3. ἀλλὰ ταῦτα μὲν ὑπὸ τούτων·
ὁ μέντοι θεὸς οὔτ' ἂν μάτην ἐποίησεν τὸν ἄνθρωπον· ἔστι γὰρ σοφός,
οὐδὲν δὲ σοφίας ἔργον μάταιον· οὔτε διὰ χρείαν ἰδίαν· παντὸς γάρ
ἐστιν ἀπροσδεής, τῷ δὲ μηδενὸς δεομένῳ τὸ παράπαν οὐδὲν τῶν
ὑπ' αὐτοῦ γενομένων συντελέσειεν ἂν εἰς χρείαν ἰδίαν. ἀλλ' οὐδὲ
διά τινα τῶν ὑπ' αὐτοῦ γενομένων ἔργων ἐποίησεν ἄνθρωπον. οὐδὲν
γὰρ τῶν λόγῳ καὶ κρίσει χρωμένων οὔτε τῶν μειζόνων οὔτε τῶν
καταδεεστέρων γέγονεν ἢ γίνεται πρὸς ἑτέρου χρείαν, ἀλλὰ διὰ τὴν
ἰδίαν αὐτῶν τῶν γενομένων ζωήν τε καὶ διαμονήν. 4. οὐδὲ γὰρ ὁ
λόγος εὑρίσκει τινὰ χρείαν τῆς τῶν ἀνθρώπων γενέσεως αἰτίαν, τῶν
μὲν ἀθανάτων ἀνενδεῶν ὄντων καὶ μηδεμιᾶς μηδαμῶς παρ' ἀνθρώπων
συντελείας πρὸς τὸ εἶναι δεομένων, τῶν δὲ ἀλόγων ἀρχομένων
κατὰ φύσιν καὶ τὰς πρὸς ὃ πέφυκεν ἕκαστον χρείας ἀνθρώποις ἀπο-
πληρούντων ἀλλ' οὐκ αὐτῶν⁶ τούτοις χρῆσθαι πεφυκότων· θέμις
γὰρ οὔτε ἦν οὔτε ἐστὶ τὸ ἄρχον καὶ ἡγεμονοῦν ὑπάγειν εἰς χρῆσιν
τοῖς ἐλάττοσιν ἢ τὸ λογικὸν ὑποτάττειν⁷ ἀλόγοις, οὖσιν πρὸς τὸ
ἄρχειν ἀνεπιτηδείοις. 5. οὐκοῦν εἰ μήτε ἀναιτίως καὶ μάτην
γέγονεν ἄνθρωπος (οὐδὲν γὰρ τῶν ὑπὸ θεοῦ γενομένων μάταιον
κατά γε τὴν τοῦ ποιήσαντος γνώμην) μήτε χρείας ἕνεκεν αὐτοῦ τοῦ
ποιήσαντος ἢ⁸ ἄλλου τινὸς τῶν ὑπὸ θεοῦ γενομένων ποιημάτων,
εὔδηλον ὅτι κατὰ μὲν τὸν πρῶτον καὶ κοινότερον λόγον δι' ἑαυτὸν
καὶ τὴν ἐπὶ πάσης τῆς δημιουργίας θεωρουμένην ἀγαθότητα καὶ
σοφίαν ἐποίησεν ὁ θεὸς ἄνθρωπον, κατὰ δὲ τὸν προσεχέστερον
τοῖς γενομένοις λόγον διὰ τὴν αὐτῶν τῶν γενομένων ζωήν, οὐκ
ἐπὶ μικρὸν ἐξαπτομένην εἶτα παντελῶς σβεννυμένην. 6. ἑρπετοῖς
γάρ, οἶμαι, καὶ πτηνοῖς καὶ νηκτοῖς ἢ καὶ κοινότερον εἰπεῖν πᾶσι
τοῖς ἀλόγοις τὴν τοιαύτην ζωὴν ἀπένειμεν θεός, τοῖς δὲ αὐτὸν ἐν
ἑαυτοῖς ἀγαλματοφοροῦσιᵃ τὸν ποιητὴν νοῦν τε συνεπιφερομένοις καὶ
λογικῆς κρίσεως μεμοιραμένοις⁹ τὴν εἰς ἀεὶ διαμονὴν ἀπεκλήρωσεν

12. ᵃ Cf. Gen. 1: 26

---

12. ⁴ τῷ p corr. c: τὸ A   ⁵ οἷόν τε pc: οἴονται A   ⁶ ἀλλ' οὐκ αὐτῶν
Schwartz: α τῶν A: ἀλλ' οὐ τῶν A¹   ⁷ ὑποτάττειν c: ὑποτάττο// A:
ὑποτάττον A¹   ⁸ ἢ p: ἦτ' (τ in ras.) A   ⁹ μεμοιραμένης A:
corr. pcn

own use nor (*b*) for the sake of anything else about which he is concerned, but (*c*) that his offspring may continue in existence as long as possible, thus consoling himself for his own death by a succession of children and descendants and in this way thinking to make the mortal immortal.[1]

3. This is what is done by men. As for God, he did not make man in vain; for he is wise, and no work of wisdom is vain. But (*a*) he did not make man for his own use; for he does not need anything, and in the case of one who has no needs at all, nothing which he has created can contribute anything to him for his own use. But (*b*) neither did he make man for the sake of any other of his created works. For (*c*) none of the beings, whether superior or inferior,[2] who are gifted with reason and discernment has been created or is created for the use of another but only for the continued survival of such creatures themselves. 4. Indeed reason can find no use which is the cause of the creation of men. The immortals are in need of nothing and require no provision at all from men for their existence; irrational creatures are by nature subordinate and satisfy men's needs in whatever way the nature of each ordains but are not naturally destined themselves to make use of men. For it never was right, nor is it now, that what rules and leads should be used by lesser beings or that what is rational should be subordinated to irrational creatures since the latter are not fit to rule.

5. If man, then, was not created purposelessly or in vain (for nothing created by God is vain at least as far as the original intention of the creator is concerned), and was not created for the use of the Maker himself or of any other of God's creations, it is clear that in terms of the primary and more general reason God made man for his own sake and out of the goodness and wisdom which is reflected throughout creation; but, in terms of the reason which has more immediate bearing on those created, God made man simply for the survival of such creatures themselves that they should not be kindled for a short time, then entirely extinguished. 6. For God has assigned this fleeting form of life, I think, to snakes, birds, and fish, or, to speak more generally, to all irrational creatures; but the Maker has decreed an unending existence to those who bear his image in themselves, are gifted with intelligence, and share the faculty for rational discernment,

---

12. [1] A clear reflection of the sentiment expressed by Plato, *Symp.* 206 c, 207 e.
　　[2] Probably angels (cf. the 'immortals' below) and men.

ὁ ποιήσας, ἵνα γινώσκοντες τὸν ἑαυτῶν ποιητὴν καὶ τὴν τούτου
δύναμίν τε καὶ σοφίαν νόμῳ τε συνεπόμενοι καὶ δίκῃ τούτοις συν-
διαιωνίζωσιν ἀπόνως, οἷς τὴν προλαβοῦσαν ἐκράτυναν ζωὴν καίπερ
ἐν φθαρτοῖς καὶ γηΐνοις ὄντες σώμασιν. 7. ὁπόσα μὲν γὰρ ἄλλου
του χάριν γέγονεν, παυσαμένων ἐκείνων ὧν ἕνεκεν γέγονεν, παύ-
σεται εἰκότως καὶ αὐτὰ τὰ γενόμενα τοῦ εἶναι καὶ οὐκ ἂν διαμένοι
μάτην, ὡς ἂν μηδεμίαν ἐν τοῖς ὑπὸ θεοῦ γενομένοις τοῦ ματαίου
χώραν ἔχοντος· τά γε μὴν δι' αὐτὸ τὸ εἶναι καὶ ζῆν καθὼς
πέφυκεν γενόμενα, ὡς αὐτῆς τῆς αἰτίας τῇ φύσει συνειλημμένης καὶ
κατ' αὐτὸ μόνον τὸ εἶναι θεωρουμένης, οὐδεμίαν οὐδέποτε δέξαιτ'
ἂν τὴν τὸ εἶναι παντελῶς ἀφανίζουσαν αἰτίαν. 8. ταύτης δὲ ἐν τῷ
εἶναι πάντοτε θεωρουμένης, δεῖ σῴζεσθαι πάντως καὶ τὸ γενόμενον
ζῷον, ἐνεργοῦν τε καὶ πάσχον ἃ πέφυκεν, ἑκατέρου τούτων ἐξ ὧν
γέγονεν τὰ παρ' ἑαυτοῦ συνεισφέροντος καὶ τῆς μὲν ψυχῆς οὔσης
τε καὶ διαμενούσης ὁμαλῶς ἐν ᾗ γέγονεν φύσει καὶ διαπονούσης ἃ
πέφυκεν (πέφυκεν δὲ ταῖς τοῦ σώματος ἐπιστατεῖν ὁρμαῖς καὶ τὸ
προσπῖπτον ἀεὶ τοῖς προσήκουσι κρίνειν καὶ μετρεῖν κριτηρίοις καὶ
μέτροις), τοῦ δὲ σώματος κινουμένου κατὰ φύσιν πρὸς ἃ πέφυκεν
καὶ τὰς ἀποκληρωθείσας αὐτῷ δεχομένου μεταβολάς, μετὰ δὲ τῶν
ἄλλων τῶν κατὰ τὰς ἡλικίας ἢ κατ' εἶδος ἢ μέγεθος τὴν ἀνάστασιν.
9. εἶδος γάρ τι μεταβολῆς καὶ πάντων ὕστατον ἡ ἀνάστασις ἥ τε
τῶν κατ' ἐκεῖνον τὸν χρόνον περιόντων ἔτι πρὸς τὸ κρεῖττον
μεταβολή.

13. Ἐπὶ δὲ τούτοις τεθαρρηκότες οὐ μεῖον ἢ τοῖς ἤδη γενομένοις
καὶ τὴν ἑαυτῶν ἐπισκοποῦντες φύσιν, τήν τε μετ' ἐνδείας καὶ
φθορᾶς ζωὴν στέργομεν ὡς τῷ παρόντι βίῳ προσήκουσαν καὶ τὴν
ἐν ἀφθαρσίᾳ διαμονὴν ἐλπίζομεν βεβαίως· ἣν οὐ παρὰ ἀνθρώπων
ἀναπλάττομεν μάτην ψευδέσιν ἑαυτοὺς βουκολοῦντες ἐλπίσιν,
ἀπλανεστάτῳ δὲ πεπιστεύκαμεν ἐχεγγύῳ, τῇ τοῦ δημιουργήσαντος
ἡμᾶς γνώμῃ, καθ' ἣν ἐποίησεν ἄνθρωπον ἐκ ψυχῆς ἀθανάτου καὶ
σώματος νοῦν τε συγκατεσκεύασεν αὐτῷ καὶ νόμον ἔμφυτον ἐπὶ
σωτηρίᾳ καὶ φυλακῇ τῶν παρ' αὐτοῦ διδομένων, ἔμφρονι δὲ[1] βίῳ
καὶ ζωῇ λογικῇ προσηκόντων, εὖ εἰδότες ὡς οὐκ ἂν τοιοῦτον
κατεσκεύασεν ζῷον καὶ πᾶσι τοῖς πρὸς διαμονὴν ἐκόσμησεν, εἰ μὴ

13. [1] δὲ Wilamowitz: τε A

so that they, knowing their Maker and his power and wisdom and complying with law and justice, might live without distress eternally with the powers by which they governed their former life, even though they were in corruptible and earthly bodies.

7. Everything that is created for the sake of something else may itself reasonably be expected to cease existing when those for whose sake it was created cease existing; it cannot survive purposelessly, since what is purposeless can have no place among the things created by God. As to that which was created simply for the sake of existing and living in accordance with its own nature, there can be no reason for it ever to perish entirely since the very reason for its existence is comprehended by its nature and is seen to be simply and solely this—to exist. 8. Since, then, the reason is seen to be this, to exist for ever, the living being with its natural active and passive functions must by all means be preserved; each of the two parts of which it consists makes its contribution: the soul continues to exist undistracted in the form in which it was created, and it works at the tasks which suit its nature (which consist of ruling the bodily impulses and of judging and assessing by proper standards and measures what constantly impinges on a man); the body is moved by nature to what is suitable for it and is receptive to the changes decreed for it, including, along with the other changes affecting age, appearance, or size, also the resurrection. 9. For the resurrection from the dead and the transformation for the better which will affect those still alive at that time constitute a form of change and indeed the last of all.

13. Encouraged by these expectations, no less than by the changes which have already occurred, and examining our own nature, we are content with life in this needy and corruptible form as suited to our present mode of existence, and we firmly hope for survival in an incorruptible form. This is not a delusion which we have got from men by feeding ourselves vainly on false hopes; but we have put our confidence in an infallible security, the will of our Creator, according to which he made man of an immortal soul and a body and endowed him with intelligence and an innate law to safeguard and protect the things which he gave that are suitable for intelligent beings with a rational life. We full well know that he would not have formed such an animal and adorned him with all that contributes to permanence if he

διαμένειν ἐβούλετο τὸ γενόμενον. 2. εἰ τοίνυν ὁ τοῦδε τοῦ παντὸς δημιουργὸς ἐποίησεν ἄνθρωπον ἐπὶ τῷ² ζωῆς ἔμφρονος μετασχεῖν καὶ γενόμενον θεωρὸν τῆς τε μεγαλοπρεπείας αὐτοῦ καὶ τῆς ἐπὶ πᾶσι³ σοφίας τῇ τούτων θεωρίᾳ συνδιαμένειν ἀεὶ κατὰ τὴν ἐκείνου γνώμην καὶ καθ᾽ ἣν εἴληχεν φύσιν, ἡ μὲν τῆς γενέσεως αἰτία πιστοῦται τὴν εἰς ἀεὶ διαμονήν, ἡ δὲ διαμονὴ τὴν ἀνάστασιν, ἧς χωρὶς οὐκ ἂν διαμείνειεν ἄνθρωπος. ἐκ δὲ τῶν εἰρημένων εὔδηλον ὡς τῇ τῆς γενέσεως αἰτίᾳ καὶ τῇ γνώμῃ τοῦ ποιήσαντος δείκνυται σαφῶς ἡ ἀνάστασις. 3. Τοιαύτης δὲ τῆς αἰτίας οὔσης, καθ᾽ ἣν εἰς τόνδε παρῆκται τὸν κόσμον ἄνθρωπος, ἀκόλουθον ἂν εἴη τὸν τούτοις κατὰ φύσιν ἢ καθ᾽ εἱρμὸν ἑπόμενον διασκέψασθαι λόγον· ἔπεται δὲ κατὰ τὴν ἐξέτασιν τῇ μὲν αἰτίᾳ τῆς γενέσεως ἡ τῶν γεννηθέντων ἀνθρώπων φύσις, τῇ δὲ φύσει τῶν γενομένων ἡ τοῦ ποιήσαντος ἐπὶ τούτοις δικαία κρίσις τούτοις τε πᾶσι τὸ τοῦ βίου τέλος. ἐξητασμένων δὲ ἡμῖν τῶν προτεταγμένων ἐπισκεπτέον ἑξῆς τὴν τῶν ἀνθρώπων φύσιν.

14. Ἡ τῶν τῆς ἀληθείας δογμάτων ἢ τῶν ὁπωσοῦν εἰς ἐξέτασιν προβαλλομένων ἀπόδειξις τὴν ἀπλανῆ τοῖς λεγομένοις ἐπιφέρουσα πίστιν οὐκ ἔξωθέν ποθεν ἔχει τὴν ἀρχὴν οὐδ᾽ ἐκ τῶν τισι δοκούντων ἢ δεδογμένων, ἀλλ᾽ ἐκ τῆς κοινῆς καὶ φυσικῆς ἐννοίας ἢ τῆς πρὸς τὰ πρῶτα τῶν δευτέρων ἀκολουθίας. 2. ἢ γὰρ περὶ τῶν πρώτων ἐστὶ δογμάτων καὶ δεῖ μόνης ὑπομνήσεως τῆς τὴν φυσικὴν ἀνακινούσης ἔννοιαν ἢ περὶ τῶν κατὰ φύσιν ἑπομένων τοῖς πρώτοις καὶ τῆς φυσικῆς ἀκολουθίας καὶ δεῖ τῆς ἐπὶ τούτοις τάξεως, δεικνύντας τί τοῖς πρώτοις ἢ τοῖς προτεταγμένοις ἀκολουθεῖ κατ᾽ ἀλήθειαν, ἐπὶ τῷ μήτε τῆς ἀληθείας ἢ τῆς κατ᾽ αὐτὴν ἀσφαλείας ἀμελεῖν μήτε τὰ τῇ φύσει τεταγμένα καὶ διωρισμένα συγχεῖν ἢ τὸν φυσικὸν εἱρμὸν διασπᾶν. 3. ὅθεν, οἶμαι, [χρῆν]¹ δίκαιον περὶ τῶν προκειμένων ἐσπουδακότας καὶ κρίνειν ἐμφρόνως θέλοντας εἴτε γίνεται τῶν ἀνθρωπίνων σωμάτων ἀνάστασις εἴτε μή, πρῶτον μὲν ἐπισκοπεῖν καλῶς τῶν πρὸς τὴν τοῦδε δεῖξιν συντελούντων τὴν δύναμιν καὶ ποίαν ἕκαστον εἴληχεν χώραν καὶ τί μὲν τούτων πρῶτον τί δὲ

did not want this creature to be permanent. 2. The Creator of our universe made man that he might participate in rational life and, after contemplating God's majesty and universal wisdom, perdure and make them the object of his eternal contemplation, in accordance with the divine will and the nature allotted to him. The reason then for man's creation guarantees his eternal survival, and his survival guarantees his resurrection, without which he could not survive *as man*. From what we have said it is clear that the resurrection is demonstrated by the reason for man's creation and the will of the Creator.

3. Since such is the reason for which man was brought into this world, the next logical step would be to examine the argument which naturally and inevitably follows these points. In this inquiry the examination of the nature of mortal men follows the investigation of the reason for their creation; and the discussion of the Creator's just judgement upon them and the end of life which comes upon them all follows the examination of the nature of those created. Since we have completed the first part of our inquiry, let us take the next step and investigate the nature of man.

14. To offer proof of true doctrines or of the various arguments set before us for investigation, proof that will provide unshakeable certainty for what is said, one ought not to begin from some point external to the debate or with opinions and doctrines of other men but with the universal and natural axiom[1] or the logical sequence which links secondary with primary principles. 2. For either it is a matter of primary doctrines and only a reminder is needed to stir up the natural axiom, or it is a matter of the natural consequences derived from primary doctrines and of natural logical sequence and all that is needed is to take the points up in order, showing what actually follows from the primary principles or the preceding arguments, so as not to neglect the truth or the sure demonstration of it, nor to confuse the natural order of arguments and the distinctions between them, nor to break the natural logical sequence.

3. Consequently it is right, I think, for those who are concerned with such matters, and who want to judge wisely as to whether there is a resurrection of human bodies or not, first to take careful note of the force of the arguments which contribute to the demonstration of this teaching, to see what place each has been allotted, and to consider which of them is first, which the second or third, or

---

14. [1] The technical Stoic term (*SVF* ii. 104, 154, 473) for notions which the human mind is naturally disposed to have.

δεύτερον ἢ τρίτον τί δ᾽ ἐπὶ τούτοις ὕστατον· 4. ταῦτα δὲ διαταξαμένους χρὴ πρώτην μὲν τάξαι τὴν αἰτίαν τῆς τῶν ἀνθρώπων γενέσεως, τοῦτ᾽ ἔστιν τὴν τοῦ δημιουργήσαντος γνώμην καθ᾽ ἣν ἐποίησεν ἄνθρωπον, ταύτῃ δὲ προσφυῶς ἐπισυνάψαι τὴν τῶν γενομένων ἀνθρώπων φύσιν, οὐχ ὡς τῇ τάξει δευτερεύουσαν, διὰ δὲ τὸ μὴ δύνασθαι κατὰ ταὐτὸν ἀμφοτέρων γενέσθαι τὴν κρίσιν, κἂν ὅτι μάλιστα συνυπάρχωσιν ἀλλήλαις καὶ πρὸς τὸ προκείμενον τὴν ἴσην παρέχωνται δύναμιν. 5. διὰ δὲ τούτων, ὡς πρώτων καὶ τὴν ἐκ δημιουργίας ἐχόντων ἀρχήν, ἐναργῶς δεικνυμένης τῆς ἀναστάσεως, οὐδὲν ἧττον καὶ διὰ τῶν τῆς προνοίας λόγων ἔστι λαβεῖν τὴν περὶ ταύτης πίστιν, λέγω δὲ διὰ τῆς ἑκάστῳ τῶν ἀνθρώπων ὀφειλομένης κατὰ δικαίαν κρίσιν τιμῆς ἢ δίκης καὶ τοῦ κατὰ τὸν ἀνθρώπινον βίον τέλους. 6. πολλοὶ γὰρ τὸν τῆς ἀναστάσεως λόγον διαλαμβάνοντες τῷ τρίτῳ μόνῳ τὴν πᾶσαν ἐπήρεισαν αἰτίαν, νομίσαντες τὴν ἀνάστασιν² γίνεσθαι διὰ τὴν κρίσιν. τοῦτο δὲ περιφανῶς δείκνυται ψεῦδος ἐκ τοῦ πάντας μὲν ἀνίστασθαι τοὺς ἀποθνήσκοντας ἀνθρώπους, μὴ πάντας δὲ κρίνεσθαι τοὺς ἀναστάντας· εἰ γὰρ μόνον τὸ κατὰ τὴν κρίσιν δίκαιον τῆς ἀναστάσεως ἦν αἴτιον, ἐχρῆν δήπου τοὺς μηδὲν ἡμαρτηκότας ἢ κατορθώσαντας μηδ᾽ ἀνίστασθαι, τοῦτ᾽ ἔστι τοὺς κομιδῇ νέους παῖδας· ἐξ ὧν³ δὲ πάντας ἀνίστασθαι τούς τε ἄλλους καὶ δὴ καὶ τοὺς κατὰ τὴν πρώτην ἡλικίαν τελευτήσαντας καὶ αὐτοὶ δικαιοῦσιν, οὐ διὰ τὴν κρίσιν ἡ ἀνάστασις γίνεται κατὰ πρῶτον λόγον, ἀλλὰ διὰ τὴν τοῦ δημιουργήσαντος γνώμην καὶ τὴν τῶν δημιουργηθέντων φύσιν.

15. Ἀρκούσης δὲ καὶ μόνης τῆς ἐπὶ τῇ γενέσει τῶν ἀνθρώπων θεωρουμένης αἰτίας δεῖξαι τὴν ἀνάστασιν κατὰ φυσικὴν ἀκολουθίαν ἑπομένην τοῖς διαλυθεῖσι σώμασιν, δίκαιον ἴσως πρὸς μηδὲν ἀποκνῆσαι τῶν προτεθέντων, ἀκολούθως δὲ τοῖς εἰρημένοις καὶ τὰς ἐξ ἑκάστου τῶν ἑπομένων ἀφορμὰς ὑποδεῖξαι τοῖς ἐξ αὐτῶν συνιδεῖν μὴ δυναμένοις καὶ πρό γε τῶν ἄλλων τὴν τῶν γενομένων ἀνθρώπων φύσιν, ἐπὶ τὴν αὐτὴν ἄγουσαν ἔννοιαν καὶ τὴν ἴσην παρέχουσαν περὶ τῆς ἀναστάσεως πίστιν. 2. εἰ γὰρ πᾶσα κοινῶς ἡ τῶν ἀνθρώπων φύσις ἐκ ψυχῆς ἀθανάτου καὶ τοῦ κατὰ τὴν γένεσιν αὐτῇ συναρμοσθέντος σώματος ἔχει τὴν σύστασιν καὶ μήτε τῇ

---

14. ² ἀνάστασιν Schwartz: αἰτίαν A   ³ ἐξ ὧν Schwartz: ἐξ //ν A:
ἐξὸν A¹

which the last of them all. 4. Those marshalling these arguments must place in the first rank the reason for the creation of men —that is, the will of the Creator according to which he made man—and then link with it intimately the examination of the nature of created men, not because this argument is second in rank but because it is impossible to pass judgement on both at the same time, even though they are as closely united with each other as possible and have equal weight for our subject. 5. Once the resurrection has been clearly demonstrated by these arguments, which are primary and grounded in the work of creation, it is possible to gain assurance on this matter no less by reasons having to do with providence—I mean, through a consideration of the reward or punishment owing each man in accordance with just judgement and the end that befits human life. 6. For there have been many who, in treating the doctrine of the resurrection, presented only the third argument to support their reason for it, thinking that the resurrection must take place because of the judgement. This is clearly shown to be false from the fact that all men who die arise, whereas all who arise are not judged. For if only justice exercised at the judgement were the cause of the resurrection, then even those guilty of no error or incapable of virtue—that is, very young children—would not arise. Since they admit, however, that all will arise, including those who died in infancy as well as all others, the resurrection does not take place primarily because of the judgement but because of the will of the Creator and the nature of those created.

15. Although the reason derived from a consideration of the creation of men suffices by itself to demonstrate by a natural line of argument that the resurrection follows upon the dissolution of the body, it is still right, I think, to evade none of the issues raised but, pursuing what has been said, to lay out the basic points arising from each line of deduction for those who cannot grasp them themselves, and to discuss especially the nature of created men, since an investigation of it brings us to the same conclusion as before and provides equal confirmation of the resurrection. 2. For if human nature universally considered is constituted by an immortal soul and a body which has been united with it at its creation; and if God has not separately assigned a creation and existence and course of life of this kind to the soul as such or to the body but to men who are made up of both, so that they might spend their life and come to one common end with the parts from which they are created and exist; then it is necessary, since all there is is one living being composed of two parts, undergoing

φύσει τῆς ψυχῆς καθ' ἑαυτὴν μήτε τῇ φύσει τοῦ σώματος χωρὶς
ἀπεκλήρωσεν θεὸς τὴν τοιάνδε γένεσιν ἢ τὴν ζωὴν καὶ τὸν σύμ-
παντα βίον, ἀλλὰ τοῖς ἐκ τούτων γενομένοις[1] ἀνθρώποις, ἵν', ἐξ ὧν
γίνονται[2] καὶ ζῶσι, διαβιώσαντες εἰς ἕν τι καὶ κοινὸν καταλήξωσιν
τέλος, δεῖ, πάντως ἑνὸς ὄντος ἐξ ἀμφοτέρων ζῴου τοῦ καὶ πάσχοντος
ὁπόσα πάθη ψυχῆς καὶ ὁπόσα τοῦ σώματος ἐνεργοῦντός τε καὶ
πράττοντος ὁπόσα τῆς αἰσθητικῆς ἢ τῆς λογικῆς δεῖται κρίσεως,
πρὸς ἕν τι τέλος ἀναφέρεσθαι πάντα τὸν ἐκ τούτων εἱρμόν, ἵνα
πάντα καὶ διὰ πάντων συντρέχῃ πρὸς μίαν ἁρμονίαν καὶ τὴν αὐτὴν
συμπάθειαν, ἀνθρώπου γένεσις, ἀνθρώπου φύσις, ἀνθρώπου ζωή,
ἀνθρώπου πράξεις καὶ πάθη καὶ βίος καὶ τὸ τῇ φύσει προσῆκον
τέλος. 3. εἰ δὲ μία τίς ἐστιν ἁρμονία τοῦ ζῴου παντὸς καὶ συμ-
πάθεια, καὶ τῶν ἐκ ψυχῆς φυομένων καὶ τῶν διὰ τοῦ σώματος
ἐπιτελουμένων, ἓν εἶναι δεῖ καὶ τὸ ἐπὶ πᾶσι τούτοις τέλος. ἓν δὲ
τέλος ἔσται κατ' ἀλήθειαν, τοῦ αὐτοῦ ζῴου κατὰ τὴν ἑαυτοῦ σύστασιν
ὄντος, οὗπέρ ἐστιν τέλος τὸ τέλος. τὸ αὐτὸ δὲ ζῷον ἔσται καθαρῶς,
τῶν αὐτῶν ὄντων πάντων ἐξ ὧν ὡς μερῶν τὸ ζῷον. τὰ αὐτὰ δὲ
κατὰ τὴν ἰδιάζουσαν ἕνωσιν ἔσται, τῶν διαλυθέντων πάλιν ἑνωθέντων πρὸς τὴν τοῦ ζῴου σύστασιν. 4. ἡ δὲ τῶν αὐτῶν ἀνθρώπων
σύστασις ἐξ ἀνάγκης ἑπομένην δείκνυσιν τὴν τῶν νεκρωθέντων καὶ
διαλυθέντων σωμάτων ἀνάστασιν· ταύτης γὰρ χωρὶς οὔτ' ἂν ἑνωθείη
τὰ αὐτὰ μέρη κατὰ φύσιν ἀλλήλοις οὔτ' ἂν συσταίη τῶν αὐτῶν
ἀνθρώπων ἡ φύσις. 5. εἰ δὲ καὶ νοῦς καὶ λόγος δέδοται τοῖς
ἀνθρώποις πρὸς διάκρισιν νοητῶν, οὐκ οὐσιῶν μόνον ἀλλὰ καὶ τῆς
τοῦ δόντος ἀγαθότητος καὶ σοφίας καὶ δικαιοσύνης, ἀνάγκη,
διαμενόντων ὧν ἕνεκεν ἡ λογικὴ δέδοται κρίσις, καὶ αὐτὴν διαμένειν
τὴν ἐπὶ τούτοις δοθεῖσαν κρίσιν· ταύτην δὲ διαμένειν ἀδύνατον, μὴ
τῆς δεξαμένης αὐτὴν καὶ τὰ[3] ἐν οἷς ἐστι διαμενούσης φύσεως. 6. ὁ
δὲ καὶ νοῦν καὶ λόγον δεξάμενός ἐστιν ἄνθρωπος, οὐ ψυχὴ καθ'
ἑαυτήν· ἄνθρωπον ἄρα δεῖ τὸν ἐξ ἀμφοτέρων ὄντα διαμένειν εἰς ἀεί,
τοῦτον δὲ διαμένειν ἀδύνατον μὴ ἀνιστάμενον. 7. ἀναστάσεως γὰρ
μὴ γινομένης, οὐκ ἂν ἡ τῶν ἀνθρώπων ὡς ἀνθρώπων διαμένοι
φύσις· τῆς δὲ τῶν ἀνθρώπων φύσεως μὴ διαμενούσης, μάτην μὲν
ἡ ψυχὴ συνήρμοσται τῇ τοῦ σώματος ἐνδείᾳ καὶ τοῖς τούτου

---

15. [1] γενομένοις c et (ex γενωμένοις) n et (ex γεννωμένοις) s: γεννωμένοις A:
ἡνωμένοις Wilamowitz, Schwartz   [2] γίνονται c et (ex γεννῶνται) s: γεννῶνται A: ἥνωνται Wilamowitz, Schwartz   [3] τὰ Wilamowitz: τῆς A

all the experiences of soul and body, and actively carrying out whatever requires the judgement of the senses and of reason, that the entire concatenation of such phenomena leads to one end so that all these things—the creation of man, the nature of man, the existence of man, the deeds and experiences and way of life of man, and the end which suits his nature—might be fully integrated into one harmonious and concordant whole.

3. If there is one harmony and concord of the entire living being, including the things that spring from the soul and the things that are done by the body, then the end of all these phenomena must also be one. And the end will truly be one if the same living being whose end it is remains constituted as before. The living being will be genuinely the same if everything remains the same which serves as its parts. And these will remain the same in a union appropriate to them if what has undergone dissolution is again united to reconstitute the living being. 4. The reconstitution of the same men demonstrates how the resurrection of dead bodies that have undergone dissolution must logically follow; for without it the same parts would not be united with one another in a way that conforms with their nature, nor would the same men be reconstituted as they were.

5. If understanding and reason have been given men to discern intelligibles, not only substances but also the goodness, wisdom, and justice of him who endowed men with these gifts, it is necessary that, where the realities because of which rational discernment has been given are permanent, the discernment itself which was given to be exercised on them should also be permanent. But it cannot be permanent unless the nature which received it and the faculties in which it resides are permanent. 6. It is man—not simply soul—who received understanding and reason. Man, then, who consists of both soul and body must survive for ever; but he cannot survive unless he is raised. 7. For if there is no resurrection, the nature of men *as men* would not be permanent. And if the nature of men is not permanent, in vain has the soul been attuned to the needs and feelings of the body, in

πάθεσιν, μάτην δὲ τὸ σῶμα πεπέδηται πρὸς τὸ τυγχάνειν ὧν
ὀρέγεται, ταῖς τῆς ψυχῆς ἡνίαις ὑπεῖκον καὶ χαλιναγωγούμενον,
μάταιος δὲ ὁ νοῦς, ματαία δὲ φρόνησις καὶ δικαιοσύνης παρατήρησις
ἢ καὶ πάσης ἀρετῆς ἄσκησις καὶ νόμων θέσις καὶ διάταξις καὶ
συνόλως εἰπεῖν πᾶν ὅτι περ ἐν ἀνθρώποις καὶ δι' ἀνθρώπους καλόν,
μᾶλλον δὲ καὶ αὐτὴ τῶν ἀνθρώπων ἡ γένεσίς τε καὶ φύσις. 8. εἰ δὲ
πάντων καὶ πανταχόθεν ἀπελήλαται τῶν ἔργων τοῦ θεοῦ καὶ τῶν
ὑπ' ἐκείνου διδομένων δωρεῶν τὸ μάταιον, δεῖ πάντως τῷ τῆς
ψυχῆς ἀτελευτήτῳ συνδιαιωνίζειν τὴν τοῦ σώματος διαμονὴν κατὰ
τὴν οἰκείαν φύσιν.

16. Ξενιζέσθω δὲ μηδεὶς εἰ τὴν θανάτῳ καὶ φθορᾷ διακοπτομένην
ζωὴν ὀνομάζομεν διαμονήν, λογιζόμενος ὡς οὐχ εἷς τοῦ προσρήμα-
τος ὁ λόγος, οὐχ ἓν τῆς διαμονῆς τὸ μέτρον, ὅτι μηδὲ τῶν διαμενόντων φύσις μία. 2. εἴπερ γὰρ κατὰ τὴν οἰκείαν φύσιν ἕκαστον
τῶν διαμενόντων ἔχει τὴν διαμονήν, οὔτ' ἐπὶ τῶν καθαρῶς ἀφθάρτων καὶ ἀθανάτων εὕροι τις ἂν ἰσάζουσαν τὴν διαμονήν, τῷ μηδὲ
τὰς οὐσίας τῶν κρειττόνων συνεξισοῦσθαι ταῖς καθ' ὑπόβασιν
διαφερούσαις, οὔτ' ἐπὶ τῶν ἀνθρώπων τὴν ὁμαλὴν ἐκείνην καὶ[1]
ἀμετάβλητον ἐπιζητεῖν ἄξιον, ἅτε δὴ τῶν μὲν ἐξ ἀρχῆς γενομένων
ἀθανάτων καὶ διαμενόντων μόνῃ[2] τῇ γνώμῃ τοῦ ποιήσαντος
ἀτελευτήτως, τῶν δὲ ἀνθρώπων κατὰ μὲν τὴν ψυχὴν ἀπὸ γενέσεως
ἐχόντων τὴν ἀμετάβλητον διαμονήν, κατὰ δὲ τὸ σῶμα προσλαμ-
βανόντων ἐκ μεταβολῆς τὴν ἀφθαρσίαν· 3. ὅπερ ὁ τῆς ἀναστάσεως
βούλεται λόγος· πρὸς ἣν ἀποβλέποντες τήν τε διάλυσιν τοῦ σώματος
ὡς ἑπομένην τῇ μετ' ἐνδείας καὶ φθορᾶς ζωῇ περιμένομεν καὶ μετὰ
ταύτην τὴν μετ' ἀφθαρσίας ἐλπίζομεν διαμονήν, οὔτε τῇ τῶν
ἀλόγων τελευτῇ συνεξισοῦντες τὴν ἡμετέραν τελευτὴν οὔτε τῇ τῶν
ἀθανάτων διαμονῇ τὴν τῶν ἀνθρώπων διαμονήν, ἵνα μὴ λάθωμεν
ταύτῃ συνεξισοῦντες καὶ τὴν τῶν ἀνθρώπων φύσιν καὶ ζωὴν
οἷς μὴ προσῆκεν. 4. οὐ τοίνυν ἐπὶ τούτῳ δυσχεραίνειν ἄξιον, εἴ
τις ἀνωμαλία θεωρεῖται περὶ τὴν τῶν ἀνθρώπων διαμονήν, οὐδ'
ἐπειδὴ χωρισμὸς ψυχῆς ἀπὸ τοῦ σώματος†[3] μερῶν καὶ μορίων
διάλυσις τὴν συνεχῆ διακόπτει ζωήν, διὰ τοῦτ' ἀπογινώσκειν χρὴ
τὴν ἀνάστασιν. 5. οὐδὲ γὰρ ἐπειδὴ τὴν κατὰ συναίσθησιν ζωὴν

16. [1] καὶ Wilamowitz: τὴν A   [2] μόνη del. Wilamowitz, Schwartz
[3] post σώματος lacunam indicavit Schwartz

vain has the body, in obedience to the reins of the soul and
guided as by bit and bridle, been shackled to prevent it from
getting whatever it desires, vain is understanding, vain is wisdom
and the observance of justice or the exercise of every virtue and
the enactment and codification of laws—in a word, vain is everything admirable implanted in men and effected by men, or rather,
vain is the very creation and being of man. 8. But if vanity in the
works of God and the gifts granted by him is ruled out entirely,
it is absolutely necessary that the body should be permanent in a
way that conforms with its own nature and should exist eternally
with the deathless soul.

16. No one should be surprised if we call existence cut short by
death and corruption 'permanence'. Reflect on the fact that there
is no single meaning of the term and that there is no single
definition of 'permanence', since the nature of the things which are
permanent is not even one. 2. If then each of the things that are
permanent has a permanence of a kind that conforms to its
nature, one could not expect to find in the case of those who are
purely incorruptible and immortal a kind of permanence like
that of other creatures, since the substances of superior beings are
not like inferior substances; nor is it worth while in the case of
men to look for the undisturbed and changeless permanence
that characterizes superior beings; for the latter were created
immortal from the beginning and were made to survive for ever
simply by the will of God, whereas men were created to survive
unchanged only in respect to the soul, but in respect to the body
to gain incorruptibility through a transformation. 3. That is
what our teaching concerning the resurrection means. Setting
then the resurrection before our eyes, we await the dissolution of
the body as a concomitant of a needy and corruptible existence,
and hope for a permanent incorruptibility to follow it. We do not
regard our death as the same as the death of irrational creatures,
nor do we regard the permanence of men as the same as the
permanence of the immortals, that we may not inadvertently
equate the nature and existence of men with beings that are not
fit objects of comparison.

4. One ought not to have qualms about the fact that a certain
lack of continuity characterizes the 'permanence' of men, nor
ought one to deny the resurrection just because separation of soul
from the body, dissolution of parts and members, interrupts the
flow of life. 5. The natural suspension of the senses and the native

διακόπτειν δοκοῦσιν αἱ κατὰ τὸν ὕπνον φυσικῶς ἐγγινόμεναι
παρέσεις τῶν αἰσθήσεων καὶ τῶν φυσικῶν δυνάμεων, ἰσομέτροις
χρόνου διαστήμασιν ὑπνούντων τῶν ἀνθρώπων καὶ τρόπον τινὰ
πάλιν ἀναβιωσκόντων, τὴν αὐτὴν παραιτούμεθα λέγειν ζωήν· παρ᾽
ἣν αἰτίαν, οἶμαι, τινὲς ἀδελφὸν τοῦ θανάτου τὸν ὕπνον ὀνομά-
ζουσιν,ᵃ οὐχ ὡς ἐκ τῶν αὐτῶν προγόνων ἢ πατέρων φύντας γενεα-
λογοῦντες, ἀλλ᾽ ὡς τῶν ὁμοίων παθῶν τοῖς τε θανοῦσι καὶ τοῖς
ὑπνοῦσιν ἐγγινομένων, ἕνεκα γε τῆς ἠρεμίας⁴ καὶ τοῦ μηδενὸς
ἐπαισθάνεσθαι τῶν παρόντων ἢ γινομένων, μᾶλλον δὲ μηδὲ τοῦ
εἶναι καὶ τῆς ἰδίας ζωῆς. 6. εἴπερ οὖν τὴν τῶν ἀνθρώπων ζωὴν
τοσαύτης γέμουσαν ἀνωμαλίας ἀπὸ γενέσεως μέχρι διαλύσεως καὶ
διακοπτομένην πᾶσιν οἷς προείπομεν, οὐ παραιτούμεθα τὴν αὐτὴν
λέγειν ζωήν, οὐδὲ τὴν ἐπέκεινα τῆς διαλύσεως ζωήν, ἥτις ἑαυτῇ
συνεισάγει τὴν ἀνάστασιν, ἀπογινώσκειν ὀφείλομεν, κἂν ἐπὶ ποσὸν
διακόπτηται⁵ τῷ χωρισμῷ τῆς ψυχῆς ἀπὸ τοῦ σώματος.

17. αὕτη γὰρ τῶν ἀνθρώπων ἡ φύσις ἄνωθεν καὶ κατὰ γνώμην τοῦ
ποιήσαντος συγκεκληρωμένην ἔχουσα τὴν ἀνωμαλίαν, ἀνώμαλον
ἔχει τὴν ζωὴν καὶ τὴν διαμονήν, ποτὲ μὲν ὕπνῳ ποτὲ δὲ θανάτῳ
διακοπτομένην καὶ ταῖς καθ᾽ ἑκάστην ἡλικίαν μεταβολαῖς, οὐκ
ἐμφαινομένων ἐναργῶς τοῖς πρώτοις τῶν ὕστερον ἐπιγινομένων.
2. ἢ τίς ἂν ἐπίστευσεν μὴ τῇ πείρᾳ δεδιδαγμένος, ἐν ὁμοιομερεῖ καὶ
ἀδιαπλάστῳ¹ τῷ σπέρματι τοσούτων καὶ τηλικούτων ἀποκεῖσθαι
δυνάμεων†² ἢ τοσαύτην³ ἐπισυνισταμένων καὶ πηγνυμένων ὄγκων
διαφοράν, ὀστέων φημὶ καὶ νεύρων καὶ χόνδρων, ἔτι δὲ μυῶν καὶ
σαρκῶν καὶ σπλάγχνων καὶ τῶν λοιπῶν τοῦ σώματος μερῶν; οὔτε
γὰρ ἐν ὑγροῖς ἔτι τοῖς σπέρμασι τούτων ἔστιν ἰδεῖν οὐδὲν οὔτε μὴν
τοῖς νηπίοις ἐμφαίνεταί τι τῶν τοῖς τελείοις ἐπιγινομένων ἢ τῇ τῶν
τελείων ἡλικίᾳ τὰ τῶν παρηβηκότων ἢ τούτοις τὰ τῶν γεγηρα-
κότων. 3. ἀλλὰ δὴ καίτοι τῶν εἰρημένων τινῶν μὲν οὐδ᾽⁴ ὅλως
τινῶν δὲ ἀμυδρῶς ἐμφαινόντων τὴν φυσικὴν ἀκολουθίαν καὶ τὰς τῇ
φύσει τῶν ἀνθρώπων ἐπιγινομένας μεταβολάς, ὅμως ἴσασιν ὅσοι

16. ᵃ Homer, *Iliad* 14. 231, 16. 672, 682, *Odyssey* 13. 79–80

16. ⁴ ἠρεμίας A¹ : ἐρημίας A   ⁵ διακόπτεται A : corr. pc
17. ¹ διαπλάστῳ A : corr. n m. al.   ² post δυνάμεων lacunam indicavit
Schwartz supplens ἀρχὴν   ³ τοσαύτην Wilamowitz, Schwartz : τῶν ταύτην
A : τῶν ταύτῃ A¹   ⁴ οὐδ᾽ Rhosus : οὐθ᾽ A

faculties in sleep also appear to interrupt the conscious life, when men go to sleep at regular intervals of time and, so to speak, return to life again. Yet we are not unwilling to call it the same life. That is why, I think, some call sleep the 'brother of death', not that they are providing a genealogy for beings descended from the same ancestors or parents, but because similar passive states affect both the dead and those asleep, at least in so far as they are tranquil and are conscious of nothing that goes on around them or, rather, are not even conscious of their own existence and life. 6. If then we are not unwilling to call that human life the same life which is filled with discontinuity from birth to dissolution and interrupted in the ways we have indicated above, then neither should we exclude the life which follows dissolution and ushers in the resurrection with it, even though it has been interrupted for a time by the separation of the soul from the body.

17. Since then this human nature has been allotted discontinuity from the outset by the will of the Maker, it has a kind of life and permanence characterized by discontinuity and interrupted sometimes by sleep, sometimes by death, and by the changes that take place at each stage of life. And the later conditions do not exhibit themselves clearly in the first stages of its development. 2. Who would have believed, if he had not been taught by experience, that in undifferentiated and formless semen lay the origin of such numerous and vital faculties or of so great a variety of substances which could unite and form a solid whole, I mean bones, nerves, and gristle as well as muscle, flesh, entrails, and the other parts of the body? For it is impossible to see any of these things in the semen while it is still liquid; nor do any of the peculiar features of those who have matured make their appearance in children, or the features of adults in those who have just matured, or the features of the aged in adults. 3. But even though some of the developments mentioned exhibit not at all, or some only faintly, the natural sequence of human growth and the transformations which affect man's nature, still anyone who is not

μὴ τυφλώττουσιν ὑπὸ κακίας ἢ ῥαθυμίας περὶ τὴν τούτων κρίσιν,
ὅτι δεῖ πρῶτον μὲν γενέσθαι τῶν σπερμάτων καταβολήν, διαρθρω-
θέντων δὲ τούτων καθ' ἕκαστον μέρος καὶ μόριον καὶ προελθόν-
των εἰς φῶς τῶν κυηθέντων ἐπιγίνεται μὲν ἡ κατὰ τὴν πρώτην
ἡλικίαν αὔξησις ἥ τε κατ' αὔξησιν τελείωσις, τελειωθέντων δὲ
ὕφεσις τῶν φυσικῶν δυνάμεων μέχρι γήρως, εἶτα πεπονηκότων τῶν
σωμάτων ἡ διάλυσις. 4. ὥσπερ οὖν ἐπὶ τούτων,[5] οὔτε τοῦ σπέρ-
ματος ἐγγεγραμμένην ἔχοντος τὴν τῶν ἀνθρώπων φυὴν[6] ἢ μορφὴν
οὔτε τῆς ζωῆς τὴν εἰς τὰς πρώτας ἀρχὰς διάλυσιν, ὁ τῶν φυσικῶς
γινομένων εἱρμὸς παρέχει τὴν πίστιν τοῖς οὐκ ἐξ αὐτῶν τῶν φαι-
νομένων ἔχουσι τὸ πιστόν, πολὺ μᾶλλον ὁ λόγος ἐκ τῆς φυσικῆς
ἀκολουθίας ἀνιχνεύων τὴν ἀλήθειαν πιστοῦται τὴν ἀνάστασιν,
ἀσφαλέστερος ὢν καὶ κρείττων τῆς πείρας πρὸς πίστωσιν ἀληθείας.

18. Τῶν πρῴην ἡμῖν εἰς ἐξέτασιν προτεθέντων λόγων καὶ τὴν
ἀνάστασιν πιστουμένων πάντες μέν εἰσιν ὁμογενεῖς, ὡς ἐκ τῆς
αὐτῆς φύντες ἀρχῆς· ἀρχὴ γὰρ αὐτοῖς ἡ τῶν πρώτων ἀνθρώπων ἐκ
δημιουργίας γένεσις· ἀλλ' οἱ μὲν ἐξ αὐτῆς κρατύνονται τῆς πρώτης
ἀρχῆς ἐξ ἧσπερ ἔφυσαν, οἱ δὲ παρεπόμενοι τῇ τε φύσει καὶ τῷ βίῳ
τῶν ἀνθρώπων ἐκ τῆς τοῦ θεοῦ περὶ ἡμᾶς προνοίας λαμβάνουσιν
τὴν πίστιν· ἡ μὲν γὰρ αἰτία, καθ' ἣν καὶ δι' ἣν γεγόνασιν ἄνθρωποι,
συνεζευγμένη τῇ φύσει τῶν ἀνθρώπων ἐκ δημιουργίας ἔχει τὴν
ἰσχύν, ὁ δὲ τῆς δικαιοσύνης λόγος, καθ' ὃν κρίνει θεὸς τοὺς εὖ ἢ
κακῶς βεβιωκότας ἀνθρώπους, ἐκ τοῦ τούτων τέλους·[1] φύονται μὲν
γὰρ ἐκεῖθεν, ἤρτηνται δὲ μᾶλλον τῆς προνοίας. 2. δεδειγμένων δὲ
ἡμῖν τῶν πρώτων ὡς οἷόν τε, καλῶς ἂν ἔχοι καὶ διὰ τῶν ὑστέρων
δεῖξαι τὸ προκείμενον, λέγω δὲ διὰ τῆς ὀφειλομένης ἑκάστῳ τῶν
ἀνθρώπων κατὰ δικαίαν κρίσιν τιμῆς ἢ δίκης καὶ τοῦ κατὰ τὸν
ἀνθρώπινον βίον τέλους, αὐτῶν δὲ τούτων προτάξαι τὸν κατὰ
φύσιν ἡγούμενον καὶ πρῶτόν γε διασκέψασθαι τὸν περὶ τῆς κρίσεως
λόγον, τοσοῦτον μόνον ὑπειπόντας φροντίδι τῆς προσηκούσης τοῖς
προκειμένοις ἀρχῆς καὶ τάξεως ὅτι δεῖ τοὺς ποιητὴν τὸν θεὸν τοῦδε
τοῦ παντὸς παραδεξαμένους τῇ τούτου σοφίᾳ καὶ δικαιοσύνῃ τὴν
τῶν γενομένων ἁπάντων ἀνατιθέναι φυλακήν τε καὶ πρόνοιαν, εἰ

17. ⁵ τούτῳ A: corr. Schwartz ⁶ φυὴν Wilamowitz (cf. 18. 5): ζωὴν A
18. ¹ τέλους A¹: τε A

blinded by evil or indolence in assessing these matters knows that first there must be the sowing of the seeds; then, when these are articulated in their various parts and members and the embryos are brought forth into the light, there ensues the growth of the first stage of life and the maturing which attends it; then, when maturation is complete, there comes a decline of the native powers until old age; and when bodies have been worn out, their dissolution takes place.

4. In these circumstances, when the semen has imprinted on it neither the form or shape of men nor the dissolution of life into its basic constituents, the chain of natural events provides confirmation of things unconfirmed by the phenomena themselves. Still more so does reason, in seeking the truth on the basis of what naturally follows, confirm the resurrection, since it is more trustworthy and more secure than experience in providing confirmation of truth.

18. All of the arguments previously brought forward for our investigation to confirm the resurrection are of the same kind, since they spring from the same basic idea; for their principle is the origin of the first men by creation. Some arguments gain their force from the first principle itself out of which they arise; others gain confirmation from God's providence[1] on our behalf, by following out the investigation of the nature and way of life of men. For the reason in accordance with which and because of which men were created, when considered along with the investigation of the nature of men,[2] has its force from the fact of creation; the argument from justice, according to which God judges men who have lived well or ill, has its force from the investigation of their end; for it is from this investigation that such arguments arise, though they depend particularly on the doctrine of providence.

2. Now that we have brought forward evidence as well as we can for the primary arguments, it would be well to demonstrate our thesis also by the secondary arguments, I mean, through a consideration of the reward or punishment due to each man in accordance with just judgement and of the end that befits human life;[3] and of these arguments it would be well to place in the first rank the one which naturally precedes and to investigate first our teaching concerning the judgement, presupposing only this to clarify the point of departure and order which suit the issues before us: (a) that those who accept God as Maker of our universe must ascribe to his wisdom and justice a concern to guard

18. [1] Cf. 14. 5 above.   [2] Cf. 12–17 above.   [3] Cf. 14. 5 above.

γε ταῖς ἰδίαις ἀρχαῖς παραμένειν ἐθέλοιεν, ταῦτα δὲ περὶ τούτων
φρονοῦντας μηδὲν ἡγεῖσθαι μήτε τῶν κατὰ γῆν μήτε τῶν κατ᾽
οὐρανὸν ἀνεπιτρόπευτον μηδ᾽ ἀπρονόητον, ἀλλ᾽ ἐπὶ πᾶν ἀφανὲς
ὁμοίως καὶ φαινόμενον μικρόν τε καὶ μεῖζον διήκουσαν γινώσκειν
τὴν παρὰ τοῦ ποιήσαντος ἐπιμέλειαν. 3. δεῖται γὰρ πάντα τὰ
γενόμενα τῆς παρὰ τοῦ ποιήσαντος ἐπιμελείας, ἰδίως δὲ ἕκαστον
καθ᾽ ὃ πέφυκεν καὶ πρὸς ὃ πέφυκεν· ἀχρείου² γὰρ οἶμαι φιλοτιμίας
τὸ κατὰ γένη³ διαιρεῖν νῦν⁴ ἢ τὸ πρόσφορον ἑκάστῃ φύσει κατα-
λέγειν ἐθέλειν. 4. ὅ γε μὴν ἄνθρωπος, περὶ οὗ νῦν πρόκειται λέγειν,
ὡς μὲν ἐνδεὴς δεῖται τροφῆς, ὡς δὲ θνητὸς διαδοχῆς, ὡς δὲ λογικὸς
δίκης. εἰ δὲ τῶν εἰρημένων ἕκαστόν ἐστιν ἀνθρώπῳ κατὰ φύσιν καὶ
δεῖται μὲν τροφῆς διὰ τὴν ζωήν, δεῖται δὲ διαδοχῆς διὰ τὴν τοῦ
γένους διαμονήν, δεῖται δὲ δίκης διὰ τὸ⁵ τῆς τροφῆς καὶ τῆς διαδοχῆς
ἔννομον, ἀνάγκη δήπου, τῆς τροφῆς καὶ τῆς διαδοχῆς ἐπὶ τὸ συναμφότερον φερομένης, ἐπὶ τοῦτο⁶ φέρεσθαι καὶ τὴν δίκην, λέγω δὲ
συναμφότερον τὸν ἐκ ψυχῆς καὶ σώματος ἄνθρωπον, καὶ τὸν
τοιοῦτον ἄνθρωπον γίνεσθαι πάντων τῶν πεπραγμένων ὑπόδικον τήν
τε ἐπὶ τούτοις δέχεσθαι τιμὴν ἢ τιμωρίαν. 5. εἰ δὲ κατὰ τοῦ
συναμφοτέρου φέρει τὴν ἐπὶ τοῖς εἰργασμένοις δίκην ἡ δικαία
κρίσις καὶ μήτε τὴν ψυχὴν μόνην δεῖ κομίσασθαι τὰ ἐπίχειρα
τῶν μετὰ τοῦ σώματος εἰργασμένων (ἀπροσπαθὴς γὰρ αὕτη καθ᾽
ἑαυτὴν τῶν περὶ τὰς σωματικὰς ἡδονὰς ἢ τροφὰς καὶ θεραπείας
γινομένων πλημμελημάτων) μήτε τὸ σῶμα μόνον (ἄκριτον γὰρ
τοῦτο καθ᾽ ἑαυτὸ νόμου καὶ δίκης), ὁ δὲ ἐκ τούτων ἄνθρωπος τὴν
ἐφ᾽ ἑκάστῳ τῶν εἰργασμένων αὐτῷ δέχεται κρίσιν, τοῦτο δὲ οὔτε
κατὰ τήνδε τὴν ζωὴν εὑρίσκει συμβαῖνον ὁ λόγος (οὐ γὰρ σῴζεται
τὸ κατ᾽ ἀξίαν ἐν τῷ παρόντι βίῳ διὰ τὸ πολλοὺς μὲν ἀθέους καὶ
πᾶσαν ἀνομίαν καὶ κακίαν ἐπιτηδεύοντας μέχρι τελευτῆς διατελεῖν
κακῶν ἀπειράτους καὶ τοὐναντίον τοὺς κατὰ πᾶσαν ἀρετὴν ἐξητασ-
μένον τὸν ἑαυτῶν βίον ἐπιδειξαμένους ἐν ὀδύναις ζῆν, ἐν ἐπηρείαις, ἐν
συκοφαντίαις, αἰκίαις τε καὶ παντοίαις κακοπαθείαις) οὔτε δὲ μετὰ
θάνατον (οὐδὲ γὰρ ἔστιν ἔτι τὸ συναμφότερον χωριζομένης μὲν τῆς
ψυχῆς ἀπὸ τοῦ σώματος, σκεδαννυμένου δὲ καὶ αὐτοῦ τοῦ σώματος
εἰς ἐκεῖνα πάλιν ἐξ ὧν συνεφορήθη καὶ μηδὲν ἔτι σῴζοντος τῆς

---

18. ² ἀχρείου Stephanus : ἃ χρή· οὐ A   ³ κατὰ γένη Schwartz : κατάγειν A
⁴ διαιρεῖν νῦν : διεριννυν A : διαιρει νυν A¹   ⁵ τὸ add. A¹   ⁶ τοῦτον A :
corr. Stephanus

and provide for all created things—at least if they want to be consistent with their own first principles—and (b) that those who hold these opinions about these matters must think of nothing either on earth or in heaven as unattended to or unprovided for, but must recognize that the Maker's care extends to everything, the invisible as well as the visible, the small and the great. 3. For all created things need the care of their Maker, each one in its own way, in accordance with its own nature and its own end. But I think that it would be a task of useless ostentation to propose now to divide up the various species or draw up a catalogue of what is suitable for each kind.

4. Since man, however, the subject of this treatise, is a needy creature, he requires food; since he is mortal, he requires a succession of offspring; since he is rational, he requires justice. Each of the things mentioned is natural to man: he needs nourishment for the sake of life, and needs a succession of offspring for the sake of the permanence of his species, and needs justice for the lawful regulation of nourishment and the succession of offspring; consequently it is surely necessary, since nourishment and the succession of offspring have to do with a composite creature, that justice also has to do with this creature, I mean man, the composite of soul and body; and it is necessary that such a man should be held accountable for all his deeds and receive reward and punishment because of them. 5. Just judgement requites the composite creature for his deeds. The soul alone should not receive the wages for deeds done in conjunction with the body (for the soul as soul is free from passions and untouched by the faults which arise in connection with bodily pleasures or with food and nurture);[4] nor should the body alone be requited (for the body as body cannot make assessment of law and justice); it is man, the combination of both, who receives judgement for each of his deeds. Our inquiry finds that this does not happen in our lifetime; for in this present life just requital is not maintained, since many atheists and doers of every kind of lawlessness and evil live out their lives without suffering any hardship, whereas those who have shown their behaviour to be an exercise in every kind of virtue live lives full of distress, abuse, calumny, suffering, and all kinds of misery. Nor does it happen after our death; for the composite creature no longer exists when the soul is separated from the body and when the body itself is again dispersed among the elements from which it came and no longer preserves anything of its previous form or shape, still less any memory of its actions.

18. 4 Cf. 21. 8 below.

προτέρας φυῆς ἢ μορφῆς, ἢ πού γε τὴν μνήμην τῶν πεπραγμένων),
εὔδηλον παντὶ τὸ λειπόμενον, ὅτι δεῖ κατὰ τὸν ἀπόστολον τὸ
φθαρτὸν τοῦτο καὶ σκεδαστὸν ἐνδύσασθαι ἀφθαρσίαν,ᵃ ἵνα ζωο-
ποιηθέντων ἐξ ἀναστάσεως τῶν νεκρωθέντων καὶ πάλιν ἑνωθέντων
τῶν κεχωρισμένων ἢ καὶ πάντῃ διαλελυμένων, ἕκαστος κομίσηται
δικαίως ἃ διὰ τοῦ σώματος ἔπραξεν εἴτε ἀγαθὰ εἴτε κακά.ᵇ

19. Πρὸς μὲν οὖν τοὺς ὁμολογοῦντας τὴν πρόνοιαν καὶ τὰς αὐτὰς
ἡμῖν παραδεξαμένους ἀρχάς, εἶτα τῶν οἰκείων ὑποθέσεων οὐκ οἶδ'
ὅπως ἐκπίπτοντας, τοιούτοις χρήσαιτ' ἄν τις λόγοις καὶ πολλῷ
πλείοσι τούτων, εἴ γε πλατύνειν ἐθέλοι τὰ συντόμως καὶ κατ'
ἐπιδρομὴν εἰρημένα. 2. πρὸς δέ γε τοὺς περὶ τῶν πρώτων διαφερομένους ἴσως ἂν ἔχοι καλῶς ἑτέραν ὑποθέσθαι πρὸ τούτων ἀρχήν,
συνδιαποροῦντας αὐτοῖς περὶ ὧν δοξάζουσιν καὶ τοιαῦτα συνδια-
σκεπτομένους· ἆρά γε πάντῃ καθάπαξ ἡ τῶν ἀνθρώπων παρῶπται
ζωὴ καὶ σύμπας ὁ βίος, ζόφος δέ τις βαθὺς κατακέχυται τῆς
γῆς ἀγνοίᾳ καὶ σιγῇ κρύπτων αὐτούς τε τοὺς ἀνθρώπους καὶ τὰς
τούτων πράξεις, ἢ πολὺ τούτων ἀσφαλέστερον τὸ δοξάζειν ὅτι τοῖς
ἑαυτοῦ ποιήμασιν ἐφέστηκεν ὁ ποιήσας, πάντων τῶν ὁπωσοῦν
ὄντων ἢ¹ γινομένων ἔφορος, ἔργων τε καὶ βουλευμάτων κριτής.
3. εἰ μὲν γὰρ μηδεμία μηδαμοῦ τῶν ἀνθρώποις πεπραγμένων
γίνοιτο κρίσις, οὐδὲν ἕξουσι πλεῖον τῶν ἀλόγων ἄνθρωποι· μᾶλλον
δὲ κἀκείνων πράξουσιν ἀθλιώτερον οἱ τὰ πάθη δουλαγωγοῦντες
καὶ φροντίζοντες εὐσεβείας καὶ δικαιοσύνης ἢ τῆς ἄλλης ἀρετῆς, ὁ
δὲ κτηνώδης ἢ θηριώδης βίος ἄριστος, ἀρετὴ δὲ ἀνόητος, δίκης δὲ
ἀπειλὴ γέλως πλατύς, τὸ δὲ πᾶσαν θεραπεύειν ἡδονὴν ἀγαθῶν τὸ
μέγιστον, δόγμα δὲ κοινὸν τούτων ἁπάντων καὶ νόμος εἷς τὸ τοῖς
ἀκολάστοις καὶ λάγνοις φίλον "φάγωμεν [δὲ]² καὶ πίωμεν, αὔριον
γὰρ ἀποθνήσκομεν".ᵃ τοῦ γὰρ τοιούτου βίου τέλος οὐδὲ ἡδονὴ κατά
τινας, ἀλλ' ἀναισθησία παντελής. 4. εἰ δὲ ἔστι τις τῷ ποιήσαντι
τοὺς ἀνθρώπους τῶν ἰδίων ποιημάτων φροντὶς καὶ σῴζεταί που τῶν
εὖ ἢ κακῶς βεβιωμένων ἡ δικαία κρίσις,³ ἤτοι κατὰ τὸν παρόντα

18. ᵃ Cf. 1 Cor. 15: 53   ᵇ Cf. 2 Cor. 5: 10
19. ᵃ 1 Cor. 15: 32 (cf. Isa. 22: 13)

19. ¹ ἢ add. A¹   ² δὲ A: om. c.   ³ δικαία κρίσις Schwartz (cf. 19. 5):
διάκρισις A

What follows is clear to everyone: that this corruptible and dispersible body must, according to the apostle, put on incorruptibility, so that, when the dead are revivified through the resurrection and what has been separated or entirely dissolved is reunited, each may receive his just recompense for what he did in the body, whether good or evil.

19. With those who recognize providence and accept the same first principles as we do, and then for some strange reason repudiate their own presuppositions, a man could use arguments such as these and enlarge on them should he desire to amplify what has been said here in a brief and summary form. 2. With those who disagree on the fundamentals perhaps it would be well to lay down another principle anterior to them, by raising doubts about their opinions and examining along with them such questions as these: Is then human existence and all of life of no account whatsoever? Has deep darkness been poured out upon the earth, covering both men and their deeds in ignorance and silence? Or is it not much sounder to think that the Maker stands over his creatures as a guardian over all that is or will be and a judge of both our deeds and schemes. 3. For if there is never to be a judgement upon the deeds of men, then men will have no higher destiny than that of irrational beasts; or rather, they will fare more miserably than these in subordinating the passions and having a concern for piety, justice, and every other virtue. Then the life of beasts and wild animals is best, virtue is silly, the threat of judgement a huge joke, the cherishing of every pleasure the greatest good, and the common doctrine and single law of all such men will be that dear to the licentious and abandoned: 'Let us eat and drink, for tomorrow we die.' For the end of such a way of life according to some is not even pleasure[1] but complete insensibility.[2]

4. If the Maker of men has any concern for his own creatures, and if just judgement of those who have lived well or ill is upheld, either this will be so in our present life when we are still alive and

---

19. [1] The teaching of Epicurus (*Ep.* 3. 128).

[2] A reference to Hegesias who regarded death—that is, insensibility (cf. Epicurus, *Ep.* 1. 81)—as more desirable than life for the wise man (Diogenes Laertius, 2. 86, 93–5; Cicero, *Tusc. Disp.* 1. 83–4; Epiphanius, *Pan.* 3. 2. 9) since pain is bound to outweigh pleasure.

βίον⁴ ζώντων ἔτι τῶν κατ' ἀρετὴν ἢ κακίαν βεβιωκότων ἢ μετὰ
θάνατον ἐν χωρισμῷ καὶ διαλύσει τυγχανόντων. 5. ἀλλὰ κατ'
οὐδέτερον τῶν εἰρημένων εὑρεῖν δυνατὸν σῳζομένην τὴν δικαίαν
κρίσιν· οὔτε γὰρ οἱ σπουδαῖοι κατὰ τὴν παροῦσαν ζωὴν φέρονται τὰ
τῆς ἀρετῆς ἐπίχειρα οὔτε μὴν οἱ φαῦλοι τὰ τῆς κακίας. 6. παρίημι
γὰρ λέγειν ὅτι σῳζομένης τῆς φύσεως ἐν ᾗ νῦν ἐσμέν, οὐδ' ἡ θνητὴ
φύσις ἐνεγκεῖν οἶά τε τὴν σύμμετρον δίκην πλειόνων ἢ βαρυτέρων
φερομένην⁵ πλημμελημάτων. 7. ὅ τε γὰρ μυρίους ἐπὶ μυρίοις
ἀνελὼν ἀδίκως λῃστὴς ἢ δυνάστης ἢ τύραννος οὐκ ἂν ἑνὶ θανάτῳ
λύσειεν τὴν ἐπὶ τούτοις δίκην ὅ τε μηδὲν περὶ θεοῦ δοξάζων ἀληθές,
ὕβρει δὲ πάσῃ καὶ βλασφημίᾳ συζῶν καὶ παρορῶν μὲν τὰ θεῖα,
καταλύων δὲ νόμους, ὑβρίσας δὲ παῖδας ὁμοῦ καὶ γυναῖκας, κατα-
σκάψας δὲ πόλεις ἀδίκως, ἐμπρήσας δὲ οἴκους μετὰ τῶν ἐνοικούντων
καὶ δῃώσας χώραν καὶ τούτοις συναφανίσας δήμους καὶ λαοὺς ἢ καὶ
σύμπαν ἔθνος, πῶς ἂν ἐν φθαρτῷ τῷ σώματι πρὸς τὴν τούτοις
σύμμετρον ἀρκέσειεν δίκην, προλαμβάνοντος τοῦ θανάτου τὸ κατ'
ἀξίαν καὶ μηδὲ πρὸς ἕν τι τῶν εἰργασμένων τῆς θνητῆς ἐξαρκούσης
φύσεως; οὔτ' οὖν κατὰ τὴν παροῦσαν ζωὴν ἡ κατ' ἀξίαν δείκνυται
κρίσις οὔτε μετὰ θάνατον.

20. Ἤτοι γὰρ παντελής ἐστι σβέσις τῆς ζωῆς ὁ θάνατος συν-
διαλυομένης τῷ σώματι τῆς ψυχῆς καὶ συνδιαφθειρομένης, ἢ μένει
μὲν ἡ ψυχὴ καθ' ἑαυτὴν ἄλυτος ἀσκέδαστος ἀδιάφθορος, φθείρεται
δὲ καὶ διαλύεται τὸ σῶμα, οὐδεμίαν ἔτι σῴζον οὔτε μνήμην τῶν
εἰργασμένων οὔτ' αἴσθησιν τῶν ἐπ' αὐτῇ παθημάτων. 2. σβεν-
νυμένης μὲν γὰρ παντελῶς τῆς τῶν ἀνθρώπων ζωῆς, οὐδεμία
φανήσεται τῶν ἀνθρώπων οὐ ζώντων φροντίς, οὐ τῶν κατ' ἀρετὴν ἢ
κακίαν βεβιωκότων [ἡ]¹ κρίσις, ἐπεισκυκληθήσεται δὲ πάλιν τὰ τῆς
ἀνόμου ζωῆς καὶ τῶν ταύτῃ συνεπομένων ἀτόπων τὸ σμῆνος τό τε
τῆς ἀνομίας ταύτης κεφάλαιον, ἀθεότης.² 3. εἰ δὲ φθείροιτο μὲν τὸ
σῶμα καὶ χωροίη πρὸς τὸ συγγενὲς τῶν λελυμένων ἕκαστον, μένοι
δὲ ἡ ψυχὴ καθ' ἑαυτὴν ὡς ἄφθαρτος, οὐδ' οὕτως ἕξει χώραν ἡ
κατ' αὐτῆς κρίσις, μὴ προσούσης δικαιοσύνης· ἐπεὶ μηδὲ θεμιτὸν
ὑπολαμβάνειν ἐκ θεοῦ καὶ παρὰ θεοῦ γίνεσθαί τινα κρίσιν, ᾗ μὴ

---

19. ⁴ post βίον lacunam indicavit Wilamowitz supplens ex. gr. ἔσται
⁵ φερομένων A : corr. Wilamowitz
20. ¹ ἡ seclusit Schwartz   ² ἀθεότητος A : corr. pc

follow virtue or evil or else after death when we are in a state of separation and dissolution. 5. But it is impossible to find just judgement upheld in either of the cases mentioned. For neither do earnest men gain the rewards of virtue in this present life nor wicked men the wages of vice. 6. I pass over discussion of the fact that while the nature which we now have endures, mankind cannot even bear a judgement inflicted for misdeeds which would be proportionate to their great number and seriousness. 7. For the pirate, prince, or tyrant who unjustly slays thousands on thousands could not by his one death serve sentence for his crimes. And he who has no true view of God but spends his life indulging every kind of wantonness and blasphemy, pays no attention to religion, breaks laws, violates boys as well as women, unjustly destroys cities, and burns houses with their dwellers, devastates land, and destroys in the process inhabitants, peoples, or even a whole race—how could he offer sufficient recompense in this corruptible body to serve a sentence which would fit his crimes? Death would prevent sufficient expiation, and his mortal nature would not suffice to blot out even one single crime. A judgement adequate to what is merited cannot be found either in this present life or after death.

20. For either death is a complete extinction of life, with the soul undergoing dissolution and decay along with the body, or the soul as such remains indissoluble, undissipated, and incorruptible, whereas the body undergoes decay and dissolution, with no further memory of what it has done or consciousness of what it has experienced because of the soul. 2. If human life is entirely extinguished, there will be no account taken of men who are not alive, no judgement passed on those who have lived virtuously or viciously. There will pile up again the practices of a lawless life, the swarm of ills that follow such a life, and the summit of such lawlessness—atheism.

3. If the body decays and each part which undergoes dissolution returns to its appropriate element, whereas the soul as such remains incorruptible, not even then will a judgement upon the soul take place, since justice would be absent; for it is not right to assume that any judgement will be exercised by God or issue from God if justice is absent; and justice is absent if the doer of

πρόσεστι τὸ δίκαιον. οὐ πρόσεστι δὲ τῇ κρίσει τὸ δίκαιον μὴ
σῳζομένου τοῦ διαπραξαμένου τὴν δικαιοσύνην ἢ τὴν ἀνομίαν· ὁ
γὰρ διαπραξάμενος ἕκαστον τῶν κατὰ τὸν βίον ἐφ᾽ οἷς ἡ κρίσις,
ἄνθρωπος ἦν, οὐ ψυχὴ καθ᾽ ἑαυτήν. τὸ δὲ σύμπαν εἰπεῖν, ὁ λόγος
οὗτος ἐπ᾽ οὐδενὸς φυλάξει τὸ δίκαιον.

21. Κατορθωμάτων τε γὰρ τιμωμένων, ἀδικηθήσεται τὸ σῶμα
σαφῶς ἐκ τοῦ κοινωνῆσαι μὲν τῇ ψυχῇ τῶν ἐπὶ τοῖς σπουδαζομένοις
πόνων, μὴ κοινωνῆσαι δὲ τῆς ἐπὶ τοῖς κατορθωθεῖσι τιμῆς, καὶ
συγγνώμης μὲν τυχχάνειν πολλάκις τὴν ψυχὴν ἐπί τινων πλημμελημάτων διὰ τὴν τοῦ σώματος ἔνδειάν τε καὶ χρείαν, ἐκπίπτειν
δὲ αὐτὸ τὸ σῶμα τῆς ἐπὶ τοῖς κατορθωθεῖσι κοινωνίας, ὑπὲρ ὧν
τοὺς ἐν τῇ ζωῇ συνδιήνεγκεν πόνους. 2. καὶ μὴν καὶ πλημμελημάτων κρινομένων οὐ σῴζεται τῇ ψυχῇ τὸ δίκαιον, εἴ γε μόνη
τίνοι δίκην ὑπὲρ ὧν ἐνοχλοῦντος τοῦ σώματος καὶ πρὸς τὰς οἰκείας
ὀρέξεις ἢ κινήσεις ἕλκοντος ἐπλημμέλησεν ποτὲ μὲν κατὰ συν-
αρπαγὴν καὶ κλοπήν, ποτὲ δὲ κατά τινα βιαιοτέραν ὁλκήν, ἄλλοτε
δὲ κατὰ συνδρομὴν ἐν χάριτος μέρει καὶ θεραπείας τῆς τούτου
συστάσεως. 3. ἢ πῶς οὐκ ἄδικον τὴν ψυχὴν κρίνεσθαι καθ᾽ ἑαυτὴν
ὑπὲρ ὧν οὐδ᾽ ἡντινοῦν ἔχει κατὰ τὴν ἑαυτῆς φύσιν οὐκ ὄρεξιν οὐ
κίνησιν οὐχ ὁρμήν, οἷον λαγνείας ἢ βίας ἢ πλεονεξίας [ἀδικίας][1] καὶ
τῶν ἐπὶ τούτοις ἀδικημάτων; 4. εἰ γὰρ τὰ πλεῖστα τῶν τοιούτων
γίνεται κακῶν ἐκ τοῦ μὴ κατακρατεῖν τοὺς ἀνθρώπους τῶν ἐν-
οχλούντων παθῶν, ἐνοχλοῦνται δὲ ὑπὸ τῆς τοῦ σώματος ἐνδείας
καὶ χρείας καὶ τῆς περὶ τοῦτο σπουδῆς καὶ θεραπείας (τούτων γὰρ
ἕνεκεν πᾶσα ἡ κτῆσις καὶ πρὸ ταύτης ἡ χρῆσις, ἔτι δὲ γάμος καὶ ὅσαι
κατὰ τὸν βίον πράξεις, ἐν οἷς καὶ περὶ ἃ θεωρεῖται τό τε πλημμελὲς
καὶ τὸ μὴ τοιοῦτον), ποῦ δίκαιον ἐν οἷς πρωτοπαθεῖ τὸ σῶμα καὶ
τὴν ψυχὴν ἕλκει πρὸς συμπάθειαν καὶ κοινωνίαν τῶν ἐφ᾽ ἃ κινεῖται[2]
πράξεων, αὐτὴν κρίνεσθαι μόνην, καὶ τὰς μὲν ὀρέξεις καὶ τὰς
ἡδονάς, ἔτι δὲ φόβους καὶ λύπας, ἐφ᾽ ὧν πᾶν τὸ μὴ μέτριον ὑπόδικον, ἀπὸ τοῦ σώματος ἔχειν τὴν κίνησιν, τὰς δὲ ἐκ τούτων
ἁμαρτίας καὶ τὰς ἐπὶ τοῖς ἡμαρτημένοις τιμωρίας ἐπὶ τὴν ψυχὴν
φέρεσθαι μόνην τὴν μήτε δεομένην τοιούτου τινὸς μήτε ὀρεγομένην
μήτε φοβουμένην ἢ πάσχουσάν τι τοιοῦτον καθ᾽ ἑαυτὴν οἷον πάσχειν

21. [1] ἀδικίας A : ἢ ἀδικίας A[1] : seclusit Wilamowitz   [2] κινεῖται Schwartz :
δεῖται A

righteousness or unrighteousness does not perdure; and the one who in his lifetime did each of the deeds that are judged was man —not soul as such. In short, this doctrine is worth nothing for the maintenance of justice.

21. In the rewarding of virtuous acts the body will clearly be wronged if it participates with the soul in the labours of its earnest striving but does not participate in the reward for such acts; it will be wronged if the soul has frequently gained forgiveness for some of its misdeeds in consideration of the body's need and want, but the body itself is deprived of participation in the reward for virtuous acts for the sake of which it endured the labours of this life.

2. Moreover, when misdeeds are judged, justice is not upheld in the case of the soul if it alone pays the penalty for the misdeeds it committed when the body afflicted it and drew it into the orbit of its own desires and impulses, sometimes carrying it off by surprise and deceit, sometimes dragging it along by force, and at other times finding it a compliant attendant, indulging and pampering the body's frame. 3. Or how can the charge of injustice be avoided if the soul as soul is judged for things to which its nature does not at all impel, move, or drive it, such as lust, violence, or greed, and the evils that attend them? 4. The majority of such evils arise from men not restraining the passions that afflict them; and such afflictions arise from the need and want of the body and the care and concern exercised on its behalf; for it is because of this that all possessions are acquired and, more importantly, are used; for this reason, moreover, there is marriage and all of life's activities. In these areas and in the circumstances connected with them what is blameworthy or not comes to light. Where then is justice if the soul alone is judged, when it is the body which first experiences passions and then draws the soul to participate in them and share the deeds to which the body is driven? Where is justice if the desires and pleasures, as well as the fears and griefs, in which all that is immoderate deserves blame, arise from the body, and yet the sins which result and the punishments that follow are visited upon the soul alone, which as such needs or desires none of these things and fears or is affected by nothing of the kind that affects man as man?

πέφυκεν ἄνθρωπος; 5. ἀλλὰ κἂν μὴ μόνου τοῦ σώματος, ἀνθρώπου δὲ θῶμεν εἶναι τὰ πάθη, λέγοντες ὀρθῶς διὰ τὸ μίαν ἐξ ἀμφοτέρων εἶναι τὴν τούτου ζωήν, οὐ δήπου γε καὶ τῇ ψυχῇ ταῦτα προσήκειν φήσομεν, ὁπόταν καθαρῶς τὴν ἰδίαν αὐτῆς ἐπισκοπῶμεν φύσιν. 6. εἰ γὰρ πάσης καθάπαξ τροφῆς ἐστιν ἀνενδεής, οὐκ ἂν ὀρεχθείη ποτὲ τούτων ὧν οὐδαμῶς δεῖται πρὸς τὸ εἶναι, οὐδ'³ ἂν ὁρμήσειεν ἐπί τι τούτων οἷς μηδ' ὅλως χρῆσθαι πέφυκεν· ἀλλ' οὐδ' ἂν λυπηθείη δι' ἀπορίαν χρημάτων ἢ κτημάτων ὡς οὐδὲν αὐτῇ προσηκόντων. 7. εἰ δὲ καὶ φθορᾶς ἐστι κρείττων, οὐδὲν φοβεῖται τὸ παράπαν ὡς φθαρτικὸν ἑαυτῆς· οὐ γὰρ δέδοικεν οὐ λιμὸν οὐ νόσον οὐ πήρωσιν οὐ λώβην οὐ πῦρ οὐ σίδηρον, ἐπεὶ μηδὲ παθεῖν ἐκ τούτων δύναταί τι βλαβερὸν μηδ'⁴ ἀλγεινόν, οὐχ ἁπτομένων αὐτῆς τὸ παράπαν οὔτε σωμάτων οὔτε σωματικῶν δυνάμεων. 8. εἰ δὲ τὸ τὰ πάθη ταῖς ψυχαῖς ἰδιαζόντως προσάπτειν ἄτοπον, τὸ τὰς ἐκ τούτων ἁμαρτίας καὶ τὰς ἐπὶ ταύταις τιμωρίας ἐπὶ μόνας φέρειν τὰς ψυχὰς ὑπερβαλλόντως ἄδικον καὶ τῆς τοῦ θεοῦ κρίσεως ἀνάξιον.

22. Πρὸς δὲ τοῖς εἰρημένοις πῶς οὐκ ἄτοπον τὴν μὲν ἀρετὴν καὶ τὴν κακίαν μηδὲ νοηθῆναι δύνασθαι χωρὶς ἐπὶ τῆς ψυχῆς (ἀνθρώπου γὰρ ἀρετὰς εἶναι γινώσκομεν τὰς ἀρετάς, ὥσπερ οὖν καὶ τὴν ταύταις ἀντικειμένην κακίαν οὐ ψυχῆς κεχωρισμένης τοῦ σώματος καὶ καθ' ἑαυτὴν οὔσης), τὴν δὲ ἐπὶ τούτοις τιμὴν ἢ τιμωρίαν ἐπὶ μόνης φέρεσθαι τῆς ψυχῆς; 2. ἢ πῶς ἄν τις καὶ νοήσειεν ἐπὶ ψυχῆς μόνης ἀνδρείαν ἢ καρτερίαν, οὐκ ἐχούσης οὐ θανάτου φόβον οὐ τραύματος οὐ πηρώσεως οὐ ζημίας οὐκ αἰκίας οὐ τῶν ἐπὶ τούτοις ἀλγημάτων ἢ τῆς ἐκ τούτων κακοπαθείας; 3. πῶς δὲ ἐγκράτειαν καὶ σωφροσύνην, οὐδεμιᾶς ἑλκούσης αὐτὴν ἐπιθυμίας πρὸς τροφὴν ἢ μῖξιν ἢ τὰς ἄλλας ἡδονάς τε καὶ τέρψεις οὐδ' ἄλλου τινὸς οὔτ' ἔσωθεν ἐνοχλοῦντος οὔτ' ἔξωθεν ἐρεθίζοντος; 4. πῶς δὲ φρόνησιν, οὐχ ὑποκειμένων αὐτῇ πρακτέων καὶ μὴ πρακτέων οὐδ'¹ αἱρετῶν καὶ φευκτῶν, μᾶλλον δὲ μηδεμιᾶς ἐνούσης αὐτῇ κινήσεως τὸ παράπαν ἢ φυσικῆς ὁρμῆς ἐπί τι τῶν πρακτέων; 5. ποῦ δὲ ὅλως ψυχαῖς ἡ πρὸς ἀλλήλας δικαιοσύνη προσφυὴς ἢ πρὸς ἄλλο τι τῶν ὁμογενῶν ἢ τῶν ἑτερογενῶν, οὐκ ἐχούσαις οὔτε πόθεν οὔτε δι' ὧν οὔτε πῶς

21. ³ οὐδ' Schwartz: οὔτ' A   ⁴ μηδ' Wilamowitz: οὔτ' A
22. ¹ οὐδ' Schwartz: οὔτ' A: οὔθ' A¹

5. Even if we grant that the passions characterize not simply the body, but man as such, and are right in saying so because man's life is a unity comprised of soul and body, nevertheless we shall not say that the passions belong to the soul as soul when we examine its own proper nature with clarity. 6. For if it requires no food at all, it could never reach out for what it does not need to exist, nor could it go in search of anything which it was never meant to use; neither, moreover, could it grieve for lack of money or possessions, since they have nothing to do with it. 7. Because it transcends corruption, it fears nothing at all as capable of effecting its destruction. It has no fear of hunger, disease, mutilation, disfigurement, fire, or sword because it can experience nothing harmful or painful from these things, since neither bodies nor bodily properties affect it at all. 8. If then it is out of the question for the passions to affect souls as such, then it is surely unjust and unworthy of divine judgement to visit upon souls alone the sins that arise from the passions and the punishments that follow.

22. Again, it is impossible to think of virtue and vice as applicable to the soul as a separate entity; for we know that virtues are the virtues of man just as we also know that the vice which opposes them does not belong to the soul separated from the body and existing in isolation. Is it not absurd, then, that reward or punishment for these things is to be visited upon the soul alone? 2. How could a man attribute to the soul alone courage or constancy, when it has no fear of death, wounds, mutilation, harm, injury, and the sufferings that attend these evils or the distress that arises from them? 3. How could a man attribute to the soul alone self-control and restraint, when there is no impulse which draws it to food or sexual intercourse or the other pleasures and delights and when nothing else troubles it from within or disturbs it from without? 4. How could a man attribute to the soul alone prudence when it does not have before it the requirement of doing or not doing certain things or of choosing or avoiding certain things, but rather has no natural movement or impulse at all implanted in it for the accomplishment of something required?

5. Is there any way at all in which justice can be a natural property of souls, either in their relations with each other or with some other being like them or unlike them? They do not have the resources, the means, or the way to distribute that which is equal

ἀπονείμωσι τὸ κατ' ἀξίαν ἢ κατ' ἀναλογίαν ἴσον ἐξῃρημένης τῆς εἰς
θεὸν τιμῆς, οὐδ' ἄλλως ἐχούσαις ὁρμὴν ἢ κίνησιν πρὸς χρῆσιν
ἰδίων ἢ πρὸς ἀποχὴν ἀλλοτρίων, τῆς μὲν χρήσεως τῶν κατὰ φύσιν
καὶ τῆς ἀποχῆς ἐπὶ τῶν χρῆσθαι πεφυκότων θεωρουμένης, τῆς δὲ
ψυχῆς μήτε δεομένης τινὸς μήτε χρῆσθαι τισὶν ἢ τινὶ πεφυκυίας καὶ
διὰ τοῦτο μηδὲ² τῆς λεγομένης ἰδιοπραγίας τῶν μερῶν ἐπὶ τῆς
οὕτως ἐχούσης ψυχῆς εὑρεθῆναι δυναμένης;

23. Καὶ μὴν κἀκεῖνο πάντων παραλογώτατον, τὸ τοὺς μὲν θεσ-
πισθέντας νόμους ἐπ' ἀνθρώπους φέρειν, τῶν δὲ νομίμως ἢ παρα-
νόμως πεπραγμένων τὴν δίκην ἐπὶ μόνας τρέπειν τὰς ψυχάς. 2. εἰ
γὰρ ὁ τοὺς νόμους δεξάμενος αὐτὸς¹ δέξαιτ' ἂν δικαίως καὶ τῆς
παρανομίας τὴν δίκην, ἐδέξατο δὲ τοὺς νόμους ἄνθρωπος, οὐ ψυχὴ
καθ' ἑαυτήν, ἄνθρωπον δεῖ καὶ τὴν ὑπὲρ τῶν ἡμαρτημένων ὑποσχεῖν
δίκην, οὐ ψυχὴν καθ' ἑαυτήν· ἐπεὶ μὴ ψυχαῖς ἐθέσπισεν θεὸς
ἀπέχεσθαι τῶν² οὐδὲν αὐταῖς προσηκόντων, οἷον μοιχείας φόνου
κλοπῆς ἁρπαγῆς τῆς κατὰ τῶν γεννησάντων ἀτιμίας πάσης τε
κοινῶς τῆς ἐπ' ἀδικίᾳ καὶ βλάβῃ τῶν πέλας γινομένης ἐπιθυμίας.
3. οὔτε γὰρ τὸ "τίμα τὸν πατέρα σου καὶ τὴν μητέρα" ᵃ ψυχαῖς
μόνον εὐάρμοστον, οὐ προσηκόντων αὐταῖς τῶν τοιούτων ὀνομάτων·
οὐ γὰρ ψυχαὶ ψυχὰς³ γεννῶσαι τὴν τοῦ πατρὸς ἢ τῆς μητρὸς
οἰκειοῦνται προσηγορίαν, ἀλλ' ἀνθρώπους ἄνθρωποι· 4. οὔτε οὖν
τὸ "οὐ μοιχεύσεις"ᵇ ἐπὶ ψυχῶν λεχθείη ποτ' ἂν ἢ νοηθείη δεόντως,
οὐκ οὔσης ἐν αὐταῖς τῆς κατὰ τὸ ἄρσεν καὶ θῆλυ διαφορᾶς οὐδὲ πρὸς
μῖξιν τινὸς ἐπιτηδειότητος ἢ πρὸς ταύτην ὀρέξεως. ὀρέξεως δὲ
τοιαύτης οὐκ οὔσης, οὐδὲ μῖξιν εἶναι δυνατόν· παρ' οἷς δὲ μῖξις
ὅλως οὐκ ἔστιν, οὐδὲ ἔνθεσμος μῖξις, ὅπερ ἐστὶν γάμος· ἐννόμου δὲ
μίξεως οὐκ οὔσης, οὐδὲ τὴν παράνομον καὶ τὴν ἐπ' ἀλλοτρίᾳ
γυναικὶ γινομένην ὄρεξιν ἢ μῖξιν εἶναι δυνατόν, τοῦτο γάρ ἐστι
μοιχεία. 5. ἀλλ' οὐδὲ τὸ κλοπὴν ἀπαγορεύειν ἢ τὴν τοῦ πλείονος
ἐπιθυμίαν ψυχαῖς προσφυές· οὐδὲ γὰρ δέονται τούτων ὧν οἱ
δεόμενοι διὰ φυσικὴν ἔνδειαν ἢ χρείαν κλέπτειν εἰώθασιν καὶ

23. ᵃ Exod. 20: 12 ᵇ Exod. 20: 14

22. ² μηδὲ Rhosus: μήτε A
23. ¹ αὐτὸς Wilamowitz: οὗτος A ² τῶν add. A¹ ³ ψυχαὶ ψυχαῖς A:
corr. A¹

according to desert or that which is proportionally equal,[1] except for the honour they give to God. Moreover they have no impulse or movement toward the use of things suitable to them or abstention from things alien to them. The use of things naturally suitable or abstention from the contrary characterize only those creatures whose nature it is to make use of things; but the soul needs nothing, and it does not naturally use this or that thing, and for that reason the individual activity of which one speaks in the case of bodily members cannot be found in the soul as it is constituted.

23. Furthermore there is another incongruity, the most irrational of all: to impose on men the laws which have been decreed and then to pass judgement for deeds lawfully or lawlessly done on souls alone. 2. For if the one who received the laws ought, if justice be done, to receive also the punishment for lawlessness, and if it was man and not soul as such that received the laws, then man and not soul as such must also submit to punishment for sins committed. For God did not hand down his decree to souls to abstain from things which have nothing to do with them, such as adultery, murder, theft, robbery, dishonour of parents, and in general all covetousness which arises to injure or harm our neighbours.

3. The commandment, 'Honour your father and mother', is not appropriate for souls alone, since such terms do not apply to them; for souls do not beget souls and thus earn the title of father or mother; only in the case of human beings who beget human beings are such terms in order. 4. Nor could the commandment, 'You shall not commit adultery', ever properly be expressed or imagined in reference to souls, since there is no difference among them between male and female nor any aptitude or desire for sexual intercourse. Since there is no such desire, neither can there be any sexual intercourse. Among those who have no intercourse at all neither is there that legitimate intercourse which we call marriage. If there is no lawful intercourse, neither can there be that lawless desire or intercourse which takes place with another man's wife—precisely that which constitutes 'adultery'. 5. Neither is it natural to forbid souls to steal or to covet greater possessions. For they do not require the things which men need, because of a natural lack or want, and consequently are accustomed to steal and carry off, such as gold, silver, livestock, or

22. [1] The two types of equality named here are derived from Aristotle (*Pol.* 1301ª26, 1301ᵇ31) and may be regarded as virtually identical: the 'desert' of the person determines the 'proportion' of the advantages conferred (cf. W. L. Newman, *The Politics of Aristotle*, iv [Oxford, 1902], 283, 290).

ληστεύειν, οἷον χρυσὸν ἢ ἄργυρον ἢ ζῷον ἢ ἄλλο τι τῶν πρὸς
τροφὴν ἢ σκέπην ἢ χρῆσιν ἐπιτηδείων· ἀχρεῖον γὰρ ἀθανάτῳ φύσει
πᾶν ὁπόσον τοῖς ἐνδεέσιν ὀρεκτὸν ὡς χρήσιμον. 6. ἀλλ' ὁ μὲν
ἐντελέστερος περὶ τούτων λόγος ἀφείσθω τοῖς σπουδαιότερον
ἕκαστον σκοπεῖν βουλομένοις ἢ φιλοτιμότερον διαγωνίζεσθαι πρὸς
τοὺς διαφερομένους, ἡμῖν δὲ ἀρκούντων τῶν ἀρτίως εἰρημένων καὶ
τῶν συμφώνως τούτοις τὴν ἀνάστασιν πιστουμένων τὸ τοῖς αὐτοῖς
ἐπὶ πλεῖον ἐνδιατρίβειν οὐκέτ' ἂν ἔχοι καιρόν· οὐ γὰρ τὸ μηδὲν
παραλιπεῖν τῶν ἐνόντων εἰπεῖν πεποιήμεθα σκοπόν, ἀλλὰ τὸ κεφαλαιωδῶς ὑποδεῖξαι τοῖς συνελθοῦσιν ἃ χρὴ περὶ τῆς ἀναστάσεως
φρονεῖν καὶ τῇ δυνάμει τῶν παρόντων συμμετρῆσαι τὰς ἐπὶ τοῦτο
φερούσας ἀφορμάς.

24. Ἐξητασμένων δὲ ποσῶς τῶν προτεθέντων ὑπόλοιπον ἂν εἴη
καὶ τὸν ἀπὸ τοῦ τέλους διασκέψασθαι λόγον, ἤδη μὲν τοῖς εἰρημένοις ἐμφαινόμενον, τοσαύτης δὲ μόνον ἐπιστασίας καὶ προσ-
θήκης δεόμενον, ὡς μὴ δοκεῖν τι[1] τῶν μικρῷ ⟨πρόσθεν⟩ εἰρημένων[2]
ἀμνημόνευτον καταλιπόντα[3] παραβλάψαι τὴν ὑπόθεσιν ἢ τὴν ἐξ
ἀρχῆς γενομένην διαίρεσιν. 2. τούτων τε οὖν ἕνεκεν καὶ τῶν ἐπὶ
τούτοις ἐγκληθησομένων[4] καλῶς ἂν ἔχοι τοσοῦτον ἐπισημήνασθαι
μόνον ὅτι δεῖ καὶ τῶν ἐκ φύσεως συνισταμένων καὶ τῶν κατὰ
τέχνην γινομένων οἰκεῖον ἑκάστου τέλος εἶναι, τοῦτο που καὶ τῆς
κοινῆς πάντων ἐννοίας ἐκδιδασκούσης ἡμᾶς καὶ τῶν ἐν ὀφθαλμοῖς
στρεφομένων ἐπιμαρτυρούντων. 3. ἢ γὰρ οὐ θεωροῦμεν ἕτερόν τι
τοῖς γεωργοῦσιν, ἕτερον δὲ τοῖς ἰατρεύουσιν ὑποκείμενον τέλος,
καὶ πάλιν ἄλλο μέν τι τῶν ἐκ γῆς φυομένων, ἄλλο δὲ τῶν ἐπ'
αὐτῆς τρεφομένων ζῴων καὶ κατά τινα φυσικὸν εἱρμὸν γεννω-
μένων; 4. εἰ δὲ τοῦτ' ἐστὶν ἐναργὲς καὶ δεῖ πάντως ταῖς φυσκαῖς ἢ
τεχνικαῖς δυνάμεσι καὶ ταῖς ἐκ τούτων ἐνεργείαις τὸ κατὰ φύσιν
ἕπεσθαι τέλος, ἀνάγκη πᾶσα καὶ τὸ τῶν ἀνθρώπων τέλος ὡς
ἰδιαζούσης ὂν φύσεως ἐξηρῆσθαι τῆς τῶν ἄλλων κοινότητος· ἐπεὶ
μηδὲ[5] θεμιτὸν ταὐτὸν ὑποθέσθαι τέλος τῶν τε λογικῆς κρίσεως
ἀμοιρούντων καὶ τῶν κατὰ τὸν ἔμφυτον νόμον καὶ λόγον ἐνεργούντων

24. [1] τι add. c   [2] μικρῷ πρόσθεν εἰρημένων Schwartz (cf. Plato, Leg.
969 b): μικρον / / / / / / / / / /ρημένων A: μικρον ἡμῖν / / / / εἰρημένων A¹: supra
ἡμῖν εἰρημένων add. πρόσθεν s: μικρῶς ἡμῖν εἰρημένων c   [3] καταλιπόντα
Wilamowitz: καταλιπεῖν A: καταλιπεῖν καὶ A¹   [4] ἐγκληθησομένων Schwartz:
ἐγκεισομένων A   [5] μηδὲ p: μὴ A

anything else suitable for their nourishment, shelter, or use. For everything that is sought after as useful by those who need it is of no use to an immortal nature.

6. We may leave a fuller discussion of these things to those desiring to examine each point more carefully or to take issue with their adversaries with greater zest. We are satisfied with the considerations just brought forward and the arguments which in agreement with them confirm the resurrection; consequently any further lingering over the same matters would be untimely. For we have not made it our goal to leave nothing on the subject unsaid but to show in summary form to those assembled what one ought to think about the resurrection and to adapt to the capacity of those present the arguments leading to this truth.[1]

24. Now that the issues have been to some extent examined, there remains the task of investigating also the argument from the final cause. This has already appeared in what we have said,[1] and needs further attention only to the extent that it will not seem as though I have forgotten any of the points mentioned shortly before[2] and damaged the proposal or the division of topics which I made at the beginning.[3] 2. To avoid these consequences, then, and to forestall the criticisms that would follow, it may be well to add only this observation: that every natural thing and every artefact must have an end that suits it. A universal axiom shared by all men teaches us this, and what takes place before our eyes confirms it. 3. Do we not see that there is one end for farmers and another for physicians, that there is one end for the things that grow from the earth and another for the animals which gain nourishment from the earth and are procreated in accordance with a natural chain of events?

4. If this is clear, and it is absolutely necessary for a natural end to be associated with the powers of nature or of craftsmanship and the activities to which they give rise, then mankind's end must surely be distinguished from that common to other creatures, since it has to do with a distinctive nature. Certainly it is not right to argue for the same end both for creatures who have no share in rational discrimination and for those who act in accordance with an innate rational law and can exercise prudence and justice.

23. [1] Cf. 1. 3 above.
24. [1] Cf. 13. 3, 14. 5, 15. 2–3, and 18. 1–2 above
      [2] Cf. 18. 2 above.
      [3] Cf. 13. 3 above.

ἔμφρονί τε ζωῆ καὶ δίκη χρωμένων. 5. οὔτ᾽ οὖν τὸ ἄλυπον οἰκεῖον
τούτοις ἂν εἴη τέλος, μετείη γὰρ ἂν⁶ τούτου καὶ τοῖς παντελῶς
ἀναισθητοῦσιν· ἀλλ᾽ οὐδὲ τῶν τὸ σῶμα τρεφόντων ἢ τερπόντων
ἀπόλαυσις καὶ πλῆθος ἡδονῶν· ἢ πρωτεύειν ἀνάγκη τὸν κτηνώδη
βίον, ἀτελῆ δ᾽ εἶναι τὸν κατ᾽ ἀρετήν. κτηνῶν γὰρ οἶμαι καὶ βοσ-
κημάτων οἰκεῖον τοῦτο τέλος, οὐκ ἀνθρώπων ἀθανάτῳ ψυχῇ καὶ
λογικῇ κρίσει χρωμένων.

25. οὐ μὴν οὐδὲ μακαριότης ψυχῆς κεχωρισμένης σώματος· οὐδὲ
γὰρ τὴν θατέρου τούτων ἐξ ὧν συνέστηκεν ἄνθρωπος ἐσκοποῦμεν
ζωὴν ἢ τέλος, ἀλλὰ τοῦ συνεστῶτος ἐξ ἀμφοῖν· τοιοῦτος γὰρ πᾶς ὁ
τόνδε τὸν βίον λαχὼν ἄνθρωπος καὶ δεῖ τῆς τούτου ζωῆς εἶναί τι
τέλος οἰκεῖον. 2. εἰ δὲ τοῦ συναμφοτέρου τὸ τέλος, τοῦτο δὲ οὔτε
ζώντων αὐτῶν ἔτι κατὰ τόνδε τὸν βίον εὑρεθῆναι δυνατὸν διὰ τὰς
πολλάκις ἤδη ῥηθείσας αἰτίας οὔτε μὴν ἐν χωρισμῷ τυγχανούσης
τῆς ψυχῆς, τῷ μηδὲ συνεστάναι τὸν τοιοῦτον ἄνθρωπον διαλυθέντος ἢ καὶ πάντη σκεδασθέντος τοῦ σώματος κἂν ἡ ψυχὴ διαμένη
καθ᾽ ἑαυτήν, ἀνάγκη πᾶσα κατ᾽ ἄλλην τινὰ τοῦ συναμφοτέρου καὶ τοῦ
αὐτοῦ ζῴου σύστασιν τὸ τῶν ἀνθρώπων φανῆναι τέλος. 3. τούτου
δ᾽ ἐξ ἀνάγκης ἑπομένου, δεῖ πάντως γενέσθαι τῶν νεκρωθέντων
ἢ καὶ πάντη διαλυθέντων σωμάτων ἀνάστασιν καὶ τοὺς αὐτοὺς
ἀνθρώπους συστῆναι πάλιν· ἐπειδή γε τὸ μὲν τέλος οὐχ ἁπλῶς
οὐδὲ τῶν ἐπιτυχόντων ἀνθρώπων ὁ τῆς φύσεως τίθεται νόμος,
ἀλλ᾽ αὐτῶν ἐκείνων τῶν κατὰ τὴν προλαβοῦσαν ζωὴν βεβιωκότων,
τοὺς δ᾽ αὐτοὺς ἀνθρώπους συστῆναι πάλιν ἀμήχανον, μὴ τῶν αὐτῶν
σωμάτων ταῖς αὐταῖς ψυχαῖς ἀποδοθέντων. τὸ δ᾽ αὐτὸ σῶμα
τὴν αὐτὴν ψυχὴν ἀπολαβεῖν ἄλλως μὲν ἀδύνατον, κατὰ μόνην δὲ
τὴν ἀνάστασιν δυνατόν· ταύτης γὰρ γενομένης καὶ τὸ τῇ φύσει
τῶν ἀνθρώπων πρόσφορον ἐπακολουθεῖ τέλος. 4. τέλος δὲ ζωῆς
ἔμφρονος καὶ λογικῆς κρίσεως οὐκ ἂν ἁμάρτοι τις εἰπὼν τὸ τούτοις
ἀπερισπάστως συνδιαιωνίζειν οἷς μάλιστα καὶ πρώτως ὁ φυσικὸς
συνήρμοσται λόγος, τῇ τε θεωρίᾳ τοῦ δόντος καὶ τῶν ἐκείνῳ δεδογμένων ἀπαύστως ἐπαγάλλεσθαι· κἂν οἱ πολλοὶ τῶν ἀνθρώπων
ἐμπαθέστερον καὶ σφοδρότερον τοῖς τῇδε προσπεπονθότες ἄστοχοι

5. Nor could the end proper to men be freedom from pain, for this it would share even with things entirely devoid of sensation; nor yet could their end be the enjoyment and abundance of what feeds the body and gives it pleasure. Otherwise the animal side of life must take precedence and the virtuous life be directed to no end. For such an end is proper, in my estimation, to animals and beasts, not to men who are gifted with an immortal soul and rational discernment.

25. Nor indeed is there happiness for the soul in a state of separation from the body. For we were considering the life or end, not of one of the parts which constitute man, but of the creature made up of both parts. For such is the nature of every man allotted this life of ours, and there must be some end which is proper to this form of existence. 2. If the end has to do with the composite, and if this cannot be discovered either while men are still alive here below, for the reasons so often spoken of already, nor yet when the soul is in a state of separation[1] (for man as such cannot be said to exist when the body has undergone dissolution or been completely dispersed, even though the soul as such is permanent), then the end of men must certainly be seen in some other state of the same composite creature.

3. Since this is the necessary consequence, there must surely be a resurrection of bodies that have died or even undergone complete dissolution, and the same men must rise again. Because the law of nature does not appoint an end indiscriminately for men taken in the abstract, but for the same ones who lived previous lives, it is impossible for the same men to be reconstituted unless the same bodies are united with the same souls. The same body cannot receive the same soul in any other way than by resurrection. When this takes place, the end that suits human nature is the result.

4. A man would not be wrong in saying that the end of a life capable of prudence and rational discernment is to live eternally without being torn away from those things which natural reason has found first and foremost in harmony with itself, and to rejoice unceasingly in the contemplation of their Giver and his decrees, even though it is true that the majority of men live their lives without reaching this goal, because they have been strongly and

25. [1] Cf. 19. 4–7 above.

τούτου διατελῶσιν. 5. οὐ γὰρ ἀκυροῖ τὴν κοινὴν ἀποκλήρωσιν τὸ πλῆθος τῶν ἀποπιπτόντων τοῦ προσήκοντος αὐτοῖς τέλους, ἰδιαζούσης τῆς ἐπὶ τούτοις ἐξετάσεως καὶ τῆς ἑκάστῳ συμμετρουμένης ὑπὲρ τῶν εὖ ἢ κακῶς βεβιωμένων τιμῆς ἢ δίκης.

Subscriptio: ΑΘΗΝΑΓΟΡΟΥ ΠΕΡΙ ΑΝΑΣΤΑΣΕΩΣ

profoundly affected with desire for the things of this life. 5. For the great number of those who fail to reach their appointed end does not invalidate their common destiny. Each man will be examined in these matters individually, and reward or punishment will be distributed in proportion to each for lives lived well or badly.

INDEXES

I. THE *PLEA*

(2) TERMS

Spirit (of God), 5. 3; 6. 2, 4; 7. 3; 9. 1;
   10. 2, 4, 5; 12. 3; 18. 2; 24. 2
spirit (hostile to God; cf. prince), 24.
   2; 25. 3; 27. 1

Thyestean banquets, 3. 1 (cf. 31. 1)
Word (of God), 4. 2; 6. 2; 10. 1, 2, 3,
   5; 12. 3; 18. 2; 24. 2; 30. 6

II. *CONCERNING THE RESURRECTION OF THE DEAD*

(3) QUOTATIONS AND ALLUSIONS